SAINT JOHN VIANNEY
THE CURÉ D'ARS TODAY

GEORGE WILLIAM RUTLER

SAINT JOHN VIANNEY
THE CURÉ D'ARS
TODAY

IGNATIUS PRESS   SAN FRANCISCO

Cover design by Marcia Ryan.
Cover photograph: Face of the Cure d'Ars
as seen by the sculptor Cabuchet,
his friend and contemporary.
Photograph by Antoine Mappus,
originally published by Xavier Mappus
52, avenue Foch Le-Puy, Paris.
Reproduced with permission.

To the memory of my grandfathers
John William Albinson
Adolphe Rutler

CONTENTS

FOREWORD

There are possibly two types of readers who will not read this book: those who think they already know everything important about the Curé d'Ars and those who do not want to know anything about him at all. Both will suffer a serious loss.

To be fair, I might well have passed up the opportunity myself, for neither reason — only because of the press of events — had I not known the author. Although it will be said of him, Father George Rutler is not another Gilbert Keith Chesterton. No one is ever really another anyone. Father Rutler does write in Chestertonian paradoxes and with that convert's insight and "orthodoxy", but he brings to whatever he treats what I suspect will one day be called a Rutlerian dimension. Such a dimension I can describe only as the Curé responded to the question of the sweet lady asking him how she should go to heaven. "Straight as a cannonball", Father Rutler tells us Father John Vianney told her.

Those who would read this book should really know of this special dimension that Father Rutler provides. Otherwise they could miss the startling insights in his matter-of-factness, as when he tells us the Curé of Ars "did not mind being called shabby, but he turned sullen when those who had never met him called him dirty".

Everyone who thinks Vianney already well-known will find, not simply new information, but what has new meaning for each discoverer. That meaning may well differ for each reader. The descriptions of the Curé's encounters with Satan and "his lesser angels" and of the hours in the confessional were my own personal crucial rediscoveries.

Neither Bernanos' dramatic *Sun of Satan* nor Blatty's melodramatic *Exorcist,* each of which introduced so many modern readers to the *notion* of a devil in real life, gives us quite the sense of "the terror and the wonder" of what can happen to *us* as do the quiet passages descriptive of what happened to the Curé, beginning in 1824 and perduring until a year before his death. Father Rutler gives short shrift to the tendency to mythologize the events and to diagnose Father Vianney as paranoid, and he provides solid evidence for dismissing this tendency. He also attributes less importance to melodramatic activities of the devil than to the devil's "hauntings" as "a *via negativa* to salvation". As such, the Curé's experiences become far more familiar to our daily experience, and far more instructive.

No one who has read a page of any life of the Curé of Ars can be unaware of his commitment to the confessional. Father Rutler writes interestingly of the stories told of the Curé's inspirations while in the confessional, but these hold far less for me personally than does the sheer tenacity of the man in refusing to invert his priorities. When I first took the Curé seriously, I was a very young priest who also took quite seriously the tremendous potential given a priest in "hearing confessions". (Despite that popular terminology, I believe we were just as concerned about reconciliation then as we have been since the name change.) I had none of the Curé's devotion or heroic piety, and I could not have stayed in the confessional all day if I had wanted to. A busy pastor would have sent me packing on other business. But I did see hearing confessions and absolving sins as a major priority.

In reading Father Rutler's account of the Curé at work in the confessional, I have been reminded, not of a truth I have never forgotten, but of the zeal I once practiced on behalf of that truth. Periodically, as Archbishop of New York, deprived to a degree of opportunities available to my priests, I still "hear confessions", and at times with some frequency, as when I am conducting a retreat. Too many weeks at a time go by, however, when I foolishly permit too many other duties to preoccupy me and to take questionable priority over this fundamental priestly act and privilege.

Others will make their own discoveries or rediscover once-cherished insights. I suspect, however, that the two described above as most meaningful for me will prove meaningful for many. The exposé of Satan will enhance understanding for many of what it means to be God's pilgrim in today's world. The insights into the apostolate of the Curé as confessor will be a reminder for all that Vatican II by no means abolished sin.

Appendices 1 and 2 are extraordinary bonuses in this extraordinary book. How uncommon to be truly helped in understanding what is of such common concern: the cultural context within which a saint lived and moved and had his being. How exceptional to illustrate the applicability of a saint's teaching to today's world by having the Holy Father himself do the applying.

An important, fascinating work by an important, fascinating author.

+ *John Cardinal O'Connor*
Archbishop of New York

Chapter I

FACTS AND ILLUSIONS

The Historical Approach

A writer whose reputation has not faded in the last hundred years said that a certain biography of Saint Jean Marie Baptiste Vianney was not historical enough. It was devotional, but of a devotion that passes over the common sort of facts needed for an earthly sense of the subject. He did not mean that the devotional approach must be contrary to facts, but that in one way this biography assumed the reader knew enough about the subject, and that in another way the facts were not especially important. But anything important has to be factual, and anything factual has to be particular.

Particularity is the ground of devotion, at least from the Christian point of view, because Christianity is the account of how God became particular. There was a period — one period of thirty-three years, to be precise, and a moment — or three hours of a Friday, to be quite precise, when God was as specific with us as he ever was. That is called salvation history, and not simply salvation, because it happened. So nothing Christian can be loose with history; there can be no dichotomy between the historical approach and the devotional approach.

Christ prayed in the presence of his apostles: "I am remaining in the world no longer, but they remain in the world, while I am on my way to thee. Holy Father, keep them true to thy

name, thy gift to me, that they may be one, as we are one"
(Jn 17:11). The "one-ness" is the character of holiness, the
effective cooperation of the human intellect and will with the
intellect and will of God. When human thought and desire
wander off on their own, they begin the meander called sin.
This is a plain fact of history. A sinner is evidence of Christ by
default, as someone lost is a sign of a place where one is not
lost. But a saint is particular evidence of Christ by example.
"The saints have not all started well", said the Curé d'Ars,
"but they have all finished well." The sinner and the saint may
have the same name; a saint, after all, is a sinner who has
perfectly accepted forgiveness. A biography of a saint should
not exaggerate if it is to do justice to the acceptance.

Legends and Myths

Legends are exaggerations, and that is why they are not
myths. Myths do take truth seriously. Hobbes did not appreciate the distinction in his own day; so he wanted to eliminate
all metaphors from conversation. But that could only have
eliminated the conversation. The myths in Christianity are
not mere myths, the way there are mere legends. A Christian
myth gets into history; a legend tries to get out of it. The
problem with devotional literature of a certain sort is that it is
only legendary; it keeps circling above what is going on
without getting involved in it. Anyone can rightly claim that
such material is not true material.

Myths are told of intuitions too broad for linear, or explicit,
language. They are about the number of "days" God took to
create the world before there were days; the beguiling "speech"

by which the "serpent" mocked the dignity of the first man and woman before there were strangers to provide a human disguise for Satan. But this figurative language describes what was involved, not who was involved. For myths are about events; individuals figure in them as ciphers rather than as personalities. If you try to personalize myths, they become legends. Someone who becomes larger than life ceases to live. We do well to speak of "Christ" because that describes who Jesus is; we would do just as well not to speak of a "Christ event" because that makes Jesus into an abstraction. This is worth mentioning here, before taking up the life of the Curé d'Ars, because the life of a saint has to be treated with the precision used for the life of the Christ of the saints. They are part of the same history.

The coming of God to earth in the Incarnation was an event among other events, and it involved a man; it is not mythical for that reason. There was a birth, but if there were only an idea of a birth, the baby would be no more significant than the crib. There have been many resurrections of ideas and cultures, and they form the substance of magnificent myth; but there has been only one resurrection of a man. If I want to discover the resurrection of classical thought in the twelfth century, I can try to get a sense of a dark ignorance that rolled away; and then I will understand that it was not a resurrection but a revival. But if I want to discover the Resurrection of Christ, I can try to find a stone that rolled away, and I will understand that it was not a revival but a resurrection. The Resurrection resurrected a man; explaining it as a metaphor distorts it into a fable. The apostles in the upper room did not see a figure of speech; they saw a figure with wounds that made them speechless. A pure myth would have marked his hands and feet with diamonds or roses; the myth would then be about the indomitability of virtue, but Christ himself would be a subjective symbol. Yet Christianity is all about the wounds. And that is why it has threatened sentimentalists who fear real wounds.

Saint Paul said that the saints live wasted and tragic lives if Christ is not truly raised from the dead. It does no good to say they were wrong about Christ but wrong in a respectable way. That they were good is not good enough. They were nothing if they were not right. Vianney was specific about Christ. He knew that great teachers pass on teachings, but that Christ passes on himself. He does this through the saints. And so the saints are solid and specific. But the language we use about divinity will have to be different from the biography of a human. To say God "walked" in the garden in the cool of the evening is a startling myth of God's involvement with creation, and I say "myth", not because the transcendent God is aloof, but because he has no legs. To say Adam walked and that Vianney walked is a misleading legend unless it means that they left footprints as we would. Whether or not God actually walked in the Garden of Eden in the evening is irrelevant to his existence, but whether or not God in Christ walked in the Garden of Olives at any time decides whether or not there was a Christ; and whether or not Adam and Vianney walked decides whether or not they were like us. When God is described as high and lifted up on a throne with his train filling the temple, we know he is the real God; to describe Adam that way would mean he was not a real man. The Scriptures say much about what God looks like because, to natural sense, he looks like nothing at all; but the same Scriptures say little about the first man and woman because they looked like every man and woman.

It did not occur to the evangelists to describe Christ's appearance, because he looked like them. The miracle was his appearing. That he had appeared was far more absorbing than how he appeared. He had "no form nor comeliness that any should desire him" (Is 53:3); he was, after all, Christ and not Apollo, and the admission becomes the essential proclamation and boast. Apollo never was and never will be, so he can be as glorious as legends will have him; Christ always was and always will be, so he must be marred and acquainted with grief as circumstances did have him. Discourse on the life of historical figures is regulated by this economy; they are temporal facts and not illusions.

Anyone can add to stories that never happened; Pandora can have a cottage in any corner of the world, but Eve can only dwell in Eden. You or I can change to eels the snakes twisting the hair of the Gorgons, but the hair of Samson has to be his own hair. If I set out to describe the Saint of Ars, I cannot place him in India to make him seem more exotic, and I cannot have him telling witty stories in rococo drawing rooms to make him more entertaining. It is true of him as it is true of his Christ. It would not matter in a dream if Atropos, who never was, cut the thread of life with shining shears or a crystal sword; but the centurion, who was, jabs the holy Side with a lance and nothing but a lance. Ceyx floats toward Halcyone over any diaphanous sea; Christ comes to Peter on the waters of Galilee. In the corridors of evening slumber Syrinx will sigh upon the woodland reeds whatever songs our reveries want; but Christ pipes one sure tune in one sultry place.

Vianney was too recent for many impossible legends to crop up about him. And given the age in which he lived, the legends would have been torn down fast enough, for if his contemporaries failed to be scientific about religion, they were very religious about science; to perform a miracle was considered almost a sign of incompetence by progressivists, and hagiography was blasphemy to the rationalist piety of the day. But if legends do attach themselves to the lives of saints, we should not be surprised. It is a way of acknowledging that saints are more than just heroes. For the most part, notables are chronicled instead of hymned. I am unaware of any description of congressmen, however remarkably honest, flying through the air on their own; even the most eloquent university presidents have not been alleged to carry their heads through the streets. The greatest heroes are honored for having done what they did, and not for doing more. But saints are sometimes said to have done more than they did, and this is because they were more than they were. Saint Paul said, and not as a syllogism, "It is no longer I who live, but Christ who lives in me" (Gal 3:20).

Heroes are better than we are; saints are better than themselves. That is, saints become the ultimate pragmatists by making themselves totally available to God's original design for men. The hero imposes his will on nature as an act; the saint imposes God's will on nature as a state. In the case of the hero, heroism is a deed; it is a way of being for the saint. "We have a treasure, then, in our keeping, but its shell is of perishable earthenware; it must be God, and not anything in ourselves, that gives it its power" (2 Cor 4:7).

There is nothing wrong in enjoying legends for their own sake, but the facts about the saints are more wonderful than any fable could be. Saint Dorothy's apples, Saint George's dragon, Saint Nicholas' bags of gold are charming so long as they only charm. But they are something like the tinting of old black-and-white motion pictures by a new computer process: when a producer saw one of his old films colored that way, he said it was like pouring syrup on roast beef. To make Saint Thérèse of Lisieux prettier than she was would diminish her great beauty; to parade Saint Maximilian Kolbe as stronger than he was would mock his courage. You might say that Saint Jean Vianney would become less brilliant than he was by any story that made him brighter than he was. It is good to remember that images of the saints should be severe and serious things, tokens of hard reality. And medals of the saints are not like the charms worn by people who do not know about the saints; holy medals ward off charm.

The Nature of True Devotion

The truth of the saints is this: the human intellect and will become more human by becoming more divine. The ancient Fathers used bold language to say it in mystical prose; but they balanced their words as skilled acrobats, and they did not mean that men become gods, as clumsy pantheists have thought. Divinity cannot be some kind of vapor leaking into creation. Humans do not become godlike, though the grace of holiness can make them a place for God. There is no contradiction, and nothing less than a great affirmation, in saying two things at once: that saints become more human by becoming more divine and that saints become truly holy by becoming human. This is a mystery which modern people misunderstood to their tragic loss. Vianney confided an old secret to his arrogant new world: "All the saints are not saints in the same way;

there are some saints who would not have been able to live with other saints . . . all do not take the same path. Nonetheless, all arrive at the same place."

In depicting the saints, there are bad and good portraits. It may be that Vianney scorned his portraitists, not because they drew bad likenesses, which they usually did, but because they liked him. Hagiography may flatter saints but, when it does, it insults them; an affectionate picture of a man who is detached from the world can make him seem disconnected. In true devotion, though, to like a subject can give a good likeness. Strachey's word portraits of his eminent Victorians were no truer for being written with venom. In the case of the saints, you either have to attach yourself to their detachment, and let sympathy become empathy, or you have to reject it until scepticism becomes satire. But either is more apt to give some sense of a soul than the clinical indifference which claims to be objective. No one can remain indifferent to an object and get an impression of it.

The one pertinent consideration is the validity of the impression. Though it should not be shaped by less than history, it may take its form from a calculus behind history; it may be under the influence of a tale more delicate and shining than the most fabulous enchantment; it may have met the truth of myth and the object of legend. The saints impress by possessing their own heart's desire within themselves. If the prophets have prefigured a truth to come, the saints have postfigured a truth that came and stayed. When the wise have lived to foretell the way of God with man, the lives of the saints are its very telling. Here is how the saints make such an impression, and no unbeliever has dared completely to deny it. The atheist denies God, but he ignores the saints; he would not do that had he not been influenced by a need to ignore them. The need assumes a paradoxical and even compulsive quality, like the nihilist insisting it is true that there is no truth and like the atheist believing that there is nothing to believe. But the saints continue to live visible lives. As the sacraments are outward and visible signs of an inward and spiritual grace, the saints are living sacraments; they are sacraments of the sacraments. And no story about them, no display of their souls' architecture, can be so grand and schematic as living their story with them. The voice of Ars said it: "At the Holy Altar I had the most singular consolations. I was looking at the Good God."

Both Feet on the Ground

Saint Jean Vianney grew up in the France of the Enlightenment. He is most usually known as the Curé d'Ars. Curé means pastor, or one who cares for or cures, and that is what he spent most of his life doing in his obscure parish near Lyons. There is a scene that comes to mind, the one that has been painted dozens of times and bronzed as a statue: the young priest arriving at Ars. He is telling a boy who has led the way that now he will show him the way to heaven. He may not have pointed his finger to the sky as the statue shows, though the gesture is characteristic, and his silhouette true to form. Language like that does not come easily to facile lips, and a grand wisdom lies in considering why so unprepossessing a man used it. The boy, in any case, lived long enough to believe that the Curé had kept his promise.

I am not saying Vianney entered heaven by pointing to it;

he got to heaven by keeping both feet on the ground. This is the sane balance of the saints, the wisdom of the serpent affixed to the innocence of the dove; without it, wisdom becomes sophistry, and innocence is bleached by naïveté. But Vianney did often point to heaven, and it is not too fanciful to say that his finger rubbed against its gates. It has to be that way, for if heaven is out of reach it is also out of truth. The most pragmatic people have shown that is not so, and even Christ, who came from farthest away, said that his home is within people. This can only mean that the road to heaven is along the route to souls, and that to lose a soul is also to lose everything besides a soul. Vianney is a witness; "Paradise is in the heart of the perfect, who are truly united to our Lord; hell in that of the impious; purgatory in the souls who are not dead to themselves."

Nothing to Attract Attention

To begin, what did he look like? It is not a superficial question, provided we ask it superficially. If we ask it as though it were the most revealing thing, then looks will deceive. But what he looked like may lead to what he looked at. Pope Pius XI spoke of his "long white hair which was to him a shining crown", by which he meant that something reflected on him so comfortably that the reflection became a radiance. With the humility of certain stout men, John XXIII remarked the "thin face hollowed with fasting"; had they been weighed together, the Pope and the Curé might have averaged out to a normal weight. But in the scale of things normality is as rare as sanctity. Vianney's contemporary, the Abbé Monnin, was not beneath Olympian rhetoric but the most extravagant feature in his description of the Saint was the very lack of anything extravagant to say; he was "pallid and angular, his body frail, his height below average, his walk heavy, his manner timid and awkward, his whole appearance rather common and lacking distinction". Apart from his ascetical air and piercing eyes, "there was nothing about him to attract attention". To the disappointment of the sensualist, he was not superhuman, and no arid amount of intellectual snobbery could find anything subhuman. He was human after all. And that is the first quality of the saints: they are human after all. After all temptation to fly with false gods, after all distraction from a promised destiny, after all moral detours have stopped at dead ends, after all substitutes for belief have carved towering superstitions, after all denial that a human is other than an animal or a quirk of evolution, after all that, the saints still are human. They are humans after all, and they are the only real humans after all that. Catholicism has held the principle through every transitory analysis: normality and sanctity are the same. Saintly normality is conspicuous in the glare of sin. There was nothing frightening about the Curé: he was singular in his normality, even abnormally normal to the eyes of disordered personalities. His walk was heavy, but it was the only walk in a crippled age; and this was a mystery to rationalists who thought fallen man was graceful. Vianney's one eccentricity was to have latched onto God in a world unhinged.

The remains of his body lie in a glass case over an altar at Ars, the face waxed, the hands exposed and shriveled. Anglo-Saxons find this custom of displaying the saints odd, and even offensive. It is a crystal-clear exposition of death, and more cerebral people prefer to keep the most graphic facts of life opaque; they do not want to think of death as a fact of life. The graphic display of a corpse is the one kind of exhibitionism still generally considered degrading. But what seems morbid to the mundane conscience is vital to the transcendent conscience. One gets muddled trying to combine the two the wrong way: sacramentalism is a right kind of transcendent earthiness, but materialism issues in a vapidity. The embalmed relics of Lenin and Mao are shadowy and grotesque parodies of the saintly cults. The totalitarian and the saint both recumbent should attack any fair sense of equipoise. If the Curé and the cruel sleep the same sleep in their glass coffins, it must mean their waking lives were indifferent options; and so, then, would dying be an indifferent matter. Vianney's steady footfall would not have seemed so heavy had he believed that. Few really do believe it, in spite of their protestations. And this accounts for the remarkable fact, so remarkable that it is paid the compliment of being taken for granted: when it comes time to die, most people would rather not.

A Man with a Face

The Saint was born to peasant farmers, had difficulty getting through seminary, worked in one parish forty-one years, behaved in such a manner that crowds thought him holy, and having lived through various social upheavals, died in 1859. There are books to supply the details, and one cannot hope to match François Trochu's definitive work. When Bernard Nodet dedicated his own anthology of the Saint, he called Trochu "for more than thirty years the mind of Ars". I want to attend to a subject that is something of a valediction to the times:

how a saint, and specifically a saint who in a rebellious and antireligious culture "covered the whole of France with incomparable glory", might have significance for our own age, which has moved beyond moral rebellion to moral inertia.

The appeal of the time was to liberty, equality, and fraternity; its clamor and manifestations were vicious enough, but they have become worse now. What once waved on placards and was the fire of hearts now drifts over sullen populations as an incantation of isolation, indifference and conformity. The old revolutionary appeal was to a new human order of the ages, headier than any bucolic motto of Virgil, laying down a flag for the new anthropological confidence to trample over on the way to a blinding horizon. Adventurism that powerful began with errancy as progress and drifted into errancy as error. The modern superman was as fictional as the Catholic saint is factual. But beginning with the dazzling enticements of the Enlightenment, and excited by romanticism, the quest of the superman took on the aura of reality and gradually became the passion of sham science in twisted chambers. The "applied biology" schemes of Rudolf Hess and Margaret Sanger, his suburbanized counterpart, are only examples among the worst later mockeries of authentic human perfection.

Saints do not surrender to dissolute social pathology. Sanctity itself is the acute contradiction of sham, and its very opposition makes modern queasiness with spiritual perfection positively cowardly. The modernist prejudice does take flight from virtue in the weakest of ways, by avoiding the saints. A psychologically driven, biographically obsessed culture exposes its intellectual pretentiousness by its refusal to acknowledge the psychological and historical phenomenon of sanctity. Vianney's Age of Reason was the archetypal assertion of the mistake, and Vianney was one who proved it wrong.

We are speaking of a real man with a real face. The insistence of the preacher persists in his case: for "our hands have handled" him. Thousands saw him and spoke with him and watched what he did. I say it again; this was a real man with a real face. He told a fluttery visitor: "The Queen of Sheba expected too little, but you, Madame, expected too much." Some overestimate what is revealed; others underestimate what is concealed. Saints can look like anyone else. Perfection lies in symmetry and not in caricature. Saul was "a head and shoulders taller than any of his fellow-countrymen"; he would have been fellow to no one had he been ten heads taller. Vianney was monumentally unspectacular that way. But he was not alone in this; freethinkers shrank from the long Jesuitical shadow of Saint Ignatius, who was a little under five feet two inches tall, about the height of Vianney. An ordinary appearance holds the most ponderous secrets; a hard face is the easiest to decipher and a soft face is the hardest to like, but the ordinary face is the confidential profile of all antecedents and homelands. Lincoln was told a beard would give him more character; Warren G. Harding had a nobler head. Eliot wrote better than Sitwell, but he looked like the bank clerk he was, while she looked like the cathedral she was not. And that is why great religious art is of necessity allegorical; a plaster statue cannot capture so free a thing as the freedom of a saint, and the best way icons represent the limitless dimensions of grace is by being totally flat. In the last analysis, only a most delicate grace may discern the barrier between banality and perfection. Banality in itself can be the very depth of imperfection: the more vindictive Henry VIII became, the more he resembled soft ice cream. A man who met both said Lenin

describing his massacres looked mild, while Gladstone was
positively fierce when served sherry in the wrong glass. Part
of the dreadfulness in real tyrants is the way they make wickedness seem as ordinary as the saints make goodness. It is worse
than legalizing a crime; it is more like legalizing everything.
The mind must be acute beyond normal perception to detect
in the pedestrian Saint of Ars a man walking the highest road.

Holiness is not godlike, and so they say some men have
entertained angels unaware. The nature of God requires something other than godlikeness of his creatures. God does not
look like himself; as perfect Being, he is himself and is thus an
analogous world's single incapacity for simile. He is the I AM
and not the I AM LIKE. His own revelation conceals him;
humans can fancy to see him in sunsets and stars, but when he
reveals himself in human form humans do not recognize him.
They become like Matthew Arnold, who wanted to replace
theology with poetry and lost the point of both. Listeners
arrayed on the Palestinian hills said no man ever spoke as Jesus
spoke; none suggested no man ever looked as he looked. In
the garden he was mistaken for a gardener, and on the Emmaus
road he was treated as any other man passing by. The deepest
mystery for man is not God as a perfect circle, or God as a
golden triangle, but God with a human face. The Shroud of
Turin, for instance, shows a scratched and swollen face, which
is not what one expects of perfection. But that again is the
clue; perfection cannot be like anything, because its perfection overwhelms analogy. As a saint, Vianney was not godlike:
he was godly. To be godlike would mean that he lacked the
capacity for God. The lesson was learned in Eden a hard way
and is repeated in each human life. "Ye shall be like gods" can
only mean ye shall not be gods. The dark vow dragged our

ancestors onto a creaking stage where the castles and countries were painted canvas and cardboard compared to God's lost acre.

"The saints are like so many mirrors in which Christ contemplates himself." The Curé's language was Pauline; the saints are able " . . . to catch the glory of the Lord as in a mirror, with faces unveiled, and we have become transfigured into the same likeness, borrowing glory from that glory, as the Spirit of the Lord enables us" (2 Cor 3:18). When Vianney's face looked incandescent in later years, the light still was from within a common-looking face; the combination, in the words of one witness "was enough to turn crowds to salutary thoughts". Churchill called himself a worm, but a glow-worm. That has to be truer of the saints, who have moved from mortal glory into the expanse of holy freedom itself. The saints not only shine; they can shine the light. The glory of God is man fully realized, said Saint Irenaeus. The glory of God is pure light, the source of each filtered ray, "white as snow" (Mt 17:2; Mk 9:2) and "whiter than snow" (Ps 51:7). It is a way of saying that perfection cannot properly be psychoanalyzed. That has been tried countless times with flagrant failure. "Psychobiography" does not work with Christ. The psychologist Binet-Sanglé attributed his long nights of prayer to insomnia, his long Galilean walks to dromomania, and his long desert fasts to sitophobia. Yet there was nothing manic about his mania, and, from the evidence of the Passion, he was phobic only about fear. A scientist who will not be scientific about limited evidence may have to pretend he is scientific about fantasy. Then we would have a pseudoscience like Dr. Soury's depiction of Christ at the age of twelve confounding the doctors in the temple as the delirious victim of encephalitis. The one objective analysis of the Perfect Man is that he had a "messiah complex". But, without patronizing the more earnest efforts of men to discern the Son of Man, a messiah is entitled to one.

The psychological eye may be little more successful when it glances at the saints of Christ. Analogies of complexes and conditions will be inadequate conventions for them. There are no two saints alike; the diversity of holiness is a riot of color emanating from the pure light of grace which "enlightens every soul born into the world" (Jn 1:9) Of the Resurrection, John Donne wrote: "He was all gold when he lay down, but rose/ All tincture...." Originating in Christ, the ordinariness of the saints is a highly colorful commonplaceness making the saint as intensely individual as the sinner is a conformist. All grace is original, while all sin is derivative, and even original sin is a corruption of original good.

The Revolution through which Vianney lived was the touchstone of modern psychological conflict, spinning the land like a carousel of bleeding horses and crying clowns. In the light of the Dark Ages, which gave birth to many bright brains, and of the Age of Reason, which covered the pavement with many dead brains, each time the Catholic Church seemed to be having a breakdown, it was having a breakthrough. As they appear with human faces and take stands in such times, the saints will be misread in many ways. But so long as Pure Light animates them, we can say that we have seen them. "In his apostles", said the Curé, "[Christ] gazes upon his zeal and his love for the salvation of souls; in the martyrs he gazes upon his patience, his sufferings and his grievous death; in the hermits he sees his obscure and hidden life; in the virgins he admires his stainless purity, and in all the saints his limitless love; so that in admiring the virtues of the saints, we are only admiring the virtues of Jesus Christ."

Nonchalant Supernaturalness

If Christ had been a myth, his appearance would have been described in detail; the New Testament is so historically accurate that it does not bother to do that. It would be too fantastic to pretend this was an oversight. I think it was more in the order of intimacy. Most of the people who photograph the Eiffel Tower are not Parisians. In an extreme circumstance I might join a war to protect the Statue of Liberty but, being a New Yorker, it would not occur to me to visit it. Intimacy is hardly intimate if it does not breed a certain casualness. The saints are that way about everything. The paradox, the violence they work on absentminded logic, is in the way they are beyond nature while not being above it. Grace and not irony accomplishes this; and by grace I mean intimacy with the Creator of nature. So supernaturalness is the remedy for that self-consciousness which is the illusion of the atheist. It is the sublime nonchalance by which the soul learns to feast with God instead of taking his picture.

One lesson of Ars is not to think "being natural" is all there is to nature. The saints know a truth that sin keeps secret: the human spirit is robbed of its natural dignity when it is content to be only natural. Evil claims to be natural, and this is the heart of its deceit. Sin rarely declares itself as sin, and the sinner tends to claim some high motive and some pink-and-white complexion for each decay. Each enslavement to sin calls itself a new form of liberation as it tightens its chains. Rare is the tyrant who does not cloak his extravagant selfishness in the titles of altruism and affected goodwill. Pope Pius XII addressed this in *Humani generis:* "Now the human intellect, in gaining the knowledge of such truths, is hampered both by the activity of the senses and the imagination, and by evil passions arising from original sin. Hence men easily persuade themselves in such matters that what they do not want to believe is false or at least doubtful." Saints live the economy of intellect more realistically and so are more at home with nature than naturalists claim to be. It is the gift which comes from being as supernatural as natural. Consequently the naturalist goes through life like a perpetual tourist, the saint like a casual native ready any moment to go somewhere else.

The aphorism says that a man wrapped in himself makes a small package; by addendum, a man unwrapped makes the largest of all packages. A soul undone by humility, contemptuous of egoism's grasp, becomes the world's embrace. I mean that the saint fulfills the potential of human nature: cognition and free will. A simple man such as Vianney doing the great things he did is a case of grace acting upon nature through humility. Aristotle said that if the art of shipbuilding were in the wood, we would have ships by nature. Human design and craft unlock nature's potential; inspired humility unlocks nature itself. The shy but serious question of whether God has a plan in mind when he animates nature, a question so high that it can freeze cool logic, which knows that things are but not why they are, will be answered by Saint Jean Vianney in his portion of the universe or it will be answered by no one anywhere.

Things Difficult to Believe

Vianney did things thought to be impossible, and he did them
with an innocent blatancy. Some may be hard for us to
believe if we are not scientific enough to recognize the limits
of science. Henry IV called James I the wisest fool in Europe
for knowing what he did not know; it is a talent helpful in
understanding the Curé d'Ars. Had he lived a thousand years
ago he would unquestionably be classed with old artful legends.
But that does something of an injustice to the ancients who
usually knew when their legends were legendary. The wild
exploits of their gods were confected as tributes to them, and
those who heard them exquisitely said or sung had a benign
tongue in cheek. Similarly, the "little flowers" of the old saints
were artificial flowers, and deliberately artificial because they
were first crafted by the contemporaries of the saints who had
seen the real flowers. Wax flowers are not meant to put florists
out of business, and they do not mean that gardens are mirages.
When a thing imitates, it publicizes more what is being imitated.
But while seeing is not altogether believing, one would have
believed nothing about Vianney if nothing had been seen. He
was seen performing miracles. Any gloss on them is not so
real or splendid as what he manifestly did. Sometimes it is
unctuously said that the real miracle of Ars was the faith of the
people; the same thing is said about Lourdes. But faith is a
faculty; it is not a miracle. Only miracles are miraculous and if
they do not happen then faith in them is not faith but illusion.

It may be that God made Vianney unusually prodigious
supernaturally to save the nineteenth century from the worst
consequence of its amnesia of heaven, its slipshod materialism.
Vianney's visions and night visitations, his conversations with

saints and angels, had more reliable witnesses than an honest judge and jury would need for a natural verdict. Materialists who were good enough to trust their own empiricism became his most ardent disciples once they discerned what was going on. The more annoying figures were the romanticizers who tested his humility, and the credulous who provoked his temper. The sceptics were far easier to deal with. The one obstacle between them and him was distance. When the credulous got near, they saw only what they wanted to see; when the sceptics approached they found what they had hoped not to see. And what puzzled the sceptics most was the signature of Providence known as a smile. An animal cannot smile as humans do, and no human has smiled wider than the great smile of Ars. In the epilogue of his first Gifford lecture on neuropsychology, Sir John Eccles wrote; "I believe that there is a Divine Providence operating over and above the materialist happenings of biological evolution . . . we must not dogmatically assert that biological evolution in its present form is the ultimate truth. Rather we should believe it is the main story and that in some mysterious way there is guidance in the evolutionary chain of contingency." The guiding mystery left its traces in the massive peace on the countenance of Vianney.

If in his commonplaceness he looked like any notable, curiously enough he could have been the twin of Voltaire. And drained of blood they would have passed for matched mannequins. The one photograph we have of Vianney was taken when he was dressed for burial, carried pale into the glare of the garden when he could no longer object to having his picture taken. Under the open summer sun the irony of him and the paramount rationalist was more apparent than ever. Neo-classical France had been dotted with busts of

Voltaire, who had let Houdon and a host of others grave his image as he wrote against idols. Voltaire sat for everything Vianney stood against, but that is beside the point. The point is that Vianney in death most resembled Voltaire in life because a final shadow had wiped away the smile that long had distinguished him from Voltaire's sneer.

When Vianney died, the spiritual vitality that had been his wonder was spread out, held against the light, and handled by investigators and prosecutors. It was examined according to what were then the 142 canons of the apostolic process by which the Catholic Church proves saints and disproves fakes. Pope Benedict XIV intricately ordered it in the eighteenth century; the process, though, was much older, the first ritual canonization being that of Bishop Ulrich of Augsburg by Pope John XV at a synod in the Lateran in 993. It worked swiftly for Vianney. Pope Pius IX did not wait the required ten years before opening the investigation in 1866. In 1872 he was given the title Venerable. In 1905, Pius X named him patron of parish priests in France; and on the Feast of All Saints in 1925, Pius XI publicly declared that he enjoys the Beatific Vision. He is a saint and universal patron of parish priests, intercessor before God for the Church on earth, and model for all who attend the call to holiness.

After the records are approved and sealed, any assertion of the historicity of Ars is still largely meaningless unless it helps to explain the purpose of what happened there. In the same sense that the miracles of Christ were signs pointing to what he was accomplishing in time for the reorientation of mankind toward the will of God, and were not displays for some lesser gain, so Vianney's signs were didactic. He called himself an old wizard and sometimes feigned idiocy to discourage sightseers who were tempted to believe in him when he only wanted them to believe him.

He wanted them to believe in something basic, the City of God, as believable as Paris or Ars or the hat on one's head. He made the Eternal City so tangible to rustics who had not seen a city that cosmopolitans came by carriage and train to learn such civility. Vianney would have been less than Catholic if he had spoken a language only for farmers or, for that matter, a language only for the landlords of farmers; but he spoke to them all in a tongue so direct that the way from anyplace to Ars became the way entire from Genesis to Revelation.

Whether there is more to Carlyle's dictum that man wags the tail of history, or to Tolstoy's that history wags the tail of man, man and history got a better grip on each other when the Curé d'Ars wagged the tail of the devil. The devil has located God and knows who he is, and he wants to keep that a secret from the children of God. The indiscretion of the saints is the way they shout the secret from the rafters of the world. They themselves are the secret, and they shout loudest when they are silent. The Church, by the authority given to Peter and his successors, calls Jean Vianney a saint because in him was the Christ of History, speaking broken French and flapping along in worn French shoes on the soiled edge of France's gilded age, but Christ all the same.

Chapter 2

MAN COME OF AGE

In the Time of Monumental Adolescence

The Saint of Ars was born in the village of Dardilly, in the same Lyons region of his future parish, on May 8, 1786. He was very young when the Revolution came, but precocious enough to know something was wrong. What he did not fully sense, his parents made sure to tell him; for the Revolution of the masses was, to such people who make up the masses, at first bewildering and then a thing horrible in its concept and dreadful in its approach. The new social order censured the Church in 1792 with the superciliousness of a committee censuring the sky; but to the general surprise of the people, the Church in France outwardly at least did seem to do what it was told. Less successful was the previous year's effort to exact oaths to the Civil Constitution of the Clergy. The word "civil" had calcified so that it came to mean the state instead of the people, and the civilized became statistics, and the statistics became victims.

This was one of the frequent fits of public temper that afflict the social reconstructionists and flood their brains with a dream half-waking and half-asleep, a stuffy kind of hallucination. As the Terror raged from September 1793 to July 1794, mobs more than men chanted a new hymn in the gory squares, a boast: the eternal childhood of the soul had come of age. Perhaps it had, but if it had, then we who look back on it

36

must now be living a gaudy senility. The other possibility is that the materialist spirit, waved like a bloody shirt in the revolutionary plazas of terrified France, was a form of ugly adolescence, a kind of food fight in the school hall that turned grotesque, with a world watching and humans flung against the stones. The adolescent does not understand that he is adolescent: the essence of his condition is to think that anyone younger or older is a kind of perimeter or commentary on his age, which he thinks is the one and only age. The length of the affliction varies. It was quite short when Alexander mounted his ivory saddle and Saint Joan buckled herself in the armor. Adolescence was brief then because life was brief, like Bede's famous sparrow flying through one window of the hall and right out the other. When life became longer in the industrial age, adolescence became even shorter because life became crueler: when six-year-olds were paid pennies to throw silk in factories and when ten-year-olds dragged coal through mines, then it did not exist at all. When the length of life is short, it is hard to mark the passage from growing up and being grown; when the regimen of life is hard, it is harder to draw a line between growing up and burning out. In the time of the French Revolution, life was short and hard. Dr. Johnson said the prospect of hanging concentrates the mind wonderfully. In the Revolution everyone concentrated. Though revolutions tend to be the briefest of undertakings, revolutionaries assume monumental airs and indulge the adolescent conceit of perpetuity. They do not know with the old people of every age the awful secret of rebellions. Quite simply, it is that the harsh second stage of most revolutions is a revolt against the revolutionaries because they have become revolting.

In the adolescent public mood of 1792, the blade sliced the

king with a crisp cruelty of which older and more arthritic moods are incapable. A year later the young muscles of new France flexed themselves against adult Austria, Prussia, Italy, England, and Sardinia. The gauntlet was tossed with the awkward defiance of the rampant teenager, and with the teenager's obligatory solemnity. With, then, the most unco-ordinated pomp, Man Come of Age in the Age of Reason took arms against any nation and any people that still believed in the Fatherhood of God. The first act of Man Come of Age was to idealize paganism, to make the cradle stories of culture into creeds, and to turn the pagan nursery into a kind of cathedral. The revolutionary reverted to the draperies and dialect of old Greece, reviving the forest and sky myths that men and women of an earlier age had outgrown. He did it furtively at first, as the pubescent youth does when he steals into the attic to play with relics of the boyhood he pretends has vanished. But he did it, and he declared when it was done that the old things were new things, and that the toys of an idler time were the gods of the great new frenzy.

Daubermesnil and le Pelletier, inventors of new anti-Christian cults, were only two who played the grown-up game. Committees were appointed to erect kinds of worship resembling a higher form of life as the intellectuals thought it must have been before Christianity had infantilized it. Readers might get a sense of the dream if they recall Gulliver in the stratospheric culture of the Houyhnhnms. It perdures in the hearts of various cultists who advertise their theories in airport lobbies and the like. But the deists who predominated in these movements attendant on the French Revolution were more sophisticated in their eclecticism; their ancient allusions were more informed, if still not very accurate. They had a readier familiarity with the old sages they envied. And it was a massive project to copy them. If their rationalism lacked common sense, it did not lack energy. The revival of things thought to be classical and precise meant more than Wedgwood pots, Doric porticoes, and girls with names like Chloe. It went so far as to streamline the unevenness of Christianity's sum, based as it is on the Trinity. The First Directory of the Revolution believed three to be a vulgar number, and this is the sort of creed that, by being a prejudice founded in nothing more substantial than the mind, cannot be overturned. Various nature-worship cults were devised to replace the Mass; they were imposed on the masses for their improvement and edification with a flagrant contempt for the common man, an elite contempt matching that of the most strident liturgical fanatic today. There was a pedantic boisterousness about it, which inadvertently would have made Jesus Christ the wrongest man who ever lived by depicting him as one of the wisest men who ever lived; Benoist-Lamothe, for instance, thought he was increasing Christian prestige by ranking Jesus with Plato. The lurid cross and empty tomb belonged on a heap with the crude refuse of Bacchus and the exhausted wineskins of Olympus. Even the Sabbath week was changed to an even decade of days; the number ten was more sensible to wild prejudice than the number seven. This seems to have been the most unpersuasive of the new assumptions: the decadist might be more reasonable than the sabbatarian, but the decadist who happens to be a worker does not get to relax as much. And rest was the one Commandment kept holy by the most licentious.

In later years, Vianney's obsession with strict keeping of the Sunday observance, one issue that would bring him close

to open blows with his parishioners, was informed by these
experiences. Reason running wild is amusing to look at from
a distance; it is not so amusing when you are running with it.
It seems perfectly reasonable. The simpler spectators, untutored in the new philosophy, had the advantage of detachment:
at first they gaped and then openly laughed at the bizarre
ceremonials. Worship popularized by self-conscious populists
is never widely popular. If Robespierre's "Oration on the
Supreme Being" brought yawns in 1794, the locals must have
made choicer remarks when the "Panthéonistes" donned styl-
ized togas to recite poetry to an oak tree. Whether or not this
sort of thing prefigures some modern conventions is not mine
to say, but the scene was repeated in the early days of Bolshe-
vism when dynamos were publicly worshipped. This temptation to be silly about solemnities and solemn about silliness is
a minor mockery the tempter rarely fails to toss in the way of
individuals with more education than sense.

The movement toward new and false gods was partially
caused by the paucity of recent saints. France in the last
generations before the Revolution had hardly been a verdant
grove of mystical vision. In some ways the mental furnishing
of the Church had been as elegantly angular as a Louis Seize
chair. Said Chateaubriand, "priests in their pulpits avoided
naming Jesus Christ and talked instead of the Legislator of
Christians". The revolutionaries thought they were bringing
in a newer and more reliable stability after the Church had
succumbed to a confusing revulsion within itself. The anticlerical elite only made an anthem of the rationalism that had
already been whispered by clerics. If the priests of the times
had not worshipped isosceles triangles, neither had they said
much about the Holy Trinity; if they knew Christ was more

than Plato, they had not well explained why. But they had greased the slide from theism through deism to the shriveled surrender of the will called atheism.

Neglect of doctrine had become a means of ascending the bureaucratic pole of peer respectability. Hilaire Belloc has remarked in his book on the French Revolution that the Church was "not concerned to defend itself but only its method of existence". And consequently, a kind of gentleman's agreement was established whereby the Church's ministers were honored by the court and the encyclopedists, or by the media and the intelligentsia, as we might say, so long as they did not insist too hard on matters of faith and morals. The pattern is no less blatant today, for but one example, in the temptation of Catholic universities to dilute their religious identity for the sake of government subsidies. And because the hierarchy over the years of social absorption had come to be drawn from that part of society that held the prevailing rationalist views, it was hard for them to detect any temporizing or betrayal in their conformity. As Belloc writes in his limpid way:

> It did not shock the hierarchy that one of its Apostolic members should be a witty atheist; that another should go hunting upon Corpus Christi, nearly upset the Blessed Sacrament in his gallop, and forget what day it was when the accident occurred. The bishops found nothing remarkable in seeing a large proportion of their body to be loose livers. . . . Unquestioned also by the bishops were the poverty, the neglect, and the uninstruction of the parish clergy; nay . . . the abandonment of religion by all but a very few of the French millions . . . was a thing simply taken for granted.

Taking all that in, I cannot think Belloc does less than overstate the case in saying the Revolution's quarrel with the Church was against this negligent form of the Church and not against the Christian life genuinely lived. It is true that there is nothing in Catholicism that is hostile to democratic life and republican order; it is even truer that the Catholic systematics of natural law, human dignity, and social order are the most amiable constituents of solid democratic polity. But to make this point, Belloc may have exaggerated the moral neutrality of republican theory in the Enlightenment. He does say that only the course of years will show whether or not this particular theory and Catholicism were irreconcilable tangents. But we may say that the years since he wrote are enough to show how they were indeed irreconcilable, and that while democracy and Christianity are compatible, the materialist underpinnings of the eighteenth-century republicanism sowed the seeds of modern secular humanism with its web of antisocial enormities. The heaps of corpses in the twentieth century are the consequence of the rationalists' false confidence. It is too much not to see the philosophical dimensions of the Revolution's anticlericalism. For one thing, its friends among the clergy were not, for the most part, the priests of high moral and dogmatic principles but rather the men who forfeited those principles. And it was instead as it had been in England when the only bishop among the bishops who fought against the Reformation was the only saint among the bishops. The call to liberty, equality, and fraternity was a call to things decidedly other than spiritual freedom, redemption, and communion: it was a predatory idealism that exploited a philosophical quarrel with Catholicism itself, a contention deeper than shallows of political and social complaint. Sentiments behind the revolutionary slogans longed for something more disquieting than a new liberty for man; the object of the Revolution was a new man, and if a precise statement of what that meant came to be understood only gradually, it was already in the minds of the ideologues at the desks of the revolutionary tribunals and in the crasser evidences of the pseudoreligious cults.

The philosophical spirit of the Revolution will not be found in indignation at the failure of the Church to be the Church any more than it was inspired by disgust at the failure of Versailles to be Versailles. The Revolution sought to undo any possibility of the Church being the Church Catholic. Its assault on the creeds of Catholicism became intrinsic to the climate of Revolution at whatever moment talented and convincing minds looked at the sky and claimed to see an Architect where once was lifted up a Father. In that miasmal instant they became builders, builders of a new age for a new man, they said; and when they were done, the building was an orphanage, and Man Come of Age was an orphan.

Yet if the Court of Heaven was obscured long before 1789, the sense of the courtliness of heaven lingered. Even Voltaire watching a procession tipped his hat to the Blessed Sacrament; he said it was what one gentleman does to another. There was, I think, more to the etiquette than that: it is said that he declined the same Sacrament on his deathbed only because he would not contaminate God's blood with his own. So something of the old religion remained, a kind of instinctive acquiescence, bereft of the intelligent systematic of Catholic formulations but imbued in the culture even when it was excised from the cult. Call it religiosity rather than religion, a power that touches rather than binds; yet it was naïve of the

Revolution to assault a mood whose very tenuousness is the ground of its tenacity.

Even independent personalities, who dislike being told by their priests what to do, dislike others telling their priests what to do. They dislike even more the ransacking of their churches; those who do the least to embellish them seem to dislike that the most. And the most impetuous rebels were the first to feel the cracks opening under their own rebellion as they watched the mock enthronement of a gaudy woman on the altar of the Cathedral of Our Lady. Mobs are predictable: they are mobs precisely because they have no will of their own. One can predict of mobs when they will back off, at least for a moment, like crests of waves breaking on the shore. They are not following a command; they obey a silent law which on a grander scale becomes the ageless law of the tides. When resistance to the Revolution's attacks on the Church threatened the Revolution itself, the state decided, as it often has before and since, that if the Faith cannot be crushed it should be appropriated, emptied, and left on newly combed sand as a decorative shell, a nautilus many-chambered but dry, which will be anything but the Roman Church.

It could not happen so long as there was a Pope. The committeemen who made themselves the voice of the silent decided that the nation should do without him, as the Tudors had claimed centuries before, and as the "sacristan of Europe", Joseph of Austria, threatened with little effect on his own terms. They dusted off the Gallican Articles, which national-ist theologians had used in the seventeenth century for lesser claims against the Holy See, and a puppet Gallican church independent of Rome was wished into some vague semblance of life. Its chief bishop was a pawn named Grégoire whose political enthusiasms are evident in David's painting of the Tennis Court Oath; his religious ambience has long been an unattractive subject of morality plays, the peculiar pastoral spirit that lays down the sheep for the life of the shepherd. Macaulay's lines on Cranmer serve this Gallican:

> Saintly in his professions, unscrupulous in his dealings, zealous for nothing, bold in speculation, a coward and a time-server in action, a placable enemy and a lukewarm friend, he was in every way qualified to arrange the terms of the coalition between the religious and the worldly enemies of the Papacy.

Grégoire was the cleric who would not be the priest: to him it was no apostasy but a solution. But it was a solution Solzhenitsyn pondered in his Lenten letter to a Soviet bishop:

> Why are communications which come down to us from the highest level of the Church so conventionally serene? Why are all church documents so benignly placid, as if published among the most Christian of people? While one serene epistle follows another, might not the very need to write them vanish in some stormy year: there will be no one to address them to, no flock will remain outside the Patriarchate's Chancellery.

The Start of the Terrors

When Jean Vianney was growing up, the secret of the Church was hid in houses; it had been tossed out of the churches. Of course the tumult was not unprecedented. In the fourth century Saint Basil the Great described the scene as desultory:

> The laws of the Church are in confusion, we have as bishops
> men who have no fear of God rushing to higher posts and
> exalted offices.... The result is that the worse a man
> blasphemes, the fitter people think he is to become a bishop.
> There is no precise knowledge of canons, there is complete
> immunity in sinning; for when men have been placed in
> office by the favour of men they are obliged to continue
> returning favours by indulging the offenders.

In the same century Saint Lucian of Antioch, chained to the
floor of his prison cell, used his own chest as an altar to
consecrate the Body and Blood of Christ; and in the twentieth century priests in Petrograd were crucified on the doors
of their churches. Vianney's own age was but one in the
course of afflictions visited on the Body of Christ. The massacres of the Carmelites, the decimation of the vicars, were
prelude to the twentieth century, which has seen from Mexico
to Spain to China more Christian martyrs than all past centuries combined. In the Spanish Civil War more than six thousand priests, monks, and nuns were slain as Western intellectuals
applauded. But the French Revolution was the laboratory for
the later horrors: it was the first time such oppression sprang
from calculation more than from passion, from a theory more
than from the absence of thought. The heat of the Revolution's
horror was its deliberate precision: wild mobs were directed
by willful committees, and the most rapacious of these was
the Committee of Public Safety. Executions were not orgies
of abandon; they were promoted as a population reform. A
machine was invented to do the job cleanly, and its inventor
went to it himself. Long before the assembly line, rationalism
had invented the disassembly line. The rationalist let loose
behind his desk is as ambidextrous as the barbarian let loose

on his horse, shooting and riding at the same time. As the government was methodically slaughtering some fifteen thousand philosophers, aristocrats, and workers, it was establishing a National Library, a National Art Museum, and a Polytechnic Institute. I have come across a textbook that speaks of the Terror in this cool diction: "Terrible as were these excesses . . . in affairs of peace the Convention wrought greatly. It gave France the metric system of weights and measures."

Vianney learned about the priesthood in that age of mad mathematics. He could never afterward think of the priesthood as an escape from practical realities; he certainly could not think of it as but another profession. He saw abuses crying for reform, but he did not nail his complaints against church doors; he was more prone to nail himself. It happened in a slow way, and in an invisible way, but the occult crucifixion of his life worked an unspeakable resurrection in the courage of his people: "Grant me the conversion of my parish; I consent to suffer all you wish the whole of my life." As a youth in horrible times, he had once asked the definition of a priest; he was told a priest is a man who would die so that he could be one.

The old Curé of Dardilly, Monsieur Rey, a doctor of the Sorbonne, had a mind so finely honed by intimidating influences that he could see three sides to a coin. He was one of the clerical crowd that justified the Civil Constitution of the Clergy; he did sign it, but he also was strong enough to recant what he had done and took his place with the proscribed priests. Vianney would learn to say after these times had passed: "When one wants to destroy religion, one begins by attacking the priests." Monsieur Rey paid the public price for walking the way of Peter rather than that of Iscariot: he was

removed by the civil bullies and replaced by a priest of the
new dispensation, a clerical policeman of free thought assigned
to catch anyone who refused to think freely his way. The new
man was careful to vest himself in the garments of the old
religion, though he did not bother to pray as he put them on
or to give thanks as he took them off. He followed the
familiar rites, but put no heart in them; he mentioned God
when the rubrics indicated, but he did not speak about him.
He did speak much about civil responsibility, peace and justice,
and the like. The man who leaves morality aside hides his
nakedness in the mantle of moralism. He is not content to love
his enemies: he hugs them to death.

The Saint's sister Catherine, then twelve, was in her innocence among the first to detect that the new priest was one of
the humanists who in the name of humanity had set up
guillotines for humans. When the Curé began to call his
parishioners citizens instead of sons and daughters, the vil-
lagers began to avoid him; soon the local church was empty.
But the Church perdured, for the Church is what is left when
the building goes. The people gave quarter in their houses to
the priests loyal to Peter beyond the mountains.

They had a halting idea of the ancient martyrs of Lyons
who had been drowned in the Rhône, but now the faded
etchings of those days came to life. The barns took the place
of the old catacombs, as splendidly defiant of the new caesar
as the church of Saint Martin d'Ainay in Lyons, whose columns were taken from the Roman temple it surmounted. For
the children it became something of a game in the best sense,
for it was enthralling and terrible at once. Any game is best
when it is more of a contest than a scheme, and this game of
being the Church was true to the great contest of the Church's

Founder's forty days in the wilderness. To shelter a priest was to risk your life, and this gave a certain thrill to the timbre of the secret passwords. When a priest in secular disguise came in the door, he went into a dark corner and emerged rid of camouflage, splendid in wrinkled vestments at a broken board for his altar; there were those who wept at so great a sight, and among them the eyes of a boy of six were wide as saucers.

Childhood

The boy they called the "fat one" tramped through the fields and hollows of Chêne-Rond and Chante-Merle, happy and indulged by his family as their meager circumstances could afford. The home was the one normal factor in his environment, and he carried its contentment in him, cultivating a wry humor with jokes and simple stories that would last his life. He held impromptu rallies under the eglantines and aspens, other children sitting around as he held forth with a primitive catechism of his own. He was old inside, repeating as best he could the old things he had heard at home. While the sheep grazed, the children knit. They had been taught not to waste time. And as they knit, the guillotine banged a short trip away in a plaza at the foot of a hill and street called the Red Cross and to be known as the Place of the Terrors. Nearly two thousand workers were executed there in the name of the proletariat. In Dickens' *Tale of Two Cities* Madame Defarge knit, too. There was a nervous knitting all over in those days. Sometime it would unwind with consequences untold, but the children only knit things to wear and watched the sheep as they were told to do, without a shred of self-consciousness.

The boy Vianney had one prize possession, a small statue of the Virgin; grown men were being sent to the galleys for keeping statues like it. The Lady was part of the children's game. When the boy got tired on his long hikes, he would toss the statue ahead and run after it. Sometimes he organized processions. The Revolution had begun with a procession of Louis XVI leading the Estates General behind the Blessed Sacrament; the land was full of processions. Vianney and his companions followed along the rivulet of the Planches singing off-key the songs that no longer rang in the bare Gothic abbeys.

All the while the guillotine of Lyons kept banging down under the cold direction of Joseph Fouché, the apostate Oratorian priest whose cruelty amazed even Robespierre. Priests have a power not their own, and priests who abandon the priesthood carry with them a volatile power they cannot shed. A consecrated soul cannot be unconsecrated but only desecrated by pride and the guilt of pride. And when a desecrated priest ceases to offer worthy sacrifice, he may start to require sacrifice; for as the priestly face turns from the Messiah it meets Moloch. As a priest, Fouché had led many processions behind the Blessed Sacrament; now he led his processions into the Place of the Terrors. But he still was a priest, and the fact is awful and beyond human judgment; when a priest ceases to intercede at his altar between earth and heaven, an angel made miserable by its fall from heaven would persuade the priest to intercede between earth and hell. Fouché slaughtered 130 priests.

The children had been born among rocks; there was nothing cloying about them, nothing soft or sentimental in their scenarios. Sentimentalism may become an emotion of those who write about shepherds, especially shepherd children, without having known any. Nor were the children working out a ritual catechism, for there was little routine in their world or their own lives then. The climate had turned chill in an unfamiliar way. No longer was the air filled with disputations about eternal problems and prayers to be learned; the new climate was more of a vacuum, empty of such thought. And the atmosphere was damp even in the sun; it could not cultivate enthusiasm easily. The sound of bells was gone, no whiff of incense, no chanted versicles from the old antiphonals. The religion of the children was not culturally conditioned in that culture: priests had become scarcer and for three years or so they had not even seen a Mass. They just believed in God the way they believed in the Atlantic Ocean.

Sixty years afterward one of the girls related having had a crush on the boy Vianney, and with commensurate seriousness, the boy had replied that this could never be. Tales are told of many saints like that, as precocious prophecies and so forth. Popes are said to have been told by some bystander or colleague in seminary that they would someday be Pope; few are the seminarians who have not been vouchsafed such premonitions, if only by their mothers. Asides and conventions seem more important later on. But they are quite useless, and they can be worse. Stories of child saints, for the best of motives, can humiliate the saints, like having a parent show your baby pictures to your fiancée. Some of the descriptions of the early years of Saint Vincent Palotti, for instance, playing with rosaries and catechizing his mother and father, make one wince and almost dislike that good man from the start. It has been done to Christ himself. The subapostolic writers were determined to make any fiction about the boy Jesus scintillating, if not true: the Holy Child skips through their apocryphal scenery making clay pigeons fly and striking bullies dead. They are little more edifying than Neapolitan stories of infant prodigies reciting the Nicene Creed as they drowned in baptismal fonts, inventions that are just the exuberant crimes of zealots who need to fill the space between a man's Bethlehem and his Cana. But more transfixing than any of these curiosities is the redolent asperity with which the authentic Gospel describes the spare elegance and artless poise of the Boy of Twelve in the temple. No childhood of greatness shines with such reticence. It is all of a hush, and in the silence childhood speaks instead of children, and the stunning game of a child leading unfriendly beasts into a peaceable kingdom commences.

Vianney was a normal child, and this must mean he was not just similar to the others; he was a normative child, not typical in the usual sense yet the spare and artless type from which childhood flows. All work and no play did not make this Jean a dull boy; he was the acutest youth because all work to him was play. He played at work the way he played at prayer. It was a serious business because it was a tournament, and it was a true tournament because it was a confrontation. The philosopher could say the contest was between meaning and absurdity; the boy of Ars would not have known what that meant, and he could not have said it that way, but he played it that way. Such behavior is not only normal for children, it is perfectly normal, and thus the boy of Ars was the only child in Ars to do it.

He began even then to put aside good things in tribute to their goodness. At one point he shied from embracing his parents. A boy would be odd who did not reach such a point: it is done by boys who think they are older than they are. But in his case there was possibly more to it; it became token of a wider and invisible embrace. If he put aside some delicacies of affection, he did not put aside the affection. That became positively ubiquitous, and he could even speak of liking the shoveling he had to do in the barn. There was nothing saintly about it. Saints really are not saintly. To be boyish is to be too old to be a boy. A cheek can blush but it cannot be cheeky: that is for those who do not blush. So the burgeoning Saint of Dardilly was not saintly, and he did not conduct himself with a childlike goodness. His was rather the goodness of a child who really was a child, the kind of goodness that can be as powerful as a team of driven horses in its determination. It is very likely that Matthieu Vianney was confused and even alarmed by his son's raging goodwill and mirthful intensity. It is known that his wife, Marie Beluse, mother of six children, paid special attention to the words of this son. She pondered them privately; there is scriptural precedent for that. The children of the village who outlived him recalled that while they were obliged to love him, they positively liked him. He had become Curé of something or other when he was seven or eight and could not spell the word.

If this great gift was supernatural, it had to have something to do with the home. If environment does not create grace, it does nurture it. It can impede grace, too. If it is almost impossible to rear a saint, it is almost an instinct of the fallen world to smother one. The home and family are more important as sacred havens than as social units. In the long run, they are antisocial artifacts if they are not spiritual facts. The home is to the church what the synagogue was to the temple. And it was in the home that the votive light burned when in the church the state's mockery of the priesthood doused it.

In preindustrial Europe, an absence of the most elementary machine tools in most places and the difficulty of communication made domestic rural life little different from the agrarian economies of any part of the world in any proximate past. On that level, the peasant anywhere in Europe was more like the foreigners he could not hope to meet than the cosmopolitans who meet them all the time today. And though he rarely could read about the ancients the way we can, he could live like them more than a modern historian could imagine doing. A farmer in central France could hardly picture Persia or the Ivory Coast, and if he drew a universal map it might be no more accurate than the old ones of the world on the back of a tortoise. But he drew water from the world and labored for the yield of the land of the world with the same sweat and bare hands known to most centuries and climes. He gazed remotely at the chandeliers burning in the local château much as any rice farmer of Cathay glimpsed the weird lamps on the walls of the Forbidden City. The rise of the bourgeoisie from the twelfth century to the Revolution had made scarce impact on that scene, and the false populism of the chief revolutionaries did little to change the shape of a rake or the dictates of the almanac. The new bourgeois was an isolationist; the old farmer was a miniaturist, universal by his provincialism and free of anything so isolating as sophistication.

The House Churches

Even in those tumultuous times, the homes were more stable than anything home dwellers could envision today. And for all their problems and confusions, families then more than now were fled to, rather than from, for freedom. The frugal domesticity of the Vianneys—and the people of the countryside were careful with what they had—provided not much more than, say, Vincent de Paul or any infantryman of the Crusades had been accustomed to. But there was no regret of deprivation. I do not mean that they did not know any better. They did know better, much better than many since, which is why they did not regret what was lacking. Free of artificial appetites created by advertising, they remained consumers and not consumerists. They knew what could not be had, and they knew they could live without it. Under the recriminatory political policies of the day they could even live better without it.

More than that, there was a repose about Vianney's parents, rooted in an instinctive piety that knew the infused and supernatural virtues were livable because they lived them. Holiness is only impractical to lukewarm souls who will not practice it. When an aunt died, and one of the children complained that it meant an extra Pater Noster and Ave Maria in the evening prayers, Jean-Marie simply shrugged his shoulders: a couple of extra prayers would not make much difference. His father would have said the same thing. It was more obviously the thing to say than to wax on about the duty to pray or the benefits of praying or what extraordinary things Aunt might be seeing at that moment in unseen worlds. A couple of extra prayers. If we knew less, we would call it formalism, religion by rote. But breathing is by rote, too, and no less vital for that. In the common sense of the barnyard and the halls of heaven, if a thing is worth doing, it may be worth doing more than once. Christ said it is wrong to repeat things vainly; he did not say it is wrong to repeat. If God did not repeat, there would be nothing but miracles, for miracles are his only creations created only once. Then nothing would be miraculous, for there would be no routine creatures to marvel at them. Vitality is vital by being repetitious, like breathing; it is boring only when it tries to be unique, like counting each breath. The Church encourages multiple Kyries and children in a flushed celebration of fecundity; the astringent modern intelligence is scandalized by that exuberance the more it loses the romance of repetition. Modern industrial production is repetitious only as a stutter, not as a rhyme; so you might say the technocratic version of repetition duplicates as duplicity duplicates. Modern perversity forces infertility to reproduce through usury and eugenics, while it prevents fertility from reproducing through contraception. It is not anything like what the Divine Creator means when he says, "Do it again." The Christian cannot be bored by the repetitiousness of domesticity; the routine of the home is the heart of a great mystery, which slips into attics and warms at hearths when it has fled exhausted the great avenues of commerce. The light gleaming in kitchen windows keeps a high vigil, and the smoke from each fireplace curls upward to an invisible altar. The home is the shrine of anything that is not self-sufficient. There is but one God, and so he has a temple; but every one of us is a reproduction, and so we have homes. Everyone is also the reproduction of a Master's work, which is why no one is a duplication even as the reproduction of a species. The home is home only when it teaches about the Master who visited and cleansed the temple but lived thirty years in a house Mary and Joseph made a home.

The Vianney house, simple as it was, became home to many who had no home of their own, or who were trying to find their way home. Hospitality was expected of people then. True hospitality was assumed, and it was hospitable in that it did not think of itself as generous. And it was returned in kind: in an agrarian culture, manners are the common exchange when there is little cash. Money has a way of driving out manners. Sometimes, if not checked, affluence drives manners so far away that they have to be replaced by social convention: books on etiquette are a signal of something wrong having happened to courtesy, the way a book on how to walk implies some horrible paralysis. When any form or manner or movement is reduced to style, it becomes deformed. To be rigidly polite is a most devastating way to be rude. Formal behavior should be so formal that its very formality is instinctive; otherwise, casualness will replace casual form as the only manner, as it has nearly done today. The Vianney home had a reputation for its casual courtesy, which gave rise to a celebrated incident.

When Jean Vianney's grandfather, Pierre, was head of the household, several vagrants one night were fed and given sleeping berths over the bakehouse. One, Benoît Labre, became a saint. It was hard to predict it then, and no one did. He was more soiled than the other guests, verminous, in fact. And he seemed peculiar, with a huge rosary around his neck. He did not speak; he did not explain how he had tried to become a Trappist at Sept-Fonds. He had failed, but they had given him dispensation to wear the tunic of a novice. He wore it as a sign of honor, the way some Edwardian sons of rajahs printed on calling cards "B.A., Cambridge (failed)". He carried a wallet with him, and a Breviary, the *Imitation,* and a New Testament. A modern fundamentalist might be appalled by such fundamentalism. The "back-to-the-basics" radical activists who shun fundamentalists would have fled Labre at double speed. In fairness, I cannot think anyone would be to blame for not enjoying his company. He did possess the talent that W. H. Auden admired in Kierkegaard and without which any preaching to the Gentiles is incomplete: the ability to make Christianity seem bohemian. A certain bent of mind attached to the myriad compensations for true vitality will not understand it; materialistic attempts to live life to the full are doomed to drain life of all but existence. The bohemianism of Labre was a Christian bohemianism: he left himself nothing to live off save life itself. This detachment became heroic in a way that derelict bohemianism is not, by showing forth the theological virtues of faith and hope and love. A salvific grace taught the holy hermit to do what the eccentric recluse cannot do: Labre made sense of the senses.

He left Dardilly in the earliest part of the morning and continued his slow route. Pierre Vianney was surprised to receive a polite letter of thanks. In nineteenth-century America the vocal atheist Robert Ingersoll stipulated in his funeral instructions: "There will be no singing." There was much singing when silent Labre died at the age of thirty-five — in Rome, as if to lay at Saint Peter's doorstep an affidavit of how successfully he had failed. And the world, or that part of it that allows itself to be astonished, was much taken when Saint Benoît Labre was raised to the altars of the Church. Some impulse had made Pierre save his letter. Perhaps it was not a rare intuition, since he got so few letters that each one must have seemed a relic. But he had kept it, and in a domesticated kind of apostolic succession the blessing of the "poor soul" was passed on to Matthieu and by him to Jean-Marie. Jean-Marie, fully knowing the importance of such great things, did as he had done with many other items, including a few of his own teeth: he offered it to some visitor who wanted it. He did not often say a saint had visited Dardilly. He put it another way. One of God's more conspicuous fools had found Dardilly a place like home.

Under the Convention, as it revived the pagan worship of the state, priests were carted off by the hundreds to die in Rochefort, Oleron, and as far as Guyana. Not very distant in Ecully, a few of these *réfractaires* sequestered themselves and organized a quiet mission to the general area. The nonjurors rejected the dovelike wisdom and serpentine innocence of the civil priests. They established themselves in separate houses and took up secular trades. One of them was Monsieur Balley, a tall and elegant man whose brothers had also been ordained: one had renounced the Faith to save his head, and the other had renounced his head to save his Faith. Vianney was certain Balley was a saint. Another was Monsieur Groboz, who first had fled across the Alps into Italy, but after some *Quo vadis* returned to take a priestly stand. In the external uniforms of carpenter and cook, respectively, they made "house calls" in the whispered name of Monsieur of Nazareth, who had worked in a shop and cooked fish in Eastertide. Groboz heard Vianney's first confession "at the foot of our clock", as the Saint remembered. The boy was now eleven. Two years later, he and fifteen others made their first Communion while their fathers watched from haycarts placed outside the windows to conceal the forbidden sight of Christ's Body and Blood from the humanitarians with guillotines. Without the assistance or even attendance of Man Come of Age, Vianney had come of age on his own.

Chapter 3

THE ONCE AND FUTURE KING

Royal Sorrow

A discourse on the Curé d'Ars is only by digression a discourse on Napoleon, though by telling what Napoleon was you can get an idea of what the Curé was not. But it was Napoleon, however byzantine his intentions, who set about the legalization of the Church after coming to power in 1799, or xviii *brumaire* of year IV, to be rational. The Concordat between France and the Church became official three years later. Accounts will say it liberated the Church, that the First Consul had made peace with the Roman and apostolic fact. Little of that is true, but the agreement did wind down a rare exercise of primitive and terrible valor by the Catholic loyalists in what we might with hindsight call France's Church of Silence. Most assuredly, it did not bring peace to Bonaparte. It did not pour forth a rush of the Holy Spirit; given the ensuing political tensions, it was rather more as if some sprite had been unbottled. The famous painting at Fontainebleau shows Napoleon crowning his empress while Pius VII is relegated to a spectator's seat, but for all of Napoleon's confidence, the caution of the Pope's fingers as they give a blessing suggests that the crown will be heavy.

Vianney soon enough found himself living under an emperor who was not sure of what it meant to be a king. Not in fiction alone have men sat on the ground to tell sad tales of the deaths of kings; yet the driven Corsican, surely one of the most remarkable figures in all history, would only count the ranks dying for him. A Cistercian abbot had the boldness of humility to reproach him: "Why do you keep on allowing such slaughter?" Napoleon responded with the aphorism "To make an omelette, you have to break a few eggs." The monk's reply deserves to be remembered, too: "But so many omelettes!" Beethoven's violent rage when Napoleon made himself royal was misplaced; the problem, which the meretriciousness of the empire style flaunted, was that Napoleon was not quite royal enough. Talleyrand said it was a thousand pities so great a genius was so poorly educated, but the defect was deeper. From the isolation of his last exile, according to one elaborate tradition of General Bertrand, which may be a study in embellishment, the emperor pondered the complexities of the royal charism:

> I know men, and I tell you that Jesus is not a man. You speak of Caesar or of Alexander, of their conquests with an army faithful and entirely devoted to his memory. My armies have forgotten me even while living, as the Carthaginian army forgot Hannibal. Such is our power. A single battle lost crushes us, and adversity scatters our friends. I have so inspired multitudes that they would die for me, then the sacred fire was kindled in their hearts. I do indeed possess the secret of this magical power which lifts the soul. But I could never impart it to anyone. None of my generals ever learned it from me, nor have I the means of perpetuating my name, and love for me, in the hearts of men. Now that I am in St. Helena, now that I am alone, who fights and wins for me?

Even this melancholy effort at a deathbed *summa* distinguished him from Vianney's wide and higher information, for while

Napoleon surmised Jesus was not a man, Vianney knew that he was. In his own exile on the island of Ponza in 1943, Mussolini ruminated over Ricciotti's life of Christ with the same perplexity. The labyrinthine scandal of the God-Man does not go away: true God and true Man, and not half angel and half yahoo. In his finest moment the crushed emperor died trying to embrace a ghost of the true and risen King.

Between 1804 and 1814, Napoleon had named 924 generals and twenty-six marshals. He had promised every soldier a marshal's baton in his knapsack, but he did not comprehend how or why any king would promise his men crosses. Vianney's king hovered before Vianney's emperor. Such a Christ with laurel in his thorn had ennobled the ceremonial space before the judgment seat in Jerusalem, speaking with a voice that commanded Pilate's attention. But Christ was a woodworker and no princeling. He gave Pilate's wife the same nightmare he gave Napoleon; the historian Eusebius imagined Pilate thinking so hard about this that he killed himself. Without comment, for he feigned ignorance about most politics, Vianney believed that his king would wait upon, or haunt, his emperor as long as it took to save his soul. One could put it fairly, I think, by saying that Vianney did not mind having a *parvenu* in Fontainebleau; he objected that there was no king there. He was not a romanticizer in the worst sense because he was a romantic in the best sense. He did not have to be convinced of a glory that strengthens slaves and gives light to lands and draws men to follow their king through whole ages. He did not need a new Arthur in Avalon because he was sure there had been a Jesus in Jerusalem; the relegation to wistful legend of *quandam rex futurus rex,* the once and future king, was obviated for him by the grander romance of one who called across an unseen sea: "I am the Alpha and Omega."

This is a key to Vianney's devotion to holy sorrow, for holy sorrow is royal. That piety flourished in the tumultuous nineteenth century, after so many eggs had been cracked, as it had done after the Black Death. The Saint of Ars was free of the morbidity that tainted more degenerate forms of that particular school of devotion. When not lachrymose, when not the bathos of sentiment wallowing in itself, the cult of Christ's holy sorrow was an empathy with a king who calls people to die for him by dying first for them. There is more Christology in Christ weeping for a friend and for a city than in all the libraries dedicated to him; every Ecumenical Council and each Creed are comments on what Christ was to Lazarus and Jerusalem. But sorrow in any lower degree is an expression of failure; at least it is taken to be so. And lost with that mistake is the ability to understand the sorrow a nation feels for a departed king.

There was a monarchy in Vianney's mind, and it was of an organic type: that is, his definition of kingship was of a power within a power, an authority that exacts loyalty and obedience for reasons deeper than political expediency or social custom. True royalty is an exaltation of familiarity; the royal household is a royal family, a public domesticity. The grandeur of a king is everything plain in the kingdom shown on a large scale; it is the very opposite of exoticism, as something exotic is something extraordinary made remote. Royalty is a form of birth before it is a form of power, and the king does not work his way to the top because he has been born at the top. His singular achievement is to have done nothing to deserve it; he can only keep his throne or abdicate it, but it comes to him by a system not his own. And so he belongs to everyone because he owes nothing to himself. He certainly diminishes himself when he is appropriated by so limited a breed as the aristocracy: the king is not in "society". The monarch of all he surveys cannot be above politics for the same reason that he cannot be beneath it: he is inside it, the way a father is to his family a head that is also its heart.

In a way that makes any earthly comparison crude, this was the sort of monarchy Vianney meant. And if it is safe to say few mortal kings ever were real kings, the Saint of Ars knew of one King who was a King of Kings. An unlettered parishioner remembered, "There was in the way he pronounced the adorable name of Jesus and said 'Our Lord' an accent which could not possibly fail to strike one." And the Curé pitied anyone who did not share the sorrow of so majestic a monarch. Joseph of Arimathea had carried this king to a cave with the same slow tread as that of Celts carrying their meager kings to the highest cairn, the same muffled sound of Danes rowing the corpses of their ragged kings to the edge of the sea, the same drone of Jews carrying glistening David into the city of David and golden Solomon after him. When Christ the King was carried away from the Cross no tiaras flashed, no princes rode behind, no gilt carriages creaked, and no bagpipes wailed, but each hour of his life the Curé d'Ars could see the procession and could feel part of it, and could feel honored to have a King who would die for him.

Long after Napoleon's death, and years before the porphyry tomb would be placed in Paris for Napoleon's bones, Vianney carried the Blessed Sacrament through the lanes of Ars in a fair duplication of a coronation. Corpus Christi was his favorite feast, and he abandoned his disciplines and became almost youthfully extroverted when he held the holiest thing in the world. It was as the emperor according to rumor had expected. All the Galilean's friends behaved that way.

The Beginning of Studies

Through the government's largesse in 1802, the ten-year silence of bells broke with the clap from the great bourdons of Paris; grey gargoyles looked stunned by the bright bells of every place, even the little clanking bell of Dardilly. To Vianney's ears this was the alarm of a battlefield broader than any Egyptian plain or sweep of Austerlitz. If heaven was marching on hell, as some said, he was due to join the invasion. Balley and Groboz had been their own kind of generals; Vianney's house had been visited by blackened veterans of silent combats who said the Mass as part of an underground intelligence. That was the sort of soldier he wanted to be: a priest. Most saints had not been priests, and no parish priest had been declared a saint. The crises of these times were crises of saints, for saints alone fight the real battles; but saints need priests to help them be saints, especially priests willing to be saints. There cannot be a Church without priests. Sometimes priests themselves underestimate that. In 1986 a group of priests petitioned Pope John Paul II not to make a pilgrimage to Ars, alleging that Vianney's concept of the priesthood was wrong and unfit for the present day; the Pope's response was to proceed according to plan and preach one of his strongest assertions of the priestly charisms. Vianney preached to his own uncertain flock, "When you see a priest, you should say: 'There is the one who has made me a child of God . . . one who has cleansed me from my sins, who gives nourishment to my soul.' " So it was settled. He would be a priest but only if he might try to be a holy priest; to settle for less would be like air wanting to be air without oxygen. He would unleash the raucous peace of Christ on the stern sentinels of a suspicious age, and place the heart of the nation back in the breast of the nation. A program could not accomplish it; it required a state of being; lacking was a high and supernatural love that could be had only by being lived. "The priesthood is the love of the heart of Jesus." And the heart was pierced.

He was inclined to shrink from what he called the unspeakable honor of the priesthood, which he spoke about constantly. Or, rather, he did not exactly shrink from it but into it. Though he was never big, he had to become smaller; at the age of nineteen, to begin remote preparation for priestly studies, he was ordered to learn the rudiments of Greek and Latin seated at a child's desk in an elementary school. The bishop had instructed Father Charles Balley to assemble classes for preseminary training, and a gamut of ages was put together to take up the slack of past years. Vianney was the oldest, and a classroom to him was as exotic and suspect as an oriental mosque. There seemed to be no lobe of his brain able to register the very concept of abstract discourse. He had not dwelt among a people who thought that way, or who had time for such. He was the first to admit he had "a poor head". To punctuate the declaration, a twelve-year-old classmate named Loras punched him when he could not come up with the right answer one day, and Vianney added to the bathos by kneeling in apology. "The way to be truly wise, my children, to be even saints on earth, is to receive everything as coming directly from the hand of God. They fool themselves who see enemies and culprits in their brother Christians. Jesus Christ did not do that on the day of his passion." One of his typical traits was beginning. He who would not be photographed functioned as a daguerreotype of anyone who tried to take him on, a transparency of anyone who confronted him; each was free to develop or smash the plate. The boy Loras, "of nervous temperament", burst into tears on that occasion and eventually became a missionary bishop in Iowa. It would be considered a work of supererogation to the mind of Frenchmen, who thought Iowa was a mispronunciation of Ohio. For a time, some pious citizens of Dubuque considered introducing the cause of Loras for beatification. But the picture to remember is Jean-Marie on his knees, declaring the hardest thing for a clumsy young man to confess: that he is clumsy. This would be his posture from then on. And anyone who has seen Cabuchet's statue of the Saint as an old man in prayer, his head boxed by Satan, is looking at the pathetic scholar of Dardilly petrified into ancient elegance.

Vianney knew how to farm; he did not know how to read. He tried, studying to the point of exhaustion; when that failed, the only way he could think of to break the curse was to stop eating. We would call it misunderstood causality, but only because most of us are not farmers. True, it did not help him to read any better, and later he called his two- and three-week fasts a folly of his youth. But it was a farmer's folly, the instinct of a tiller who, more than working for his daily bread, works for his daily wheat. It was a basic perspective that relates the source of everything to the source of food. It was not great ecology, but it was great Catholicism. A famine in the brain was still a famine; to conquer it, he would make himself a famine. And it is also the instinct of a man in love with what he is doing, however troublesome it may be and however poorly he may do it. The academy was not merely academic to him; it was to be plowed and seeded. And if the harvest were poor, he would eat less. There was a reverence about his fast, a delicate etiquette not found in the most delicate places; a restaurateur would not starve himself for his customers, but a father would starve himself for his family—a real father, that is. The farmer Vianney went about it that way. Whatever else it did or did not do, it did teach him to fast.

Accounts will dramatize the Saint's dullness. He was intelligent, in fact, even very intelligent. In the major seminary he would acquit his theological studies in slightly less than two years, and his intellectual curiosity, the definitive recommendation of the creative intellect, would last him a lifetime. We are told that he often read in bed until overcome by sleep; books were among the few items on which he was willing to spend money. Even after he gave so many away he was left with some four hundred on his private shelves, well thumbed and annotated. If he was cursed in study, it was the curse of too high a regard for the printed word. It is easy to take books for granted if you have grown up in a library, but in Dardilly a book was a rare creature, a rune stone dropped from another planet. When superior witnesses said he handled books like a farmer, they were telling the truth; he was a farmer, after all, and could not get over astonishment at something that sprang from the head at all seasons and not from the soil at one season. A reverence for the printed page moved him, greater than what an average writer or collector of incunabula might feel. He probably was the only one of the literary lot who could understand why in the Bible a sacred scroll is eaten; he fasted to study because his books, out of all proportion, had become more or less a sacred food. His teachers taught literature as though it were a fine garden, when he took it for a finer farm. And to see the clumsy youth rubbing his hands over the cover of his *Gallic Wars* was a scene of almost oriental beauty, like the *sharawagi,* which shapes art out of the contradiction of the smooth and the gnarled, or like the *yin-yang* of the round stone against the sharp pine. It is no less delicate or refined in a book held by a stumbling adolescent who finds it hard to read what he reveres.

In school Vianney bore a certain resemblance to Saint Ignatius Loyola. I have not found them compared, and a certain instinct of church historians might find such a comparison bizarre. As soldiers, for instance, they were completely different: Loyola elegantly sliced the air with a Toledo blade, while Vianney preferred a plow and nicknamed the devil a rake. If there was something of Mars about Loyola, there was much of Cincinnatus about Vianney. But in spiritual matters they were soldiers of the same stripe in the same violent battle. Ignatius used a fine and sharp sword against the devil, and Jean-Marie used his bare fists, but both fought with an unearthly ferocity. In the schoolroom Ignatius endured the same humiliations, even worse than Vianney's, for Ignatius squeezed behind a schoolboy's desk at thirty-three; at the age of Christ when he conquered sin and death, the battle-scarred Ignatius was just beginning to conquer the pluperfect subjunctive. Ignatius and Vianney were the same size and seem to have shared the same stomach: the Basque often lived on a handful of chestnuts and a crust of bread, the Gaul on part of an old potato. And they habitually ate standing; biographers add that they ate quickly, which makes me wonder how they could have done otherwise. The point, I suppose, is that they were driven men, or, more accurately, they were pulling men, dragging worn and torn populations into a morning only they could imagine beyond a furtive horizon only they could see. Contemporaries did not wonder how they could get by on so little, but how they could do so much on so little. Paragons of orthodoxy, Ignatius was twice delated to the Inquisition, and Jean-Marie often had to explain himself to his fellow priests. Both saw the heart of Christ's grace in the confessional, and both had so little self-regard that as Vianney would not be photographed, Ignatius would not be painted. That would have been too easy a way to dismiss them. If someone said, "Sir, we would see Jesus", there was no cause for showing them the Sir. "Their example is the saints' sermon", said the Curé. Cabuchet's likeness of Vianney and Coello's of Ignatius had to be done after death. The two saints were also utterly incapable of memorizing the Scriptures as well as the tempter in the wilderness, but the breath of each was the Scripture entire; then again, at Pentecost the Holy Spirit did not drop books on the apostles' heads.

Meanwhile, the courts of Napoleonic Europe were becoming something like receptions at which all the guests have the same last name. Cardinal Fesch of Lyons was uncle to the emperor, albeit on the maternal side, and was careful to fly the Bonaparte honeybee. It was he who confirmed Vianney in 1807, a year in which the energetic prelate had to compensate for past years by confirming sometimes close to three thousand in a single day. The rites were not free of confusion, and the Saint was part of it, known to the archbishop only by his name on the ticket of admission and by his inscription as a candidate for Holy Orders in his twenty-first year. He had

just made a pilgrimage to the shrine of Saint Francis Regis, the
Jesuit who had done much to preserve Catholicism in south-
ern France and northern Italy during the Protestant Revolt.
Balley had suggested the pilgrimage when Vianney confided
to him at a dark moment in his studies, "I think I'd better go
home." The trip was one of the two longest he would make,
about a hundred kilometers, along which he begged for his
food. Saint Francis had died hearing confessions; the young
scholar did not ask for such grace, but he did want enough help
to learn the Latin he needed. He returned feeling absolutely
able to memorize and so sure that he might soon be able to
win souls that he took the confirmation name Baptiste; having received the gifts of the Holy Spirit, he from then on
signed himself Jean-Marie-Baptiste or Jean-Baptiste-Marie.
The Holy Spirit was upon him; at least he was under the
impression that now he could write.

A Soldier of the King

The road to priesthood was at last clear; then a messenger
came down it with not a happy message. Vianney was nearly
twenty-four, and he was being conscripted for the desultory
Spanish Campaign. It was the autumn of 1809, the year
Napoleon seized the papal states and arrested the Pope himself,
confiscating the papal archives, the ornamental papal desk,
and even the papal pen. Vianney had no crusade against
armed crusading. He was not a pacifist, if that means there are
no just wars or that peace is to be had at any price; it is unjust
to say there is no justice worth fighting for and that priceless
peace can be bought. His chagrin was of another order: the

wickedness of the emperor's maraudings aside, to be an infantryman meant not being a priest. His name had been drawn
by mistake; as a candidate for Holy Orders, he was legally
exempt. The authorities would not be persuaded that he was
a serious candidate for the "unspeakable honor", and he still
lacked enough Latin to prove it, the consolation of Francis
Regis notwithstanding. To complicate matters, his father had
already hired a substitute for his son François according to the
mercenary custom of the day. With no little complaint,
Matthieu scraped together close to three thousand francs for
the son whose vocation had dismayed him in the first place;
but the substitute must have done some sober thinking, for he
returned the money a few days later. Jean-Baptiste-Marie,
soldier of the emperor, headed for the barracks of Lyons.

Two days in the army put him in the hospital. The army
discipline did not do it—there was little enough of that in this
dispirited time—instead he had a ferocious fever. Loyola would
have called the army a farce. Vianney's interior mortifications
made regimental life a lark by comparison. What was mag-
netic in him could be attached to only one of two poles. The
discipline of abstinence, which he had honed for spiritual
battle, was repelled by the gorging for land battle. He could
not brace himself for the ascetical rigors of retreat and at the
same time arm himself for the atavistic rigors of assault. The
Saint was a soldier, even if he did not look like one. A warrior
from the Irish hills clad only in bands of bronze or a Spartan
with his plain shield was no less fierce for battle than a
modern armored tank division; but it would be wildly wrong
by any chivalric convention to pit one against the other.
Vianney was unsuited for imperial combat, though he was
suited for another war; psychologically you could say he was

too naked and enflamed for rank-and-file fighting, quite as
Charles de Foucauld would find the drinking life of a soldier
of fortune too tame for the spiritual combat he thirsted after.
The situation was more problematic in Vianney's youth, when
the doubtful national cause was exacting half a million lives
from the families of France. Vianney had to choose his uniform and could hardly wear two at the same time. Not all
holy figures have had to make the choice: Clovis and Joan of
Arc and some of the papal Zouaves had hairshirts under their
armor; but if Vianney could not in conscience be all things to
all men, he would not even be two things to all men.

Some have seen this interlude as the one blot on his stainless
career, an awkward example of how the noblest souls have
their weak moments. Others have paraded it in the cause of
pacifism; I have even come across a liturgical calendar that
listed Vianney as a "draft dodger and parish priest". It is like
calling Joan of Arc a "suffragette and cowherd", or Francis of
Assisi an "ornithologist and deacon". What inaccurately can
appear to be a desertion from Emperor Napoleon was purely
a retreat to King Christ; that is not facile, that is fact. Sometimes those who blindly charge ahead are too uncertain to
make a retreat. Parallels are bound to be flawed; the noncha-
lant system of hiring proxies, for instance, is of another time.
One thing is clear: the girl of Domrémy and the boy of
Dardilly were not pacifists; few in history have fought on
such a front as Jeanne d'Arc and Jean d'Ars. For all his de-
testation of wars, Vianney thought that if orders must be
given, they should not be given from the rear; the number of
officers killed in his battles would outnumber the enlisted
men. He intended to fight out front for the Man who said,
"*We* go up to Jerusalem" and then led the way. When ordered

to Spain after eight weeks in two military hospitals, Vianney rose for the march, still weak and without a uniform. "So be it. It is the law." He had missed the morning roll call. Captain Blanchard, the officer in charge, went through the usual remonstrations and threats of prison; then he flung a knapsack at him and pushed him out the door to catch up with the rear guard in Renaison. "Never, perhaps, have I said the rosary with such courage."

As the mountain road stretched higher, Vianney sat down exhausted. Meanwhile, a youngish woodsman had been following the scene and appeared from one of the hills: "What are you doing here?" He motioned the frightened conscript to a hamlet in the mountains. Oliver Twist was in the hands of the Artful Dodger. Things became more complicated when the mayor of Les Noës, Paul Fayot, who took every opportunity to pick the pockets of his emperor, made himself a benevolent Fagin: "You are already listed as a deserter. If you return now, you will not enter the army's ranks but rather a prisoner's cell." Resisting halfheartedly, Vianney became what the Abbé Renoud called "refractory in spite of himself". It is truer than Ronald Knox's shorthand: he "ran away . . . to escape the conscription". But Monsignor Knox also said that Vianney then went on to live a life that was "the most heroic of any which is described to us in any detail after Our Savior's". There is no hyperbole in that.

This took place in the lilac mountains around the hamlet of Les Robins, where he hid for the next two years at the farm of Fayot's widowed cousin Claudine under the pseudonym Jerome Vincent. The mayor assigned him to tutor and help with odd jobs. As a village scenario, neither vicious nor valiant but extravagantly pretty with its meadowlarks and silver rivulets, the mountain settlement was more operettic than operatic. A chorus of Franz Lehar and a row of Victor Herbert's rouged milkmaids would not have been out of place. Nor was Vianney out of place. He was technically a criminal, but neither a Robin Hood nor a cad. The hills were filled with such as he.

For want of a better word, this one long idyll of his life attests to his plain congeniality. He was as entertaining, or nearly so, as the Frenchified troubadour of Assisi, making things young and light at his touch. Later, when asked what he hoped to get from life, he replied, "Just a little friendliness. That's all." The mountain people guarded him rather as a rare pet that is hardly ever domesticated. None in Les Robins remarked any bad humor in him, and he did not even seem anxious when the snows melted and the military patrols poked their way through the woods after such as he. One day a detective's bayonet stuck the haystack he was hiding in and stabbed him; he stifled his gasp and stayed motionless: "I was never so terrified." But his one anxious pain was not being able to let his family know his whereabouts. They found out after Bonaparte celebrated his marriage to the Archduchess Marie-Louise in 1810. As part of the festivities, an amnesty was granted to military *refractaires,* who by then were an army of their own, possibly outnumbering active enlistees, and the defaulting Vianney was free to return home. The people of Les Noës found black cloth and the tailor did his best to make a soutane. Madame Fayot gave him a dozen linen napkins: "You will be a priest and your table must look good."

Back home there was no use in protesting that he had been drafted by error; his younger brother, nicknamed Cadet, enjoyed the prospect of banners and bugles and offered to take his brother's rank for three thousand francs. His father was fed up with the whole business and glad it was over. The Curé Balley summoned Jean-Marie back to classes, and the deep battle resumed. The dark spirit does not seem to have forgiven him for not having turned his desertion into apostasy. Forty years later, a woman said to be "possessed" (and Vianney was cautious about such claims) went to Ars and accused him of having stolen a grape; the Curé's response was odd. His mind wandered back to Les Robins, and he answered solemnly that he had left a *sou* under the vine. She retorted that the farmer there never got it. The strange conversation sounded like two old soldiers recreating a half-remembered battle, ignoring the blood and thunder and reliving the barracks brawls. It is possible that Vianney was arguing with more than a psychic or psychotic.

Among the many innocent failings for which the Curé faulted himself, he did not count that old "desertion"; only once did he joke about it, when the government of Napoleon III had the unwisdom to offer him a medal. Crimes in his book could only be lamentable crimes when they were sins. As meticulous as he was in his examination of conscience, there was not a shred of scrupulosity; his sense of conscience was a remarkable breath of lucid air in his age of neurotic spiritual compulsions and aversions. The observer, regardless of whatever else he takes in, surely must see a deft and perfect equipoise in the Saint: a mental balance that, as in the sublime case of Jesus Christ, is the most cheerful argument against any imputations of fanaticism. He would not raise his voice in an unimportant cause, nor would he hush it in an important one, and this is the opposite of clamor. One had the feeling that when the Curé d'Ars took an inventory of himself, he did not expose his meager sins, if there were any, as much as he shed light on them.

Chapter 4

HOW HE GOT ORDAINED

Perils of the Curriculum

His mother died a few weeks after he got home. "I can never think of her without weeping." No precise account of their reunion remains, but he was moved to remember how she died thanking God for a son who would be a priest. The son, less certain of his chances by this time, had asked her to lobby for him, if that is not an unsuitable description, when she went to God.

In the autumn of 1812, Charles Balley said a prayer and sent his pupil off to the minor seminary at Verriers. At twenty-six, Vianney was older than his teacher of rhetoric there, who had enough to worry about already. Napoleon was closing such seminaries in retaliation for the bishop's refusal to defend his claim to episcopal investiture without papal consent. But by that time, he had become his own problem. Though only middle-aged, the emperor's walk was slow, and those who watched felt something unhealthy in the way he lingered among his soldiers' corpses, as he did for hours in the field of Eylau. The cardinal of Lyons may have had the faintest breath of Becket in him, resisting his nephew in however subdued a style; his seminary stayed open. In the end, he was less than Becket and more than Wolsey, and entirely a nervous uncle; soon his nephew paid him the compliment of taking him seriously as a bishop. At least the emperor did not call Fesch what he called the apostate bishop Talleyrand: a silk stocking stuffed with dung. Nor did he call him what he called Talleyrand once leaning on the apostate priest Fouché: vice on the arm of crime.

But no entreaty could prevent the expulsion of the Sulpicians from the major seminary of Saint-Irenée in Lyons, and it was to Saint-Irenée that Vianney was headed. At Verriers, he had received good grades in application, conduct, and character; his "general knowledge" was marked very weak. Abstract philosophy might have been from Saturn and in the language of Saturn as far as he was concerned; of the Latin lectures he could scarcely understand a word. During the summer Balley told him, "You're going on." He was speaking to himself as much as to Vianney. As the weeks passed, Balley pumped up this patched tire with a few last gasps of syllogisms and gerunds. By the time Vianney arrived back at the seminary, the school was in the unsteady hands of a substitute faculty, new priests with no mind or patience to indulge clumsiness.

In the middle of the unrest menacing Church and empire, the cardinal seemed to appear *ex machina* and announced that all students would powder their hair and wear buckled shoes as in the first-rate institutions. If he meant it for morale, it did little for the morale of Vianney. One day the Curé would say priests should wear shabby soutanes and golden chasubles, but of the lesser romance of powder and buckles he was innocent. He dressed as told; there was no false humility in him. But his self-esteem was low as that of a man who, by being given a plumed hat, is reminded that he has no brain. Yet if he could be a fool for Christ, so also would he be a mannequin, if necessary. One can imagine his discomfort in the new uniform; nothing his mother or the people of Les

Noës made him had fit, and now everything the cardinal provided fit too well. He was homesick and haberdashered, a perfect agony for a misfit.

Were it not so pathetic, the seminary could have been one of the Punch and Judy shows which, suitably enough, had originated in Lyons; in the eighteenth century an unemployed silk weaver named Laurent Mourguet became a tooth extractor and used his marionettes to attract customers. But the city had been home to more than Grand Guignol. Its second-century bishop Irenaeus had been taken as a boy to hear Saint Polycarp preach, and Polycarp in turn had stood as a youth in the presence of "John and with the rest of those who had seen the Lord". Lyons was the Christian primacy of France, a grace of place that Vianney willed to continue even if it meant running the gauntlet of the liberal arts.

Catholicism has long required a serious respect for those arts. In *Christianity and Philosophy* Etienne Gilson says, "We are told that it is faith which constructed the cathedrals of the Middle Ages. Without doubt, but faith would have constructed nothing at all if there had not also been architects; and if it is true that the façade of Notre Dame of Paris is a yearning of the soul toward God, that does not prevent its being also a geometrical work. It is necessary to know geometry in order to construct a façade which may be an act of love." The scholastic curriculum was astute as psychology. Before undertaking various studies in music, arithmetic, geometry, and astronomy, the young scholar had to pass through the *trivium* of grammar, rhetoric, and logic. Even scholastics who might have been inclined to think of children as miniature adults, dressing and sketching them that way, knew the shape of learning proceeds from reading to expression and then to reasoning. In the case of Vianney, he could take care of the end of learning, that is, the knowledge of God, without the benefits of the *quadrivium,* let alone the preliminaries. But if a cathedral is built of love and geometry, someone else would have to do his geometry, though he would know just which mathematician to pick. He was a theologian of supernatural intuition and, one might say, of common sense; for common sense is so uncommon a thing itself that it may be an act of grace upon virtue in a persistent mind. But higher intuition is a function of intelligence unaided by reason, a habit proper to angels and a gift extraordinary to man.

A saint has been gifted with an understanding of the *Doxa Theou;* the Jews knew long ago that this Glory of God, more than the configuration of the beautiful and good, is the source and end of wisdom. The difference between higher understanding and simple perception already was clear in the difference between the proud decibels of any Old Testament prophet calling for his Messiah and the mournful apostrophe of Epictetus: "I desire, by the gods, to see a Stoic who is perfect, but you cannot show me one, and since you cannot do this, show me at least one who is concerned to cultivate himself for that perfection. Do me this kindness. Let an old man not be deprived of the sight of that miracle which he had vainly sought to behold." Years later, the greatest orator of the age, Lacordaire himself, went on pilgrimage to Ars to see a prodigy more perfect than Epictetus dreamed could be; and the Curé's instinctive response was to apologize for his poor French. When Vianney had been a priest for awhile, an expert in moral theology tested him with a long list of sample problems and concluded that with but one exception, the Curé had managed to give the perfect response. Like Saint

Anthony of Padua, according to his teacher, he "without worldly knowledge had such profound mystical theology that like another John the Baptist he might almost be called a lamp burning and shining". Cardinal Newman, who was better at Homer and Cicero than was Vianney, asked to have read to him a life of the poor Curé as he was dying in 1890. And Cardinal de Bonald would comment in passing, "Do you realize, your Curé sees things from a very exalted standpoint."

Others saw in him what he could not see himself; for one thing, he was not looking at himself. When he tried, he was amazed at the littleness of his mind; in turn, he exaggerated the virtues of minds more refined than his. An isolated man may be so dazzled by the wonders of science that he attributes magical powers to them; modernism is essentially that superstition on a large scale. Blinded by books and deafened by Greek pentameters and Latin iambics, Vianney sniffed a fearsome force in every alien participle. The devil did not daunt him; the examining canons of the Grand Séminaire did. To hear him describe the power of the seminary to take away his vocation was like listening to an aborigine describe the power of a Polaroid to rob his soul. When it came to the examinations, "I was almost in despair; I didn't know where to turn."

The Help of the Lady

The faculty of the seminary could have been the travelers on the road to Emmaus, discussing between themselves the meaning of recent events; meanwhile, Vianney was breaking bread at the inn. But he did it quietly; a former classmate said, "There was nothing extraordinary about Jean-Marie; he was just perfectly simple." After six months, the faculty dismissed the future patron of the world's parish priests with the lowest mark they could give; it would have been lower, but there was no lower grade, so they drew a line through it.

You might test his psychological balance by watching his reaction to the apparent ruin of his plans. He went to his mother's grave and wept. I cannot think of a more normal thing to do, and I cannot think of any act more incomprehensible to a motherless world. I mean a world bereft of confidence in maternity, and so hostile to its own nature that it thinks fertility is fruitless. His mother was only a mother; she had not brought borax out of the ground, or raised buildings from blueprints, or brought any new party to power; she had only brought life into the world. Vianney did more than weep in the graveyard. He prayed to his mother: sober and businesslike requests for help in getting through the seminary. Retrograde psychosis should be less pragmatic. Of course he was not backward at all; he was not trying to go back to the womb. It is quite clear that he was asking for a rejuvenation, beyond the obtuseness of a Nicodemus and the myopia of a Freud. He understood nature; he knew where babies come from because he knew where babies are going. He understood nature, and he saw a labyrinth in nature that can only be explored to its end maternally. Any lesser way of dealing with human nature is unnatural.

The priest must be in some measure a solitary man, and like Christ, Vianney struggled for solitude as the one clear cure for loneliness. He turned to maternal memory as a point of departure into the supernatural solitude of Christ's own Mother. For the Mother of God is nothing as a mother substitute; she is everything as the Mother. And one who turns to her becomes a child substitute. Saint John was the first. "Woman, behold thy son." Human immaturity has been more impatient with her title "Mother of God" than it has been with our title "Children of God". If souls attain heaven by becoming children, then they attain heaven by locating their mother. And she is our mother only for having carried in her womb the One who carried the world on his shoulders. The order was confirmed when the Second Vatican Council made prominent another title for the Lady: Mother of the Church. She is the only model of the Church by being the Mother; if there are other "models of the Church" then we are adopted children with surrogate mothers. At his mother's grave, Vianney knew all this if he could not conjugate it. His primitive litany was as euphonious as the highest hymns of Sophronius and Tarasius. He said, "The Holy Virgin gave birth to us twice: at the Incarnation and at the foot of the Cross."

By kneeling in the face of affliction and saying Amen, suffering moves from humiliation to humility; as humiliation is the source of loneliness, humility is the strength of solitude, which cures it. Contemporary culture finds this no more plausible than did the proud sceptics dancing in the holly groves of post-Cartesian France. But the modern mind is in the process of realizing, to its bewilderment and agony, what the *philosophes* dismissed with mandarin disdain, and it is this: anything worth an Amen has been crucified. Man and woman were worth God's own Amen at creation; it took the crucifixion of the Holy One to bring the Amen back. The brutal reality of that moment was foolishness to the ancient philosophers, who were the prototypes of the later sceptics. They hungered for the *kalon*, by which they meant the noblest realization of interior beauty and goodness, but so long as it was an idea and not a divine presence in reality it became a cliché of contentment and rectitude. Without the true sacrifice of Christ, the human race can only say Amen to superficial idealism. And this, more than anything, lies at the heart of modern banality in worship; where the majesty of Christ's sacrifice is lost, and where the Amen of the Blessed Mother is obscured, the only object left to worship is worship itself. The search for worship that is "meaningful" is a dangerous sign of fragmented perception; it betrays itself in sentimental speech and music. Vianney turned to the Blessed Mother as the one certain guide to the meaning of meaning; without her humble submission to the Divine Will as a guide, the mind cannot even know how intelligence is born. He carried that terrible beauty of submission back from his mother's grave like a trembling flame, a fragile light that flickered until it burst as a great brightness in the dark caverns of the Enlightenment.

Vianney had not so much fallen into a depression as he had plunged into it. Paul Claudel was in a similar state on a Christmas Eve when the sound of the Magnificat came crashing upon his ears and began his conversion: "when Paul spoke to me, and Augustine made things clear to me, and Gregory broke bread for me with antiphon and response, the eyes of Mary above me were there to explain it all to me." The Lady who explains all things was in that deep place of sorrow where each joy finds its root, and there Vianney must go if he would find his joy and fair love. She had followed her Son there to say Amen in the blackest noonday as she had in the dawn at Nazareth and the morning of Cana. To all those who passed by it seemed a poor reply to her Son's great voice in all its agony. But her small voice could be heard in hell. And soon a light spread from Mount Hermon to En-gedi, and it was as if the Mother and the Son were at Cana again in their supernal youth dancing to the sound of youth with hawthorn in their hair. And far away and long away a young Vianney heard the sound. From that moment he could grow old and feel old but never would he really be old. As wrote Yeats:

> This is no country for old men. The young
> in one another's arms, birds in the trees
> —Those dying generations—at their song
> The salmon-falls, the mackerel-crowded seas
> Fish, flesh, fowl, commend all summer long
> Whatever is begotten, born and dies.
> Caught in that sensual music all neglect
> Monuments of unaging intellect.

God Does the Rest

Vianney was eager to try anything now; he did not care what, for it would be a supernatural work whatever it was. Possibly he could be a lay brother. But once again Monsieur Balley gave him a crash course and presented him for the ordination examination. Again he lost his nerve; when his name was called, he went up before the row of professors and his mind went totally blank. The disaster was not total; it was not a disaster at all. The examiners had not seen such a primitive mind; it was like a cave painting or a child's slate, with a few scribbles drawn the way the Church had drawn when she first knew she was the Church. The faculty conferred and looked back at the twenty-nine-year-old with his petrified eyes. They would not stand in the way of his ordination, at least to the Minor Orders, provided he could find a willing bishop.

Balley came forward with a novel request: would the chief examiner, Canon Bochard, test Vianney back in Ecully. In French? To his credit, and as witness to a humble perspicacity that not all the years of accommodation had doused, and certainly also in deference to the sanctity of Balley, the canon agreed. In the familiar presbytery two days later, Canon Bochard tossed questions to Jean-Marie, and Jean-Marie tossed answers back. The superior of the seminary witnessed the match; meanwhile the people of Ecully lit a flood of candles in the church. Vianney's own curate would ask him one day, "Who was your master in theology?" "I had the same master as Saint Peter."

In the following months, he continued studies and assisted his Curé in the daily parish rounds. "Monsieur Balley was a saint. But there is one thing he will have to answer for before God, and that is having admitted me to Holy Orders." So would the Holy Virgin, for he was convinced she was on his side. But the war was not on the emperor's side; Russia, Austria, Germany, Sweden, England, and Spain invaded France in 1813 after the October battle of Leipzig, and Napoleon abdicated in April. Cardinal Fesch fled Lyons in a cloud of dust, and his unruffled vicar-general, with more urgent matters to occupy him, took the opportunity to consult with Balley about his hapless young man. Monsieur Courbon has been called a simple man, but he was far from a simpleton. Today he would be scientific enough to take psychological tests seriously, and even scientific enough not to take them too seriously. The interview was brisk and very merry: "Is the Abbé Vianney pious? Has he a devotion to Our Lady? Does he know how to say his Rosary?" "Oh yes! He is a model of piety." "A model of piety! Very well, I summon him to come up for ordination. The grace of God will do the rest."

In the Cathedral of Lyons on the next feast of the Visitation, July 2, 1814, he received Minor Orders and the subdiaconate at the hands of Monseigneur Simon, who had come from Grenoble. The correct ceremonies were performed and the right prayers prayed; what had to be done was done, but the future never seemed more insecure. The world itself, at least the Gallican idea of the world, had stopped turning and no one knew if or when it would start again. If there had been a thousand priests and a halcyon peace, Vianney might not even have been there. But clergy were few and important men were concerned about other things; Vianney slipped into history when history was looking the other way. At the conclusion of the ceremony, he walked in procession through the romanesque nave, under the early gothic vaults, beneath the thirteenth-century glass and past the great astrological clock, whose mechanical dove had fluttered its wings before the New World was discovered. Suetonius had heard Faustus preach on the day the first walls of this great building were blessed. Now the line moved out the doors and across to the seminary. Abbé Pierre Millon watched them pass and noticed the oldest singing the Benedictus with such vigor: "Moved by a presentiment, I applied to him its verse: *Et tu puer propheta Altissimi vocaberis!* And you, child, shall be called the prophet of the Highest! saying to myself: 'He is less learned than many of his companions, but he will do far more than they in the sacred ministry.'" We can consign that to the venerable pile of such presentiments in pious literature; but the man had said it, of that he was sure, and in this case his throwaway line was not lost.

Once again the indefatigable Balley went to work. It was one of the advantages of having had no grand achievements in life; he had not grown bored with doing things that count. This time he arranged Vianney's examination for the priesthood. Back in the presbytery of Ecully, Canon Bochard, not above irony, now called the thin young man "our theologian". But he also remarked the quality of the answers this time. No barrier remained, except to find a bishop. So the candidate began the one other long trip of his life, walking south for several August days along a hundred kilometers of dirt road to his ordination, with some food and an alb wrapped under his arm. The Austrian border guards at first did not believe his explanation and nearly turned him back. On August 12, 1815, without the attendance of friends or relations, he knelt before Bishop Simon at the Grand Séminaire of Grenoble for the imposition of hands and anointing. "How great is the priest! The priest will only be understood in heaven. Were he understood on earth, people would die, not of fear, but of love."

He used the same phrase for the Mass. If we really understood the Mass we would die, not of fear, but of love. The priest and the Mass are the same invitation God offers the world to become the world his way. Europe might be wrapped in a smoking and acrid pall, gouged from end to end by mercenary boots; but the new priest moved almost unnoticed to the altar the next day, the eve of the Assumption, to begin a new battle in a war not even Metternich knew had been declared. The priest from Dardilly, all five feet and one inch plus of him weighed down by unfamiliar vestments, offered his first Mass as two Austrian army chaplains said Mass undisturbed at adjacent altars. "The priest should have the same joy as the apostles in seeing our Lord whom he holds in his hands." An exploration began then, so universal that he would not have to see more than sixty miles of the globe to travel it, or look any farther than his own hands to hold it; intensity of creation more encompassing and confounding than a black hole in space had been seized and found to be a White Circle.

John Wesley said the whole world was his parish; Vianney could say in a more authentic way that his parish was the whole world. He could prove it in the Catholic sense because he did not mean it in a parochial sense. The whole round world would come to the Curé d'Ars because the truest importance in the round world was held in his hands: so small that it would have to be feasted on to be felt and adored to be seen. Any priest is given the gift, but Vianney accepted the gift with a holy gluttony, so greedy that he convinced people this was all that mattered. The farthest he ever walked again was the distance home. "At the sight of a steeple you can say, What's in there? The body of our Lord. Why is he there? Because a priest has passed by and said the Holy Mass."

Chapter 5

THE ROAD TO ARS

In Ecully

The greatest confessor possibly in the history of that sacrament and the man who spent three-fourths of his life in the confessional was denied faculties for hearing confessions for several months on account of his problematic academic record. When he did hear his first confession, it was that of Monsieur Balley. Henri Gheon has said that a saint always thinks he is a sinner. Whatever outrageous diatribes afflict human conversation, or whatever human violence grinds against the everlasting hills, there was one quiet day in the village of Ecully when a saint heard the confession of a saint. And we may imagine only a fraction of the stillness in the church in those moments.

Balley was his pastor; no one else would take him. It was well enough. His first baptism was on August 23, and soon a steady stream of parishioners came for his ministrations. His sister Marguerite visited and did not think he preached very well. In Sydney Smith's phrase, no one "deserves to be preached to death by wild curates". At least the number who came to hear grew, and some even listened. The rhetoricians of Lyons would have judged the sermons deadly, I am sure; the people of Ecully did not think so, though they were a little uncomfortable at the peculiar way he looked at them from the pulpit. To describe it, more than one writer has alluded to Saint Francis de Sales' ability for "seeing everyone without looking at anyone".

Vianney had this gift in the confessional, too. Penitents came to watch him look at them. He could do it through the wall. It confused Vianney as much as it amazed others, for in life he had not known such a depth of souls. And while it is possible nearly to worship the glory of a soul, as Saint Catherine of Siena said, it is also possible to want to run away from its secrets. Vianney now encountered such secrets in abundance and met temptations he had not known before. He would not count this for innocence; to him it was mere stupidity. Not that he had been unaware of grave matter: the tenacity of pride, or material and mental lusts, and hateful pettiness; but now he saw them as specimens and ways of life. Again he had a wild solution, and the remote cynic will think it naïve and the pietist may take it to mean that his temptations were vapid. Each day he said the *Regina coeli* and exclaimed six times: "Blessed be for ever the most holy and Immaculate Conception of the Blessed Virgin Mary, Mother of God! Amen."

Monsieur Balley and Monsieur Vianney sometimes walked on rainy pilgrimages to the shrine of Our Lady of Fourvière under one umbrella. Two umbrellas would have been a waste of money, and there was only one rain. If the needleworked canopy held over a tribal chief displays his idea of himself, the umbrella grasped by the old and young priests sort of unfurled what they thought of generation gaps and their place in that part of the globe stretching along the Ecully road.

As Balley was dying from gangrene in 1817, Vianney heard his confession and anointed him; the two were left alone for a few moments. The Abbé took his instruments of penance from under the pillow and handed them to his protégé: "Look, my poor child, hide these things; if they were found after my death people would imagine that I have sufficiently expiated my sins, and so they would leave me in purgatory until the end of the world." Vianney kept these for a long time with a few other memorials; his most carefully guarded relic, and perhaps the one personal possession for which he showed anything close to jealous regard, was Balley's cracked shaving mirror "because it had reflected the good priest's face". That, and a worn umbrella, can be seen in Ars today.

One would have expected the parishioners of Ecully to want Vianney for their pastor, and they did. One would also have expected the authorities to think him incompetent for even so modest a responsibility, and they did. One might have expected Vianney to have felt relieved at being denied the position, and he was: "I would not have liked to be the parish priest of Ecully; it was too big a parish." A new pastor soon arrived and made it known that he did not approve of what he called Vianney's "rigidity". Upholstered chairs were moved into the house and the food was improved. Balley and Vianney had not made much of a distinction between the presbytery and a monastery. Saint Thomas says, "It is more difficult to live well, when one has care of souls, on account of danger from without." Pope Pius XII adds that the interior life of the parish priest requires a pattern of life stricter than that of monastics, for the secular clergy are largely on their own; to extend this, the interior life of the laity should expect much the same, especially given the fact that they are increasingly called to live the Catholic life as a counterculture. The idea seems novel now, and will be an ever-increasing trial for lukewarm Catholics; it seemed so to Vianney's new pastor, Monsieur Tripier, who perhaps through no fault of his own had no Balley to foster him. Vianney could not ever be a fashionable "abbé de salon"; he shied from parties on the ground that his one cassock was too shabby. Tripier's reaction was shock that he did not have two.

A remote place in the Ain had conveniently opened. That was not a rare occurrence, for the parish had the reputation of being a punishment place for priests. Ars was not strictly a parish, but a commune of 260 farm people some thirty-five kilometers from Lyons. Hardly an inviting location at any time of the year, its previous chaplain had died from tuberculosis after twenty-three days. Since the Revolution, two of its pastors had quit the priesthood, and one ran a shop. In a phrase, it was Siberia out of season, a modest desolation of desolations, and Vianney was glad for it. The one boast of Ars was its château, the lady of which was pious, generous to a fault, and desirous of a good chaplain. As for the rest, the vicar-general told him flatly, "There is not much love of God in that parish; you will bring some into it."

Moving West

So he came to Ars in 1818, thirty-one years old, with some books and a bedstead in a cart. When he got within sight of it, having gotten lost along the way, he turned to his guide, one of the local boys: "You have shown me the road to Ars; I will show you the road to heaven." From all we know, he said it in a matter-of-fact way. Heaven is not a gargantuan dream; it was as palpable to him as his books and his bed. For one who was not a university man, he had that blazing primitive gift of which we have spoken, a universal sense of the universe in miniature, like Dame Julian's vision of the hazelnut, which "containeth all things". His working model of the world had not been chopped into departments; each thing he said and did was the same thing said and done a different way, the whole of the human experience; he could even fit it in a cart.

His part of the planet was small. He could cover it on foot. He did not visit the capital of his own country, though he sometimes spoke of the parks of Paris like a bored roué who had lolled there all his life. The short trip from Ars to Lyons would be his idea of a journey from then on. This is not to say he was a recluse. There were times when he very much wanted to be on the move and only crowds could hold him back: had he been a Franciscan he might have gone off to see the sultan, or as a Jesuit he would have sailed off the end of the Occident with Xavier. But even his pathetic attempts to get out of Ars were ways of locating some other place to stay. He was not a restless sort who wants to go someplace; he was rather more the solid sort who wants to be someplace.

Travel is nothing more than motion until it becomes a pilgrimage. The planet does not ensure against dysfunctional human wandering. In Ars, the Curé and his flock moved from west to east every twenty-four hours and around the sun every year; from the way he spoke of heaven, it was evident he knew how to move as well as how to be moved. That is to say, he was conscious of a destiny. Others might think themselves helpless pawns in the hands of an indifferent fate; he could not. The perspective of life on earth as a pilgrimage toward heaven helps explain what motivated Vianney without moving him much. It was more important to bring microscopic Ars into the cosmic dimension of Christ than to expand the village borders into the next town.

Vianney had a special kind of physics, the *meta* kind, according to which, by going west he might grow young. There is a curious human urge to move west; it is a symbol of the desire to find new things and be young where there is no past; it was symbolized in myth by the glorious sun spirit, Phoebus Apollo, who fed ambrosia to his horses before dawn and rode them westward in a chariot of diamonds and chrysolite. But the very strange people one meets in parts of California, for instance, are a clue that the west can have a disastrous effect if you think you have reached it. To think that the farthest horizon is the final limit of all that exists is a flat way of looking at a round world. Materialistic people are spiritual flatlanders, and they will not easily understand their place in a round world; they think of the west as a physical direction, whereas the saints also know of a metaphysical west that is a destiny. Looking for direction without a loftier destiny is devastating madness. And being physical without being metaphysical will inevitably mean ruin. Kierkegaard, that limited mystic, called madness the state in which one fact is as relevant as any other fact; if he was right, then the relationship between place and purpose, between time and eternity, holds no significance for the mad mind. William Watson has a stanza:

> Think not thy wisdom can illumine away
> The ancient tanglement of night and day.
> Enough to acknowledge both and both revere;
> They see not clearliest who see all things clear.

The sun is unsetting somewhere else when it is setting in the west; and fittingly it is not snuffed out from gold to dark in the blinking of an eye, but it leaves slowly in a bloody riot. The "ancient tanglement of night and day" is itself a physical metaphor of a transcendent fact: there is more to the west than the absence of an east. The saints know that most clearly and exult in it, so that maddened flatlanders who think themselves sane think the saints are mad; they have called the calendar of saints a pantheon of hysteria. But it is a calendar more accurate than one with nothing but numbers. The saints look ahead to a red sky every hour of the day, and everything they preach is in the light of the sanguine glow; it does not matter what gets the sense of destiny across: the red sun itself, or a red leaf on an autumnal heap, or a red apple in Eden. Vianney believed with all his heart that a Man had died for him in the east so that he might go west. Either we declare him a lunatic, or we declare that even Apollo with his ghost horses and chariot of golden gauze did not ride the horizon more wonderfully than the skinny young priest headed for Ars with a cart of books and a bed.

Leading the cart, his tricorner hat under his arm (it was not his habit to wear it), he had difficulty finding his way. A heavy mist covered the plateau of La Dombe, filled as it was with stagnant water. Neither smooth nor hilly, neither fertile nor barren, it was the perfect description of a nondescript place. To Vianney it was heaven and hell wrapped in a drab greatcoat; he was not arriving at anything less than, as he might say, all things visible and invisible. No signs or markers showed the direction or listed the name; he could not yet see any evidence of a church. Some children were playing along the side of the road, but it was difficult to understand their patois. Ars was as strange as Mars. One of the boys, Antoine Givre, was chosen to show him the path. This was February 9.

How Small It All Is

Canonically he was not curé, or pastor, but vicar; his pastoral responsibility for the few inhabitants was appended to his official role as chaplain to the family of the château. But Curé was his unofficial title, and it became his universal name; the parish that was not a real parish was his whole life that was not really his own. Few saints usually are called by titles homelier than saint: there are perhaps Don Bosco, Mother Cabrini, Mother Seton, and the Little Flower. But people who have not heard of Saint Jean-Marie-Baptiste Vianney have heard some reference along the line to a Curé d'Ars. The Curé knelt to pray on the boundary of Ars and saw from the small rise a little rectangular church of weathered greyish-yellow stone surrounded by a few thatched cottages. Altogether Ars had forty small houses and boasted four larger taverns.

The tower had been torn down in the Revolution, when the church served as a club for a society of freethinkers and, as it was said, a shrine for a certain Monsieur Ruf to worship the goddess Reason with occult formulas. "How small it all is. Yet this parish will not be able to contain the multitude of those who shall journey here." The wild thought came to him of a sudden and passed. He gave it little heed at the time, but it was odd enough for him to remember it. Early the next morning, Ars was surprised to hear its cracked bell ringing.

The problem was not the place's impiety; until the Revolution it had been markedly more devout than neighboring settlements. But Ars was apathetic. At his first Mass Vianney was greeted with the most crushing kind of indifference, kindly indifference. The folk patronized their spiritual father.

Too many priests had arrived, moved faceless through the streets for awhile, and gone out of their lives. The vagary of Ars, product of years without sacraments or catechesis, was *acedia,* the spiritual tepidity in which the Holy Spirit is felt more like a heavy fog than any fiery wind. Ars was one of so many hundred nameless settlements along the highways, neither inspired nor haunted, vacuums for every unmentionable neurosis. Vianney had been given a canvas as blank as if he had taken over a modern suburban housing development, one of those tracts that seemed to civil engineers a good idea at the time and that now seem like an afterthought, the disjointed and anonymous culture of the condominium and the mall. Only a few of the fifty families were not what would be called in modern parlance alienated Catholics: Cinier, Verchères, Chaffangeon, Lassagne, and the des Garets in their manor on the slope across from the settlement.

Utter boredom wearied even those who were said by superior types to lack sensibility. Their frustration quite literally unbottled itself in miserable attempts at weekend debauches. When a settlement like this held a "vogue", it was more than a dance. This must be remembered when Vianney is said to have been against dancing. He was against what Plato was against when he shunned the Corybantic revels of his day. Vianney took a stand that few adults in Ars had the moral courage to share. The censorious voice must be even more incomprehensible to the pusillanimous parents of today, who do not dare order uncivilized teenagers to turn off their radios; but it had a certain sympathy with the design of Socrates and Glaucon in dialogue on rhythm in *The Republic,* a sound of sanity in the surrounding swirl. The gaunt young people tried to play harlequin, spinning about in cast-off remnants as a fiddler tortured his worn strings. It would have been unfeeling and even cruel to stare at so seedy a scene. But at least the croaking whirl took place in the broad daylight of the public square. Things have changed now; some future historian will try to explain why our own age drinks and dances only after dark.

The fact is, these were drunken riots. Old and young alike fell sick on the local cider and cheaper wines. Vianney was not a Pharisee, to be scandalized as some modern social workers might be. He was stunned with fury to see his golden souls wrapped in tinsel. Compared to our drug culture, Vianney's social problem was modest, but no diminution of one soul could be neglected by one with so high an estimation of every soul. He placed a sign on the statue of John the Baptist: HE PAID FOR A DANCE WITH HIS HEAD. Fine humor written in a rustic hand, but no one at the start of those years expected him actually to crush the vogue, or that the people would try to crush him.

Curiosity summoned nearly all the local populace to the installation on February 13. The former superior of the minor seminary led him from the presbytery, a small comfortable two-story structure, to the shabby door of the church, where he placed a stole on his shoulders. The Curé was in his thirty-second year, and the stole added another eighteen hundred. This is the most typical recollection of him: dressed in his bulky shoes and frayed soutane under a tired but clean surplice, the traditional neckbands and the great stole. When fashion inclines to silk underwear and denim outerwear, it is well to remember a man who had it the other way, his salute to an all-seeing God. He was a priest and would dress as one, and as he never cast off the priesthood even for a day, neither would he cast off the clothes of the priest. There was no purpose in trying to be one of the boys: the boys were men. And men want priests. The men were curious about this priest; it was reported that his candle was lit in his window in the middle of the night. One of the men got up at two o'clock in the morning and crept into the church; this Curé was praying. By daybreak the word was already spreading: "This one is not like the others."

Jansenism

When he stood still, he tended to fold his hands together tightly, as though he were squeezing the parish like an orange. Sometimes he extended both hands in an effusive embrace, even surprising a visiting cardinal this way, but he was not a backslapper. One young nobleman was surprised at the unrehearsed courtliness with which he opened the confessional door; no trained footman could have done it more elegantly. His typical greeting was of a lovely cadence: *"Je vous présente bien mon respect."* Only on those occasions when he turned quickly in the pulpit could one detect some concealed discomfiture; he did not admit to wearing the hairshirt.

A glimpse gives the idea: short, and curiously jerky in his movements when rushed, like a crab scurrying across a beach, so impatient with walking that he could burst into a loping run, habitually reminding himself to keep his shoulders straight. Deep wrinkles formed early in life; the emaciated face was highly animated, registering pain and playfulness in a matter of seconds. The great gaunt people of Ars watched his installation duly impressed: this quirky figure being led to the altar, where he opened the tabernacle, and from there to the confessional, pulpit, and baptismal font. The mayor remarked, "We have a poor church but a holy priest."

The next Sunday their young Curé practically skipped into the pulpit and, after a few preliminaries, cried out in his taut and scrappy voice. The Comtesse des Garets said it always hurt her ears. "Christ wept over Jerusalem . . . I weep over you. How can I help weeping, my brethren? Hell exists. It is not my invention. God has told us. And you pay no heed . . . you do all that is necessary to be sent to it. You blaspheme the name of God. You spend your evenings in the cabarets. You give yourselves to the sinful pleasures of dancing. You steal from your neighbor's field. You do a world of things which are offenses against God. Do you think then that God does not see you? He sees you, my children, as I see you, and you shall be treated accordingly. What misery! Hell exists. I beg you: think of hell. Do you think that your Curé will let you be cast into hell to burn there for ever and ever? Are you going to cause this suffering to your Curé?"

Those who watched him grimace became afraid at least as much for him as for themselves. His exclamations could not be dismissed as generic moralizing; he gave the impression of a man calling for help for himself. Their sins offended moralists, but they hurt him. What might have passed for his oratorical massacre of the sinners of Ars was a massacre of his innocence by Ars. It was there on display, happening in the sunburned man with hollow cheeks and hair hanging this way and that. He could indeed have been a perfect madman, but he knew himself to be an imperfect priest; he saw his people's sins as a judgment against himself.

No doubt the spirit of Jansenism was still much a part of

French Catholic piety. This form of rigorism, a truncated view of human nature and creation, or what is known as de-ontological spirituality, is endemic in many modern spiritual movements; like the modern movements, its imprudence was born of a worthy reaction against aridity, formalism, and the vices of the times. Although named for the seventeenth-century bishop of Ypres, it was associated primarily with the convent of Port-Royal, whose nuns were "pure as angels and proud as devils", and had a pronounced influence even on rural France, an influence lasting long beyond its condemnation by the bull *Unigenitus* in 1713. Heresies tend to exaggerate a basic truth that has lain fallow in regular practice. For instance, distortions of the doctrine of the Blessed Trinity give rise to three fundamental errors: distorted attention to the Fatherhood of God leads to deism, as the Sonship of God as an autonomous doctrine tends to immanentism, and an exclusive cult of the Holy Spirit foments spiritualism. In reparation for years of cynicism, probabilism, and moral laxity, Jansenism tried to recast and restore Saint Augustine's doctrine of grace. Bishop Jansen had read Augustine's anti-Pelagian books at least thirty times; but in a way, he overread them, knowing all the pieces but not seeing the finished puzzle. His *Augustinus*, published two years after his death, has been called a delayed-action time bomb; if it shed light on the great Augustinian architecture, it did so as an atom bomb does. The battlements of the City of God were smashed beyond recognition.

During discourses in public audiences, John Paul II has reminded the Church of the similarity between Jansenism and Lutheranism in their misperceptions of original sin. They understood the Fall of Man to be the burial of an important part of man; consequently, they called into question the integrity of the free will. The Council of Trent told the truth of these things in the sixteenth century, as the Council of Orange had done in the sixth: as man is corrupt, but not irredeemably so, his will and reason can still lead him toward the font of redemption. In the *Credo of the People of God,* Paul VI repeated this: to be "fallen" is to be deprived of sanctifying grace, but we speak of a relative, and not absolute, deterioration. The human race is fallen, but the human race is also redeemed. The persistence of Catholic teaching on this central truth is an ornate example of the Church's unremitting stand for penance and reason against pessimism and secularism. Emotional rigorism is most agreeable to the impatient rationalist who likes to have details spelled in artificial detail, and to the impulsive pietist who suspects that anything of importance is a kind of uncontrollable spell. Jansenism has been, more than anything else, a superstition of science and a science of superstition.

In the modern experience, individuals who think they are liberated from Jansenism may be the most subtle victims of it. For Jansenism is not so much a wrong body of doctrine as it is a wrong doctrine of the body, and as long as we have bodies we will be tempted to deny the bodiliness of them. There is an example of it in the young modern agnostic who mocks any discipline of the soul while making a positively military onslaught against his flesh: I mean the young upwardly mobile professional who has not learned which end is up, who would laugh at the rigors of Port-Royal as he stands on his head in a health club. It is just as odd to think the body can be healthy by becoming superior to other bodies, as it is unhealthy to think souls can become holy by becoming superior to other souls. The notion is an obsequious form of hysteria that cannot tell the difference between a collapse and a lapse. The human race, body and soul, has been thrown into confusion by the Fall, but it has not been crushed. The change has been for the worse, *in deterius commutatum fuisse* says the Tridentine Decree; but, as we have said, that deterioration is relative and not absolute. Concupiscence derives from sin and tends to sin; still it is not sin in itself. The subtlety will be lost on the laxist Pelagian and his rigorist Jansenist rival alike, but by trying to correct the opposite mistake, each makes the same mistake of looking the wrong way as the shadow of a cross crawls out the city gate.

Jansenism's tendency to separate the "Spiritual Church" from the "Institutional Church", and its overwrought emotionalism, were somewhat modified by the small galaxy of intellectual stars it attracted. Pascal, for example, represents the school of scientists (he invented theories for the hydraulic pump and adding machine) whose sheer brilliance perceives its limits; his sensitive empiricism detected that there were things it could not know of itself. Gilson writes in *Christianity and Philosophy*:

> A person always has the right to disdain what he surpasses, especially if what he disdains is not so much the thing loved as the excessive attachment which enslaves us to it. Pascal despised neither science nor philosophy, but he never pardoned them for having once hidden from him the most profound mystery of charity. Let us be careful, therefore, we who are not Pascal, of despising what perhaps surpasses us, for science is one of the highest praises of God: the understanding of what God has made.

As a man of profound rational equipment, Pascal took an almost sensual pleasure in humbling his reason. Nothing can be more satisfying to reason than to be reasonable about it, and the definition of a rationalist is exactly one who is not reasonable about it. By chalking up an outline of reason's limits, Pascal defined its rightful patrimony. He agreed with the ethereal votaries of Port-Royal so far as to say that the defective human will is a slave of concupiscence, but the inventor of the early computer saw what the morally blinded Jansenists would not see, that the sum of slavery minus its chains is liberty. In this he had a fraternity with Montaigne: the cultivation of habits, devotional practices, and the like can raise the basest souls to grace, for grace in its prevenient form disposes the soul to cultivate these things in the first place. Doubtless he typified the best of his moral force in the "Memorial" of a mystical experience, written on a piece of paper preserved in the lining of a jacket for the rest of his life:

The year of grace, 1654,
Monday, 23rd November, Feast of St. Clement, Pope and Martyr, and of others in the Martyrology,
Vigil of St. Chrysogonus, Martyr, and others.
From about half-past ten in the evening until about half-past twelve

FIRE

God of Abraham, God of Isaac, God of Jacob, not of the philosophers and savants.
Certitude. Certitude. Feeling. Joy. Peace.
God of Jesus Christ.
My God and Thy God.
"Thy God shall be my God."

It could have been an exclamation from the pulpit in Ars, though it would have been a perpetual one. For Vianney the Shepherd had no particular moment like the conversion of Pascal the scientist. His 23 November 1654 was 8 May 1786, the day of his birth and baptism. What ultimately made Pascal uncomfortable with Port-Royal is precisely what would have made the Curé a total stranger there; he could not have abided its quiet confidence of superiority to the visible Church. The Apostolic Faith has no secrets, no inner light reserved for a brightened few; the last book of the Scriptures is Revelation, with all its seven seals open. The God of Abraham manifests himself in outer light to the darkened, but not blinded, intellect. "Remember where you stand: not before the palpable, blazing fire of Sinai, with the darkness, gloom and whirlwind, the trumpet blast and the oracular voice, which they heard and begged to hear no more. . . . No, you stand before Mount Zion and the city of the living God, heavenly Jerusalem, before myriads of angels, the full concourse and assembly of the first-born citizens of heaven, and God the judge of all, and the spirits of good men made perfect" (Heb 12:18–23).

Even Port-Royal was never just a sect, though its anti-Romanism risked becoming just that through the influence of Martineau's clique in the National Assembly during the Revolution. Pascal, it will be remembered, opens his last testament: "First of all, as a good Christian, catholic, apostolic, Roman". Vianney needed no such attestation of loyalty to the authentic ways of grace. Pascal rejoiced that he had been undeservedly favored, Vianney that he had been deservedly forgotten. A small difference, but one that only the spirit of Catholicism has been able to contain without distorting it into a dozen separate sects and schools.

But was the rigorism of the Ars sermons unhealthy in complexion if not in conviction? The preaching and some of the counsel bear its marks; Pope John Paul has remarked a residue of what he specifically calls Jansenism in Vianney's tone. Contemporary historicists who urge us to adopt the spirit of our age should hesitate to criticize the Curé for having absorbed a little of his own. His one untimely trait was the trait that kept him up with the times. The rigorism of Ars, though, did not become the religion of Ars; it did not become a religion of itself the way relativism has become the modernist's unquestioned creed. That it was only the dregs of an age and not the stream is evident in Vianney's quick modification of his moral norms around 1840 after he read the balanced works of Saint Alphonsus Liguori. He would advise the scrupulous: "Well, my child, say such and such a prayer and forget all that."

On the subject of Purgatory, he detested histrionic pathos. After hearing a preacher imitate the shrieks of the poor souls, the Curé took him aside to say he had taken liberties with the truth: the souls in Purgatory understand God's justice and are docile. He told one of his converts, Jeanne-Marie Chanay, "The souls in Purgatory can do nothing for themselves, but they can do much for their benefactors." No Jansenist said the secret of a confessor is to give light penances and do the rest himself. And no Jansenist, for that matter, combined such holy hilarity and heroic humility. The indelible hallmark of disordered ontology is a recrimination, and of such the Curé was sublimely free. In reply to Canon Camelot, who asked if he had ever lost his patience, he replied that once he had given his table "a great push"; in this answer is the exclamation of one who has crossed the narrow but steep chasm between retentiveness and serenity. He wept freely, to the astonishment of less magnanimous types who were used to holding back their tears; indeed, he wept as raucously over Ars as Christ wept over Jerusalem, and from the same passion. I do not think either merely sobbed; I think the oceans heard the sound.

The Curé was not like the others. He did not see moral acts in black and white like a checkerboard, or any grey areas like a man in mufti. He waved the natural law of moral life like a banner of crimson and gold. I suppose his extravagant strictness as a preacher and confessor was wafted by a flamboyant desire to parade the truth instead of preserving it. And to some, the heraldry unfurled that way was all golden as the sun shining in the sun; to others it was as a red flag to a bull.

His unflattering recollections of the antipapalist Constitutional church are doubly significant when we recognize the Jansenist leanings of many of its leaders. In 1828 the bishop of Belley wanted him to become pastor of the parish of Fareins, which had a legacy of fanatical Jansenist flagellants, whose mortifications seem to have mortified everyone except themselves: in one rite a live crucifixion had been attempted. Vianney, the sane flagellant, declined the offer with horror: "Pagans are more quickly converted than Jansenists."

The Sum of All Creation

Leftover vapors of rigorism may have driven him in such a punishing daily schedule. Vapors have to be blown away: they cannot be crushed. His was in fact a far different breath and a wilder ethic; a man who hates the world would not want to spend all but two hours a day awake in it. The rigors of the rigorist are a hostility to creation; the rigors of the Curé were a love for the Creator. And he preached a deep and continuing mystery that had been lost wherever the Catholic sacramental vision had been obscured: man is saved with the world and not from it.

Once again, liturgy is the gauge. The more didactic, verbal, and static it becomes, the less it bespeaks the cosmic dance that unites souls with the divine harmony. The Catholic sacramental is the channel of that harmony, and without it the sacred dance becomes a pious conference. It alone attains a compatibility between communalism and personalism, without which it can only become collectivism and eccentricity. Only in the most literal vein might one say the reform movements in northern Europe exalted the individual: more truly, they replaced a communion with a congregation, laying the pattern and psychology for what would come to be the commune. In a slow and unanticipated process, this conditioned the secular transformation centuries later from sheep with a universal shepherd to factors in a remote social computation. The sacramental person takes up a role; the desacramentalized individual takes up space. Fittingly, then, through these manifold distortions of cosmic order, the fear of hell has now been replaced by the fear of overcrowding, and the fear is most frightening in cultures with declining populations.

In personalities of genius, anxious behavior tends to be polarized between bravado and despair. Yet the sacramental vision of the saint is neither. The typical saint, if there is such a thing, is more like a Spanish bullfighter than a Swedish suicide. But his bravado is rarer than bravado: it is bravery itself. Vianney understood his social place in creation in a way the utopian socialist is too isolated from redemption to grasp. A

Slavic aphorism, attributed to Saint John Climacus, has it that "a man can be damned alone, but he can only be saved with others". Certainly from about the time of the Enlightenment, this idea began to seem remote and exotic; the failure to understand it has led to middle-class cults of self-affirmation and hostility to apostolic institutions. By these mistaken routes, people isolated from their creation hold their own maturity ransom. They accuse saints like Vianney of neurotic sublimation, and then they proceed to socialize neurosis through a sublimation of private guilt which they do not understand and will not confess.

In the sixteenth century Descartes unwittingly began the neurosis by indulging a reverie: "It is true that the visible world would be more perfect if lands and seas had more ordered shapes . . . if the rains were more regular, the lands more fertile: in a word, if there were not so many monsters and disorders." *Philosophes* tried to make the dream a tenable prospect, social biologists tried to transfuse it into the Aryan lifeblood, and modernity as a whole tried to build it in chrome and concrete. Vianney came into the world when the dream was spreading as a political dogma, as though the magical *terra infirma* of Descartes could be made firm by revolution, reformation having failed. Vianney said it could come about neither by reform nor by revolution but by redemption.

The failed reformers, alienated from the wisdom of historical experience, have become the modern secular humanists, and by that alienation from the facts of God and creation, they have absorbed the same disorientation that made the puritan puritanical. In the modern reform of a world without its God, love has been reduced to meaningful relationships and mutual respect, cuisine has become a list of calories, and the singer of the Song of Songs is fitted with electrodes in a sex clinic. No puritan ages ago or now was in love with the pure lady: he has always sniffed Vishnu and Astarte in the incense of Mary's shrines. If the Redeemer needs a mother, the reformer needs only a scheme. Vianney's Lady appeared to him in the diamonds a puritan loathes; since the time she bade her Son turn water to wine, she has offended the puritans, whose social policy turns wine to water. The sacramental vision, the great gospel preached by the Curé, was of a searing brilliance in his fragmented age: he scourged and scoured the puritanical distillation of dream from fact, of creation divorced from its Creator. The disorder of his own day has become the wider disorder of ours; the vaunted moral revolution that separated attempts at love from openness to creation has fizzled into a murky plague of infidelity and disease. The modern puritans in their anthropological helplessness wanly offer drugs and mechanical devices to mitigate the disaster, while the Church says what she has always said: the sacramental union of fecundity and faithfulness converging in the Resurrection of Christ is the reason for life and the cure for death.

Vianney's reformation of Ars reformed Ars by not reforming the people of Ars. Even his pulpit cries about sin and damnation appealed to the souls of Ars to enter the redemption already secured by the Lord and Savior. He said it simply, the bare bones of a massive construction of theological systems and expressions. But Vianney in his rustic simplicity was not an isolated phenomenon of piety out to save his own soul as an example for others. He was a player in a vast drama to which he could only point a thin finger and raise a strained voice. Yet he would have understood what supposedly greater minds have taught in more rotund declamations. Authentic theology, as Nicholas Zernov wrote, "does not think of salvation in terms of the individual soul returning to its maker; it is visualized rather as a gradual process of transfiguration of the cosmos culminating in *theosis* or deification in Christ of the members of the Church as representatives and spokesmen of the creation". The truth, perhaps lost on Descartes, was not lost on Saint Augustine; there would possibly have been no Jansenism if Jansen had understood the words of the Bishop of Hippo: "I no longer wished for a better world, because I was thinking of the whole of creation, and in the light of this clearer discernment I had come to see that, though the higher things are better than the lower, the sum of all creation is better than the higher things alone."

In the valiant Aristotelianism of his Counter-Reformation theology, Vianney managed to catch a glimpse of this equally valiant Neoplatonism; it glowed and then burst high in his devotion to the Sacred Heart. For this deep and fiery devotion reacted against a deadly rigorist tendency: I mean the Jansenist's reduction of salvation from a cosmic reality and social possibility to a juridical kind of moral election. If a Saint Gertrude and a Saint Margaret Mary could challenge that error in their own ages with this devotion, the same would happen in Ars or any place where people had hearts. The pilgrimage of Ars was saved from becoming an esoteric cult for a clear reason: the heart of Christ was not separated from the body of Christ. "The priesthood is the love of the heart of Jesus." The Curé insisted on a Catholic life, which evangelizes the self and others, participates in the entire life of the Church, and lives according to sound ecclesiology. Ars indeed would be the whole world, if only because the whole world is redeemed by the Creator who redeems Ars. "Oh my children, how good God is! What love he had and has for us! We shall not really understand it until one day in paradise." The eternal God of Abraham, God of Isaac, God of Jacob is eternally "the good God".

Chapter 6

THE PULPIT OF ARS

A Science of Opposites

Vianney spoke darkly as a defiant way of revealing a moral creation in which nothing was meant to have a permanently dark side; the world is round, after all, and spinning, and not square and stuck. Brooding imprecations warned of how sin can darken a dazzling world by making the proud heart think it is gilding a black world. The saints figure as part of the universal light which was the primary fact of the created order, and while lesser men must live in the shadow of great men, they are illuminated by the saints. To be overshadowed is to be humiliated and to endure the consequences of humiliation, which are insecurity, selfishness, and sadness. To be illuminated is to be humbled and to enjoy the privileges of humility, which are confidence, sacrifice, and hope. The Messiah declined to overshadow his apostles as any merely great figure inevitably has overshadowed his disciples; the apostles received, almost reluctantly, a radiant power. There is no other way to explain the transformation of the sluggish and obtuse men around Christ. It accounts for them being apostles more than disciples. Only one of them rejected the gift through his own huge pride and cast himself into the shadows.

The voice from the pulpit of Ars mocked humiliation. The dark part of the moon is not dark once you have been there; it is only far. The Curé had the saint's ability to reach the far part of the soul and to humble it until it flashed like summer lightning across the face of pessimists. The people of Ars chose to sit through these sermons; they had walked out on other preachers, but they stayed when the Curé spoke, not for the harangue but for the heart of the harangue. One candle flickered next to the Curé: it became a searchlight. Some would say it shone in a dark age. Whenever a civilization falters in its own intuitions, voices speak of a dark descent upon the times; but there never was a completely dark age, though each age in ways peculiar to it has occluded light. Then a light has shone more brightly for being set against the dark panel of lassitude and rebellion. It has been carried through each age like a fugitive torch held by a fleet and rampant grace, lighting lanterns in the library of a Dominican doctor, setting blazes in the banqueting hall of a Scottish queen, striking the campfires of Uganda; once it trembled on the edge of the Curé's pulpit. In each instance it was the same light, uncreated yet tangible, light from light lifted onto the Cross long ago in the world's one black moonlight.

"When the end of the world comes, each parishioner will meet his pastor and our Lord Jesus Christ will say: 'Pastor, curse them!' 'What, Lord, am I to curse the children that I have baptized to you?' 'I tell you, Pastor, curse them!' 'I, Lord, curse the children whom I have taught for you, to whom I have given your holy Body, to whom I have distributed the Bread of your Word?' The Pastor will say what he has done for them. Our Lord Jesus Christ will reply, 'Pastor, they did not listen to you enough; curse them. I command you, curse them.' Ah, my brethren, what grief for a pastor!" Then the great lamps of his eyes clouded over, and before a luminous congregation he wept.

This surprised those who had first encountered the Curé in their own houses. He had not spoken thus at their own firesides. A youth of the time, Guillaume Villiers, testified as an older man: "The majority judged him to be full of kindness, cheerfulness, and affability, though we never realized his great holiness." To the mind of a boy the Curé did not make a morbid impression.

I suppose we can say, without offending his privacy, that the pastor was venerating the very people who were trying to figure him out. He wrote no books; he shrank from any thought of lecturing on pastoral theology. Yet something of what he knew about the human condition, and especially his measure of his "own" people, could be learned from incidental remarks, such as the occasional way he referred to the parish cemetery as a sacred reliquary. But we linger ever fallibly in a land of which he knew more than he said. "The heart of man must remain until the end a *mélange* of good and bad, of vice and virtue, of light and shadow, of good grain and bad tares." The rare science of opposites was discernible in the juxtaposition of his own mannerisms, which could be agitated and even compulsive, against his manner, which was almost lordly and dismissive about current events and conditions. This pastor involved himself in ordinary circumstances in most extraordinary ways, like discussing the archangel Michael while helping farmhands to shoe a horse; today it would be like reading the Apocalypse in a gas station. Before any of the social encyclicals from *Rerum novarum* to *Laborem exercens,* frankincense mixed with chimney smoke in a mysticism that is practical because it is practiced. From the Curé's lips the very crack of doom sounded like a wisecrack, which thing was at once more plausible and more shocking.

Magnificence as Virtue

Vianney was closest to being a prince by being a peasant. Detachment from revenues made him cavalier with finances, and freedom from fashion allowed him to set it. In other than a saint this would be disastrous; in the case of the saint it is not ethereal or irresponsible to be cavalier and free. In the life of the virtues exists a chivalric flair more towering than the munificence that aims at doing a great work; the scholastic vocabulary, which has a name for nearly every article of psychological aptitude, calls it magnificence.

The magnificence of Ars was that of the prodigal's father, who ran to greet him with a flashing ring; or it was the magnificence of Thomas More, who promised his executioner merriment in heaven. Liberality is generosity with things; magnificence is generosity with generosity itself. Aquinas describes magnificence adding to liberality a magnitude that reaches to the idea of arduousness. When magnificence preens its display, the eye accustomed to taking delight in things gives delight to them. I suppose that if there is one virtue certainly lacking in the most virtuous modern socialists it is this talent of magnificence. And it is so because socialism, even in an altruistic form, is bound inescapably to the sin of envy. Its generosity is not a generosity of the self: it is a forced generosity of the selves of others. Envy may be a lamentable attitude of the capitalist, but only as a moral accident; it is the socialist's essential motivation. Lingering behind each socialist panegyric to the poor is a ritual incantation against the rich. When a socialist reforms the world, he makes charity mean a soup kitchen; he will not let it mean anything like a banquet. But essential living is meant to be a banquet, and life eternal is an eternal banquet. This cannot be realized if one is obsessed with distribution while remaining naïve about production. The functional defect of socialism is that it is not social. It has not helped the poor man by eradicating the prince; it has only made the prince poor. If it has not put a chicken in every pot, it has removed the peacock from every lawn. It has made liberality a casualty of an artifact called liberalism. Such may satisfy the motive of envy; it is irrelevant to the motive of charity, and in the collectivist bosom it engenders the very greed it scorned.

In contrast, a striking thing about the virtue of magnificence is its utter practicality and sociability. The preacher of Ars turned this paradox into a magnificent platitude by living the paradox himself. As Vianney gilded the shrines of his broken-down church, he also prescribed remedies for whooping cough. This I can imagine because one of his clerical emulators near Ars treated my own grandfather for mumps; admittedly the scars remained through life. Liberalism lacked the flair. The century of opera and opium would come to be called the Gilded Age, but it was not magnificent; its liberalism and false progressivism gold-plated a brassy sense of the self and God. How anyone could fail to see the paradox was beyond the Curé, who told a journalist: "We live in such a poor century. Although it may seem grand, think about its poverty and its opulence." And if one were to pursue the matter, the Saint of Ars would tear the veil from that bloated kind of impoverishment with the flourish of all the saints of every place. The poverty underlying physical injustice and deprivation is a poverty of the spirit, cruel in its ubiquity, for it attacks the rich and poor alike whenever the sense of direction is lost to a life. Vianney told the truth when he said that he never reproached his people; he approached them, a voice of strength strong enough to be heard above the progressivist cant, and a light bright enough to shrivel the progressivist tinsel. A progress that is not toward God is an infinite regress. *"Magnae vires et cursus celerriumus sed praeter viam"* (Saint Augustine on Psalm 31)—much strength and great speed, but all off the track. It may be a negligible sentiment to the clerical bureaucrat, but it is indelible on the last signpost to the dark places.

As Christ with the rich young man, Vianney considered even the poor people of Ars burdened in that youth's miserly way so long as their hearts were tepid. The Angelic Doctor says, when lukewarmness resides in the will, "that man has resigned himself to consent habitually to levity and neglect, or at any rate to cease fighting them. He has come to terms with deliberate venial sin . . . he has robbed his soul of its assurance of eternal salvation." From the lips of the Curé, what the sentimentalist might consider sentimental was a shattering Thomistic realism: "If one of the damned could just once say 'My God, I love you' it would no longer be hell for him." There was no shuffling of feet. When he climbed down from the pulpit there was silence. Nor was there the vulgar tribute of a standing ovation. The surrogate applause was the footsteps approaching him for absolution. They came from France and many lands: from as far as America, over eighty thousand annually near the end. Some counted over one hundred thousand. It was hard to estimate, and it would be harder to figure what the equivalent would be today, when travel is so much easier. The lame voice outran itself: "Only on the Day of Judgment will one know how many souls were saved in Ars."

Kinds of Preachers

There are two kinds of preachers, according to a venerable distinction: those who have something to say, and those who have to say something. Ars had a preacher with a whole gospel to preach, a Curé a world away from the preacher satirized by Swinburne who "for . . . tender minds . . . served up half a Christ". The pulpit involved a high act of sacrifice not detached from the altar. And here Vianney anticipated the Second Vatican Council's Constitution on the Liturgy: "The two parts which, in a certain sense, go to make up the Mass, namely, the liturgy of the word and the eucharistic liturgy, are so closely connected with each other that they form but one single act of worship." The synagogue and the temple meet in the eucharistic action, and Vianney was not one to deface the synagogue. The early fathers and Thomas à Kempis had spoken of the "Two Tables" of the Eucharist, and Vianney took up the theme in his little church: "Our Lord, who is truth itself, does not value his Word any less than he values his body. I do not know which is worse, to have distractions during the Mass or during the instruction; I do not see the difference. During the Mass you can lose the merits of our Lord's death and Passion, and during the instruction you can lose his Word." He prepared the sermons with the same intensity that characterized the preparation for Communion. Freely judging himself a poor preacher, he did not think that was any reason to preach poorly: he just preached harder. If he could not find enough time for remote and proximate preparation, he took up the most audacious of crafts: he made time.

In the early years he wrote the sermons in a painstaking longhand late at night, after the parish calls. Standing over a writing table in the sacristy, he sometimes fell asleep there. Later, when the demands of the confessional allowed no time for much study, he carried some spiritual reading around and snatched a minute or two when he could. He did not mind quoting reams from the saints: the treasury of merit, he said, was meant to be plundered. And with the sonorous ridicule of his old professors still loud in his ears, it seemed a safer course. He plundered with the appetite of a buccaneer, but with the backing of Origen: "Having received of his fullness, the prophets sang of that which they received of the fullness." So then, the Curé did not borrow his sermons: he took them without trying to cover his fingerprints. To his way of thinking, the Good Thief had set a precedent for right intention. But it cannot be said he relied on faith without works; the pulpit was a workbench, and no one knew how much that work exacted. He made it sound simple, but then only a neophyte makes anything sound as hard as it is. He never said Yahweh when he could say God. He was explaining the obvious; he was just the one man in Ars who knew it was obvious. The listeners found themselves learning theology the way the *bourgeois gentilhomme* learned prose; the deceit was gorgeous. When all seemed to no avail, he made a novena to the Holy Spirit. Some thought he preached better when he prepared less. But he never prepared less; he prepared more secretly, for his moral consultation with the world had become the remote preparation and his prayer the proximate plotting. And no reliance on grace would have helped without those long years of labor; Christ promised to give the right words in the very moment, but he did not promise to supply the stenographer.

The sleeping head of the young Curé on the writing desk remains one of the enduring recollections of Ars.

Originality and Orthodoxy

Monsieur Balley had introduced him to most of his favorite writers. And after awhile he knew them almost on a conversational basis, or so that was the impression he gave when he prayed to them. If the rabbis are correct when they say you can pray by studying, then Vianney showed that you can also study by praying. What the saints had written and told him, he turned into a village dialect that he had to master himself; here and there he added a gloss of his own. Sometimes the passion of the moment inspired some lengthier interpolation. Those were some of the lines the people remembered best. Gradually Saint Jerome and Saint Vincent began to sound like Vianney, if only because Vianney at night had been spending so much time in the land of Jerome and Vincent. Evidently then, and suffice it to say once and for all, this was not plagiarism but the commonwealth of the saints as saints alone dare to live it.

The adventure of orthodoxy has been orthodox exactly by being what anything else is not. Saint Vincent of Lerins said doctrine should be taught *non nova sed nove,* not to be changed but to be explained anew for new times. If the thought is the mind of the Church, its only originality has to be the authority of its origin. But originality of expression is another thing altogether, and it has a place in the parabolic tradition, for it gives the mind a mouth. When originality of thought and originality of expression are confused, heterodoxy may seem more adventurous than orthodoxy; but only for awhile, because the adventure leads nowhere vital. It seems striking that so many of the most brilliant Christian apologists, describing the career of orthodox doctrine, have used the same image of a charioteer careening from side to side yet never losing balance. Winston Churchill wrote of the time in his early life when he toyed with the idea of becoming a clergyman who would preach orthodox sermons in a spirit of audacious contradiction to the Established Church. Tradition requires an audacity that offends radical and reactionary alike. The radical does not like anything that has to keep balance, and the reactionary suspects anything that goes anywhere. The radical wants to get rid of truth for new time's sake, and the reactionary wants to preserve the truth for old time's sake, but neither is willing to spread the truth for all time's sake. Vianney was practically novel in the vivacity of his traditionalism; it does, after all, take a wild man to find the right path through a wilderness.

Right, however, does not necessarily mean short. Sometimes our Saint preached for upward of an hour; when some pastor complained that his own assistant had preached too long, Vianney replied, "He puts them into an ecstasy but you do not even give them time to sit down." His troublesome curate, Monsieur Raymond, was more florid in the style of the day; this delighted Vianney. The Curé often told visitors he wished he might be so grand. But then he said that about many others. His taste was untutored. It is well that he was not just a little better himself, for then he would have been much worse. I have already told of his confusion when splendid Lacordaire, the most celebrated orator of France, asked for the honor of standing in the pulpit of Ars. Vianney expressed genuine bewilderment that "the greatest in science should come to the weakest in science". The great Dominican's voice had soared time and again up the arches of the cathedral of Paris, moving the faithful to more devout resolutions and enchanting no less the curious with his poise and grace, a veritable talking manual and model of rhetoric, but he was more than that. When he began to preach from the rickety pulpit that afternoon in Ars, he turned to see the bowed head of the poor Curé in the choir. His voiced lowered; he spoke simply, and with a slight tremor in his silver voice. In the seventeenth of his conferences at Notre Dame of Paris, Lacordaire said: "Similarly sympathetic intuition between two men accomplishes in a single moment what logic could not have brought about in many years. Just so, a sudden illumination sometimes enlightens the genius."

Vianney's own notorious voice sounded like a fiddle at a barn dance, and when he got excited it got higher, as though he were running out of strings. At first he tried to memorize each sermon, a disaster; his memory was no better than his pitch. Then he would lose the train of thought and stumble over the words; the gaunt little figure would hang its powerful chin over the edge of the pulpit as if pleading for rescue, only to stare at helpless looks from below. His collected sermons have been edited, and none of this pathos is left in them; but even edited, they should not be used as models. He is the model, and the sermons are to be read with a mental image of the occasional panic of the man who preached them. He continued preaching long after most of his teeth were gone and many of his words had become incoherent. The crowds continued to grow and were largest when the old man gave up preaching sermons altogether and called greetings and petitions to the Divine Presence in the tabernacle.

Winged Michael and all his disembodied host may have been
watching for all we know. They did not have to take notes,
but some of the congregation did. The pilgrims were increasing who could write, and fortunately so, for many of his own
manuscripts were lost. There is a collection in Rome at the
Church of the Canons Regular of the Immaculate Conception.
But his first curate, the eloquent Raymond, threw the sermons on the love of God and the Eucharist into the fire.
Those seated in the church taking notes were only following
the advice of an eighth-century monk: "If you find a book by
Athanasius and have no paper on which to copy it, write it on
your shirt."

Chapter 7

COFFEE IN PARADISE

Domestic Piety

In no excess of his own language, Vianney had declared war on the devil and set about to prepare his defenses. The presbytery near the church was adequate and considered quite respectable in the simple estimation of Ars. Having decided to use just the kitchen and an upstairs bedroom, he returned with thanks the several stuffed chairs and some kitchen equipment that the comtesse had given to the parish. She did not object, for she quickly began to get a measure of her Curé. Indeed, he deliberately set out to remedy the Jansenistic veneer of her finishing school training. He introduced her to a wider reading and to more frequent Communion. Before that, she had been disposed to small prayer groups of friends out of the shade of the parish throng. To four such Vianney said, "My friends, what would you think of a child if it were to say, 'I love my father dearly, but as for my mother I have no wish ever to see her again'?" But they had only lost their breath, not their souls. The Curé soon revived them in the Church, where any real revival takes place: Catholicism is the realization and renewal of nature's first lost breath.

The chatelaine's full name was Mademoiselle Marie-Anne-Colombe Garnier des Garets, but everyone called her Mademoiselle d'Ars. She was an aristocrat in the rare sense of the word, for she had refined her refinements until they were not conspicuous. To use a phrase that is increasingly out of fashion now, she was a Christian lady. At St. Cyr she had been taught that one sign of grace is graciousness.

The des Garets had long enjoyed the esteem of the area so that the family and their rather undistinguished château, which in one form or another had stood since the twelfth century, escaped the depredations of the Revolution. Clandestine Masses had been celebrated in the chapel of the château during those years. Now sixty-four, her one brother, Vicomte François, living in Paris, the chatelain continued her routine of visits to the sick and various charitable projects. She was innocent of ostentation and did not claim to be doing other than what she thought anyone in her position should do. She may have lacked the high calling of imperial Helena and the incisive drama of Avilan Teresa. Her domestic piety bore the stamp of women whose attentions are not above normal human strength, nor is it clear that hers was an instinctive and unfailingly joyful spirit of sacrifice according to the canons of heroic virtue. But by any measure she was the woman whose price is far above rubies, though this now sounds inflationary to some provincial women who want to be merely as valuable as men.

"It appears", we find among the conclusions of Frédéric Ozanam, "that nothing great can be done in the Church without a woman having a share in it." A woman, that is, who does not trivialize gender as a profane burden and anthropological accident; a woman so confident of her spiritual motherhood that she promotes in priests a spiritual fatherhood. There are unimaginative feminists who do call the notion antique and culturally conditioned, and I admit that they are correct. But the antiquity is as old as revelation, and the culture that conditioned it is the culture of God's chosen people, who parted company with the pagans to preach it. One can disagree with it; one can also disagree with a volcano and a rainbow. But the great facts remain, and one of the facts is simply this: there are two basic ways to explain nature. One is by the sacraments and the apostolic priesthood; the other is by pantheism and sorcery. The priest and the *Te Deum* cannot be modified; they can only be replaced by occultists with songs of Orpheus and rhymes of Sappho. To deny the Catholic doctrine of nature is to embrace something hoary and superstitious.

The fixed mental habits of Madame des Garets were concerned with none of that, although her eyes had already noticed the plain truth of it in the experiments of her unfamiliar new society. In the château the echoes of an older France full of Christ and courtesy sounded amid the fading Aubussons and dusty Sèvres as she and her somewhat dessicated butler, Saint-Phal, recited daily prayers. When the new Curé returned the gift of furniture, she became privy to his strange quest. If he had set out after a more golden fleece, she would attend his adventure.

Had the other parishioners been richer, they would not have so minded their Curé's austerity. The modest prosperity of the presbytery, and especially of its kitchen, was supposed to be a source of local pride. So not to offend by advertising poverty, Vianney kept the plain canopy over the bed, but gave the pillow and mattress to a man who had none. Not that it made much difference; he often slept in the kitchen or barn. Modern Pharisees who jog to the point of collapse, cough blood for marathon medals, and starve on diet pills to fit into bathing suits may be scandalized to learn how the Curé lashed himself nightly with Monsieur Balley's knotted cord until sometimes blood flecked the wall. It is horrible, as is sin. But it is not sin. The Freudian would shake his head, the Jungian would ponder, the Rankian might envy, and those who take it for what it is would conclude that he was trying to make strong that which was weak. In the end, the "discipline" was apparently no more or less effective at killing the libido than a shock treatment is, and in the etiology of psychosis it certainly was more humane than a group dynamics session.

The Curé blamed his sins on himself, and not on his environment, or on his parents, or on a lack of enzymes, or on the trying times in which he lived. He held himself to blame as an accountable part of a creation divorced from its cajoling Creator. His moral weakness was the weakness of the world of which he was part and for which he was partly responsible. Social responsibility is not limited to the contemporary situation, for each participant in history participates, however remotely, in every other fact of history. In this luminous vision, his self-hatred was not a hatred of the self entire but of the selfish self, of the complacent ego detached from God's plan at work in history, of Pascal's *"le moi haissable"* that blocks the personality from being a vehicle for the Divine Will. Vianney's use of corporal discipline was an immense form of social bravery, a species of the sacrifice of the self for the good of the whole that constitutes great love, the habitually graceful counterforce to inhumanity.

Mortification

The concept of mortification of the senses was as threatening to the second-century Manicheans, the twelfth-century flagellants, and the seventeenth-century Jansenists as it is to the modern egoist, for while they mimicked mortification, their motive was completly different from that of the saints: mortification should be for the love of God, but in each wrong instance it has been out of a spirit of subtle pride. Properly, mortification exercises the virtues of penance, temperance, and patience, and it disposes the soul to the service of God and of neighbor. At the opposite extreme of the proud rigorists were, and are, the quietists: these are the pietistic believers who would think a feeling of personal closeness to God eliminates any need for mortification, or resisting temptations, or gaining indulgences, or making prayers of petition. In the modern idiom, the pride of the rigorist and the false mysticism of the quietist become unwholesome companions; many "consciousness-raising" techniques and many "born-again" movements are part of the same spiritual schizophrenia. A strange philosophical assumption abounds that is masochistic but not mortified, introspective but not illuminative, activist but not positively social. The modern egoist mortifies, but he mortifies others instead of the self.

Mortification helps to kill disorder in the passions, provided it does not offend health, which is a good; as such, it is more of a virtuous amalgamation than a virtue itself. As the human being is a physical, intellectual, and spiritual reality, mortification encompasses the body, mind, and spirit to be complete. In the instance of the body, the external senses are disciplined; in the instance of the mind, the internal senses of imagination and intellect are disciplined; in the instance of the spirit, the passions are disciplined. Saint Thomas made a great psychological advance in asserting the power of virtue to shape the irascible and concupiscible appetites; the Augustinian view greatly doubted the effect of the particular virtues over passionate being. But Saint Thomas carefully explored the nature of the passions, as he distinguished irascibility, or the strong drive of the sense appetite against obstacles toward a difficult good, from concupiscence, which is a less powerful movement of the will motivated by an act of the intellect toward a pleasurable good and away from injurious evil. In each case, though original sin has disordered the passion, each sense tends toward what is perceived to be a good. Mortification helps to discern the authentic good and to will in a truly free way.

So the passions themselves need not be evil and are in fact prerequisites for holiness; mortification done for the purpose of their vindication conducts the soul into the drama of holy passionate being, after the model of Christ. The Perfect Man rose in righteous anger against the hypocrites; he wept for Lazarus and the holy city; he sweat blood in high agony; with unspeakable sadness and weariness he whispered that he had no place to lay his head, and enjoined the daughters of Jerusalem to weep for a grief deeper than the sadness of one sad day; he loved a love that outlasts the world's first hate, and hated hatred with such a passion that the prince of hatred wailed to be left alone. The solemn series of events celebrated as the definitive crisis of time in the face of eternity, a crisis so perfect in the triumph of original good over derivative evil that it is known for all ages as the Holy Passion.

The benefits won in the perfect Passion can be received when inordinate passion is destroyed, for the killing of death requires many little deaths, the dying of the old man in a life of self-abnegation. If blood has to be shed by God as atonement to God, the children of God offer their own blood as an act of faith in that redemptive act: not to remedy any inadequacy in a Passion already perfect, but to become moral and social agents of it in the world for which Christ died: "I fill up in my flesh what is still lacking in regard to Christ's afflictions, for the sake of his body, which is the Church" (Col 1:24). The Saint of Ars had no desire for vicarious martyrdom, such as is urged by secular reconstructionists; to urge upon others what one is not willing to suffer oneself is willful destruction. The awful thing about Vianney's corporal mortifications was the very absence of that morbidity or compulsive behavior characteristic of the unmortified soul; absent too was the pessimism that separates the impassible stoic from the impassioned Saint. Saint Francis of Assisi practiced the same holy mortifications to the same effect: this is overlooked or deliberately ignored by many ornithologists and ecologists who admire Francis for inadequate reasons. There never was a saint who was not a mortified saint. And like Saint Francis, and unlike most bird fanciers and gardeners, Saint Jean Vianney frequently went into the fields and kissed the ground for joy.

In the Kitchen

An ebullience of the spirit is seen even in his fasting. The pot, the *marmite,* in which he cooked a few potatoes to last the week, is still on display along with his dinner bowl. The Saint lived for many years on little more than a potato or two a day and a cup of milk, which he sometimes drank while crossing the square. This fare was supplemented from time to time with a piece of burnt flour called a *matefaim,* a snack to kill hunger. The most he went entirely without food during the Ars years was an occasional three days in Lent. Unimpressed with his stamina, he casually remarked that he had tried to live on sorrel alone but "could not keep it up". The diet was not a fetish; he recognized his physicians's right to modify it. And he had the knack of Teresa in Avila, who said there is a time for penance and a time for partridge. He offered good food to guests and the children in his charge, performed a miracle by multiplying grain, and even tried to make a show of eating in public; he tried this when dining with his bishop and with some of the other clergy, but his stomach was so unaccustomed to it that he suffered great pain.

Now if this had taken place in the Sahara, where there is no food, or among the Saxons and Celts, whose cuisine has struck some as a recipe for mortification, this would have been less remarkable. A great paradox of Providence was spelled out by geography: the man without a stomach lived in the breadbasket of Europe and vineyard of the World. Granted, the poor did not get to share the best of this Lucullan harvest, but whiffs of the finest gastronomy were as much a part of the air as the air itself. As some boys run away from home to become sailors or soldiers, many boys of the Lyonnais ran away to become chefs. Even Vianney would not spurn a glass of wine when visiting, for that would have been the height of pride and an inexplicable rudeness in the land that claimed to be irrigated by three rivers: the Rhône, the Saône, and the red Beaujolais. Joan of Arc took wine in her soup, and Cardinal de Bernis was at pains to remedy his defective sacramental theology by saying Mass with a great Mersault. Some years ago, but within the living memory of many, a Frenchman shot his housekeeper caught in the act of decanting a bottle with a tin funnel, and was treated leniently by the jury, which, given the vintage, considered it a crime of passion.

Brillat-Savarin was born in Belley, the see city for Ars. This contemporary of Vianney is still considered a king of gastronomy, and his devotion to the table was shared by one of his sisters-in-law, who at the age of ninety-nine years and ten months cried out during dinner: "Quick, bring the dessert! I feel that I am going to give up the ghost!" She in fact did miss the dessert; one of the servants grieved that she would have to take her coffee in paradise. It is not hard to imagine what the Curé would have replied, but he would not have been surprised. Lyons, birthplace of the emperors Claudius and Caracalla, is no less the home of the *grands-chefs*. When it was called Lugdunum, it already had the beginning of such a reputation. Even the lion on the city's coat of arms has a tongue hanging out, and the sword in his paw is shaped something like a carving knife. The city can draw on beef of the Charollais, Dauphiny butter, pickerel and perch from La Bresse, the truffles of Valréas, and the artichokes of the Rhône. Dull would he be of soul as much as of sense who could not respect a *saucisson chaude,* a *poulet à l'ail,* or a weeping cheese St. Marcellin. Vianney was dull in nothing. He lived in the land of the earthly banquet, and if he could not feast he would fast; no son of the Lyonnais could merely eat. So our Saint practiced what might be the one culinary perfection more perfect than a great sauce, and that is no sauce at all. Coffee would come a little later, in paradise.

The Devil's Advocate might well ask if his health complaints came from his fasting. It is a fair question, and to the degree that it was so it should not be an example. Vianney knew that, and we have seen how he looked on his earlier fasts as foolish; but his idea of moderation was as extravagant as everything else in the enormous economy of his deprivations. Raucous men who devour beef and beer should not take scandal at one who dines elegantly on bread. Doctor Timécourt ordered him to eat more to prevent his "nervous affections" from becoming chronic. Ten years before his death, a physical examination concluded "science could not explain how he survived". He was given to frequent tears. His undernourishment must have hastened the loss of his teeth, and perhaps some of his hair, but his tears were not a loss. There is a spiritual tradition of the "gift of tears" among the charismatic gifts of the soul. He had these in abundance: discernment of spirits, prophecy, reading of hearts, healing. What was the source of energy enabling him to sleep less than two hours a night? These were not sleepless nights; very much were they watchful nights, and I venture to say that if he lost anything by his fasts it was the loss of love as an abstraction. Love became his solid food in no poetic way; when totally consuming, love attains a point at which it can also be consumed. "All is love." "When you are working for heaven you don't die of starvation." The wilderness manna of the Hebrews and the bread of Elijah's ravens filled more than stomachs, but they did fill the stomachs. And while a starving man will rightly prefer four sandwiches to the four freedoms, the prophets have long known that the divine image in man includes something comparable to a stomach; hunger for God is still hunger. The final bread, that which lasts, is the "other bread" that Christ saves for those who have had their fill and still are hungry. Vianney ate that bread first and needed none other.

Strength to Do More

Vianney wept with a "supernatural melancholy" as one too drunk to drink. That is why he kissed the ground beneath him and often kissed the chalice in his hands. The emptying, hymned in the Letter to the Philippians, had flooded into a fullness, the *pleroma* of Colossians, where "Christ is all in all". The expiring breath of Christ on the Cross was the first blast of Pentecost before Pentecost, and only the dead who had been emptied of life could hear it. And by fasting and other mortifications, the fellowship of Christ's disciples in all the ages has made a small emulation of that hollowness, like copying a hole by copying the hollow of the hole. "It is our emptiness and thirst that God needs", said Father Clerissac, "not our plenitude." Christ spoke of an evil that can only be driven out by fasting and prayer. When the devil spoke to Vianney, he called the Curé a "potato eater". It was his noblest insult. And Vianney was happiest on the Feast of Corpus Christi, when, with an empty stomach, he carried the Holy Bread become the Holy Body through the streets of Ars.

He could hardly bother to smell food, but, as is sometimes remarked of saints, he could smell trickery. There was the case of a farmer hiding one Sunday in a field as the Curé came along. The Saint made a straight line toward a haystack and laughed as he pulled the man out: "You are very upset to find me here, my friend. But the good God sees you always." No one in Ars was out of his scent, but for him it was more like digging up truffles than chasing foxes. When one cabaret proprietor complained about the Curé drying up business by his temperance speeches, Vianney told the man he had a point in justice, raised enough money to buy him a farm, and then shut the tavern altogether. He paid a fiddler double his normal fee not to play so close to the church. The youths howled when they found their dance canceled and taunted the Curé as he walked by; the master psychologist passed through them as though entranced by some great errand, and they dispersed "like a flock of sparrows". At the same time he created new festivals and processions and dressed the younger ones in costumes he designed himself. "Come, you must think that you are before the good God and hold the place of angels." Only about a fifth of the parish took this kind of talk seriously during the first few years.

The Saint was not successful at reviving the old custom of family prayers, which had remained dormant since the Revolution. Again, using his knowledge of human nature, he encouraged families to pray the family devotions in church alongside other families; a father would not feel so self-conscious that way. In not too long a time large numbers headed to church for night prayers and the Rosary at the sound of the Curé's bell. "My brethren, the good God looks neither at long nor beautiful prayers, but at those that come from the bottom of the heart. . . . There is nothing easier than to pray to the good God and nothing is more comforting." The plain truth is that prayer is like climbing the stairs; it is easy until you are told it should be hard. And of course sometimes it is hard; perhaps many times it is hard. But if we worry about which foot to put forward next we are far more likely to trip than if we keep climbing and focus our eyes ahead. Vianney spoke as a man to men who were under the impression that religion must be harder for men than for women; some of the men did not make their Easter Communion and thought their wives could do it for them. If by nothing else, the men were compelled by his audacity. He had a reason for every extravagant demand he made of them, and this impressed them deeply even when they had not the slightest idea of what he was about. And soon enough the Curé ceased to look like the village eccentric and loomed as the balance and unity of village life.

Vianney's faith was not at the expense of wisdom, nor was his zeal a substitute for prudence. He was the wisest and most prudent of the men of Ars, and this was a shining curiosity to men long taught that the practice of holiness was a surrender to the forces of unreason. Here was witness to the single-mindedness of monotheism against the monomania of atheism. Garrigou-Lagrange writes in the exemplary words of *The Three Stages of the Interior Life:*

> Nature is, so to speak, determined *ad unum;* it needs to be completed by the different virtues under the direction of wisdom and prudence. Great sanctity is thus the eminent union of all the acquired and infused virtues, even of the most dissimilar ones, which God alone can so intimately unite. It is the union of great fortitude and perfect meekness, of ardent love of truth and justice and of great mercy toward souls that have gone astray.

So the Curé was reeling side to side in that grand chariot of orthodoxy with a dizzying balance and sobering agility; the way he did it was on his knees. Ask the men of Ars. Their Curé could be found before dawn kneeling at the altar, arms outstretched, sometimes motionless and other times moving his lips quickly in what sounded like other tongues, or sometimes calling out phrases such as:

"My God, my all. You see how I love you and I do not love you enough."

"My God, give me the strength to do more."

"My God, here is all—take all: but convert my parish. If you do not convert my parish it is because I have not deserved it."

Chapter 8

THE GOOD GOD IS VERY GOOD

A Prophet Not without Honor

The national shortage of priests was particularly acute in the *département* of the Ain. The Carthusians of Lyons could not take care of all the vacant parishes, so Vianney was among the priests called on to give missions in obscure places: Trevoux, Saint-Trivier-sur-Moignans, Limas, Chaniens. The authorities were not prepared to call him eloquent, but they knew he was available. They ordained him only out of desperation, so out of desperation would he get to spread his work. But once he was seen and heard, he had distinct success; it came far more easily elsewhere than at home, another prophecy of Nazareth fulfilled. Other priests even began to intimate among themselves that he had a way with words, that in those missions a new diction performed the semantic wonder of coining old phrases and mouthing clichés for the first time. The crowd at the Trevoux mission of 1823 shoved so hard to get near him for confession that they nearly overturned the confessional with him in it. Unharmed, he kept it in his small repertoire of what to his native tastes were hilarious anecdotes.

When even lawyers began to wait on him for advice, some of the clergy began to think something uncommon had come into their midst. Surely his reputation as a confessor was surpassing convention. During the mission at Saint-Trivier, a rumor reached Ars that he had died. He had in fact gotten lost

on the way and fainted in the snow from hunger; the telling
thing is the assumption of Ars that he had died from exhaustion in the confessional. He spent six days in Montmerle in
1826, hardly ever leaving the church. The good-humored
pastor of Saint Bernard did not mind his congregation flock-
ing to the stranger: "I have a splendid missioner; he works
well and eats nothing." As his reputation increased, his
obliviousness to himself became a kind of holy shamelessness;
on entering the church in Limas, "I beheld the chancel full of
clergy and the body of the church packed with people of
every condition. At first I felt unnerved by the spectacle.
However I began to speak of the love of God, and apparently
everything went well: everybody wept."

Ars was not neglected during these brief trips. There are
countless stories of the visits he made to his families at all
hours. No matter where he was on mission, he returned on
foot for the Sunday celebration. He had but one cassock,
his hat, and a pair of heavy shoes. He would not wear a coat.
As for transportation, he went by carriage only when placed
in one after having collapsed from walking. Once he heard
the confession of a sick man lying down next to him, sicker
than the invalid himself. In 1837 the entire population of
Fareins poured out in welcome when he arrived to fulfill the
wish of a woman with cancer to see him at least once. Like
Pius X, he was constantly giving his clothes away; he was
known to stop behind a bush and remove his trousers from
under the soutane for a beggar. There was no telling how he
might appear on arrival anywhere: he returned to Ars one
day without his shoes.

So then, a prophet is not without honor save in his own
country and among his own people. His own country was

Ars. On the surface, parish life was more than well; between 1818 and 1824 there were more than twice as many baptisms as burials (ninety-eight). Confessions and Communions had certainly increased, and they increased together, for confession without Communion is Jansenism and Communion without confession is quietism. There was a healthy emphasis on both in Ars, and that was the problem. Slavic Christians have a saying: whenever God builds a church, Satan pitches a tent across the street. A virulent little discontent began to rise in some of the corners of Ars. By the firesides and along the paths, a grumbling began; there were those who resented being called pseudo-Capuchins by teasing visitors. The little Sin Town was getting a reputation of a little Holy Town. The more common refrain of resignation was "Our Curé is a saint; we must obey him", but a few began to call their Curé an *ingrat,* or bore.

Attendance at Mass had once again come to be expected; one way to express dissatisfaction was to yawn during the sermon. Other priests just let the men sleep during sermon time; it was something of a custom in the parishes during the long sermons, and Vianney committed the grave offense of speaking so shrilly that dozing was impossible. The ostentatious silliness became a kind of demonstration. The loud yawning was not boisterous like the organized taunts of the decadents against Athanasius or the orchestrated mockery of the Pope at Mass in Managua, but the Curé knew what was happening, and sometimes he would stop his preaching to remark: "When I am with you *I* do not feel weary." A mother, angry that her child had been denied absolution, helped start a commotion that lasted ten years. The remnant freethinkers, in danger of disenfranchisement, tried to capitalize on the unrest. Vianney detected the move immediately and did not obfuscate from the pulpit:

> If a villager has a misunderstanding with his pastor because, for the good of his soul, the latter has admonished him, the man at once conceives a hatred for the priest; he speaks ill of him; he loves to hear him criticized; he will distort everything that is said to him. Here is another who, in the priest's opinion, is not fit to approach the Holy Table: he will answer you rudely and foster resentment against you, as if you were the cause of his evil conduct. Another time it is a woman to whom you have refused absolution: at once she rebels against her confessor; in her eyes he is worse than the devil himself.

The Revolution of 1830 was almost stately in its restraints, as revolutions go, and it did not have very important repercussions in villages such as Ars; but seven residents took advantage of it to confect a local tempest. There was even a fleeting hope of restoring the old auguries of the Enlightenment. The dissidents demanded their Curé's resignation. The Curé ignored it, and after an awkward silence Vianney never reproached them afterward, though he remembered it well, and as an old man spoke of it vividly to a few friends in a way that showed the depth of his hidden hurt. In *Monsieur Ouine,* Bernanos perceived the hatred of priests to be as old as the human race, and it is no hyperbole. Even when there were no priests there was in various forms a suppurating hostility at anyone who tried to drag the agony of memory to a paradise whose gates were shut. Even when the rage is streamlined as a civilized anticlericalism, it remains an intimate affliction, revealing more of human discomfort at the consort of grace and nature than an advanced society might care to confess. So it was in Ars.

Like a chain reaction, the pent-up bitterness of some of the younger parishioners, still missing the old public vices, exploded. The presbytery was vandalized and placarded for eighteen months; excrement was flung against the door. The young Curé had crossed the generation gap. All this was going on in Ars as crowds were praising him in the other parishes. In 1823, the year of his memorable mission at Trevoux, the diocese of Belley was reestablished, and the new bishop, Monseigneur Devie, was obliged to investigate a series of wild accusations: the Curé's pallor and emaciation were from debauchery, and he had fathered the child of one of the village girls. Twenty years later, he looked back on the nasty carnival: "I thought a time would come when people would rout me out of Ars with sticks, when the bishop would suspend me, and I should end my days in prison. I see, however, that I am not worthy of such grace."

That same year he contributed the last of his small inheritance to the furnishing of a school for girls. It had one large room on the bottom floor and two upstairs, enough, he thought, to house twenty waifs and their supervisors. The two young women, Catherine Lassagne, who was a lifelong witness to the miracle of Ars, and Benoîte Lardet, who died a few years later from exhaustion, were sent by the Curé to study teaching for a short time with the Sisters of Saint Joseph at Fereins. The school began the following year and, run as it was on a shoestring, was called La Providence. As it charged no fees, it quickly became popular. In those years the roads were filled with orphans, victims of the national disarray, children given to begging or prostitution or both. Not until the Soviet *bezprisorny*, the "wolf children", who roamed the streets of Kiev and Moscow with flaming eyes in the nights after Stalin's and Molotov's engineered famines had starved off their parents, or today's vacant Western youth morally orphaned by the dissolution of the family structure and parental integrity, would there be such a pathetic judgment against a society that tries to live without God. The Curé began to collect these young, and by 1827 La Providence had to be enlarged. Without any more material resources, the Curé made a novena to the Blessed Virgin and then made some bricks; cajoling volunteers, he worked alongside the carpenters and masons, carrying the lumber and mixing the mortar. When the building was complete, he decided to admit only the destitute, yet there were so many of them alone that Catherine sometimes had to give up her own bed. Soon there were between fifty and sixty children for whom the Curé had to provide by "every imaginable transaction". What furniture of his own he still had went quickly. In jest Marie Ricotier offered five francs for each of his twelve teeth and was appalled when he began tugging at them. When La Providence's food supply ran out, he could be seen praying in the road.

The Beginning of Miracles

One of the great events in the saga of Ars occurred around 1829, when a few grains of wheat remained in the attic storage. Remembering the helpful saint at whose shrine he had prayed for his vocation, the Curé placed a small figure of Saint Francis Regis in the little mound of grain he was able to scoop together, and then gathered the children to pray with him. When Jeanne-Marie Chanay, a third teacher of bad disposition, was sent to bring the grain down, she could barely open the door. The large room was so full that grain poured down the staircase, and it was fortunate the main floor beam did not collapse. The mayor and others came to see the prodigy and had to admit that the new grain was a color different from the local variety. This was the first recognized miracle of the Curé: "The good God is very good! He takes care of his poor." And so did Vianney. The girls were taught skills to make them marriageable or to help them support themselves. The Curé tried to find each suitable work when she was old enough to leave, and none left without a small trousseau and the promise of a regular correspondence with Monsieur le Curé.

This beginning of miracles introduces a determinative part of his personality, that need for friendship that may seem incongruous with his hunger to be left alone: he had first prayed for the gift of solitude precociously at the age of eleven. The "flights" from Ars increased as his fame increased; it would seem that the solitude he sought was a solution for loneliness. As any parish priest must be, he was a social creature; and as any parish priest should be, he was an interior man. The coexistence of the two gifts makes spiritual perfection such an arduous task for a pastor, as we have heard Pius XII attest. Christ felt most futile at the height of his popularity. The poignancy of the parable of the Seeds on Barren Ground wafted over great crowds surrounding him, and his attempt to sail away alone in a boat was made when the throngs tried to put a crown on his head. Vianney did that three times, fleeing the faces and the appeals. Each time he ran away only to be turned back on the outskirts of the parish by an impulse greater than himself or the people. When he fled by night in 1843, his penitents pursued him and he returned to a cheering assembly, wearily blessing them with his veined hand; and when he tried one last time, this in 1853, they swept him back into the confessional to stay. After reading all the accounts, and taking seriously the intensity of his purpose, it is also quite clear that a will within him, which he himself discounted, would not have had it any other way. He was too innocent to be coy, but he was too holy to want to be alone. He spoke that way of the interior life of the soul: "Prayer is like two friends living together." His affection for special saints was of this order; he was on the friendliest terms with Peter, Joseph, Sixtus, Blaise, Michael, Francis of Assisi (becoming a Franciscan tertiary in 1846, which was almost like George Washington applying for U.S. citizenship), and of course Benoît Labre.

The most fascinating of these friendships was with one whose story is written on the thinnest air. Even the name of Philomena, like Veronica, may only be a title. The one thing known about her was her martyrdom at Rome. As ancient as she was, she had died in youth, sealing her youth, and the discovery of her remains by the excavation of her tomb in 1802 made her young and modern. The vagueness about her was her precise appeal; she cut a romantic figure at the start of the Romantic Age, for romance then was avant-garde and the look of the future. Monsieur Balley had taken his young charge to Lyons to meet Pauline Jaricot, the foundress of the Society for the Propagation of the Faith, who claimed to have been cured through Saint Philomena's intercession. From this encounter, Vianney's devotion took on almost exaggerated proportions, though it was a true romance so that not one part of the romance grew out of scale to any other part of it; it was perfectly gigantic and nothing so minor as a mere enlargement or inflation. Since, as the Church has recently resolved, not enough is known about her to warrant official veneration, it is appropriate to ask why Vianney praised her to such heights. It seems to me there are at least three reasons.

The first reason is that her virtual anonymity made her a convenient symbol for the general condition of sanctity, a personification of the Feast of All Saints instead of the saint of a particular feast. She was a sort of noble and holy cipher for heroic goodness; the mysterious allure was especially fit for the young, who needed something like that in the expressionless plain of Les Dombes.

The second reason may be that her indefinite gifts provided a foil in dealing with those who were too willing to attribute miracles to the Curé; "Thank Philomena, not me." She was more than a catchall: she was a flagrant and charming scapegoat lavishly decorated and let loose to wander the misty fields of Ars. "I am but a poor ignorant man who once tended sheep. Address yourselves to Saint Philomena; I have never asked anything through her without being answered." Philomena, that lovely obscurity, was his efficient intermediary and competent chargé d'affaires.

The third reason was her long silence: for seventeen hundred years she had been waiting for a Francis to her Clare, a Benedict to her Scholastica, a de Sales to her Chantal. When he stood before her shrine, the potato field of Ars was like a thin slice of paradise, and he an Adam able with her to name the animals. What Dante read into Beatrice, our Saint of Ars saw in Philomena daily in the plaster chapel he built for her. One does not need to say much to so close a friend; acquaintances discuss the weather and other superficialities, but the dignity of silence is a habit of intimacy. Part of Philomena's utility, and Catholicism directs every impractical obligation to a purpose, was her reticence. It was an eloquent device.

One day a geologist named Maissiat called on the Curé out of eclectic curiosity; at one time or another he had been a Jew, Muslim, socialist, and communard. Though he was unwilling to be a Christian, the Curé told him there was certainly no harm in kneeling before Saint Philomena's shrine; after half an hour Maissiat the syncretist was weeping orthodox tears. But the Curé explained it all with his familiar flourish. "Someone said: 'Is Saint Philomena now obeying the Curé d'Ars?' Certainly, she can well obey him, since God obeys him."

Vianney blessed the sick frequently, but with reluctance. He was no more of a professional healer than was his Master. Healing of the sick had the urgency of compassion in counterpoint to the salvific mystery of suffering, but not as an end in itself; the crookedest bodies often seemed to him to have the most upright souls. It would be an awful thing, he thought, to seek release from pain while remaining captive to pride. "The worst cross is not to have a cross." Before praying for the infirm he customarily asked them why they wanted to be well. To Françoise Lebeau of Saint-Martin-de-Commune: "My child, you can be cured, but if the good God restores your sight, your salvation will be less assured; if, on the contrary, you consent to keep your infirmity, you will go to heaven, and I guarantee that you will have a high place there." According to the testimony of her great-nephew Abbé Chopin, disclosed in 1911, she asked who would take care of her; and Vianney assured her that her eight brothers and sisters would tend to that, and then he accurately predicted the dates of each of their deaths. After many similar occurrences, he confessed that he had "forbidden" Philomena to work any more miracles in Ars: "It causes too much talk. I have asked the saint to cure souls here to her heart's content, but to heal bodies

elsewhere." But if he ever was coy, it was with her; informed
in the sacristy that a healing had taken place during Mass, he
said this was no surprise: he had "scolded" Philomena at the
altar: "Great saint, if you perform no more miracles, you
will forfeit your reputation." So the truth was out: the Curé
scolded saints instead of sinners.

But there were times when he was caught in the act of
healing without his holy friend's help. And the witnesses
knew what they saw. Standing in the aisle he noticed a boy
with a tumor on his face; it was daytime and people were
milling about. Moved by instinctive pity, he walked over and
touched the boy's face; as he removed his hand, the tumor
disappeared. His mild associate Toccanier stormed: "This time
you won't say it was Philomena!" In the ensuing clamor, he
pushed his way through the onlookers and shrank out of the
church like a child caught stealing cake: "How ashamed I was!
If I could have found a rat hole, I should have hidden in it."

Chapter 9

ARS NO LONGER ARS

The Schedule

A change could be detected in the parish even before the rumor and sight of miracles. In 1830 the high-pitched voice shouted from the pulpit, "Ars is no longer Ars!" No proof was more convincing than the farmboys saying the Rosary as they followed the ploughs. There was even less cursing in the fields. The Curé often related an incident about the farmer Louis Chaffangeon:

> A few years ago there died a man of this parish, who, entering the church in the morning to pray before setting out for the fields, left his hoe at the door and then became wholly lost in God. A neighbor who worked not far from him, and thus used to see him in the fields, wondered at his absence. On his way home he decided to look into the church, thinking that the man might be there. As a matter of fact, he did find him in the church. "What are you doing here all this time?" he asked. And the other replied: "J'avise le bon Dieu et le bon Dieu m'avise" [I look at the good God and the good God looks at me].

Or as Father Laurentin, I think, has noted, the word in dialect was "aveuse": to look and look very deeply. For Vianney, it was the highest form of prayer, and nothing needed to be added except Amen.

151

Jean Icard returned to his village in 1832 to find it "unrecognizable". When fruit was stolen, the Curé was asked to judge the case (he cut down his own trees to remove temptation); when shopkeepers had difficulty with their ledgers, he played bookkeeper; and when some preferred to bask in the bright ochre of the public square during Mass at least until the Gospel, he was the one who rounded them up. He formed sodalities and persuaded men to take part; about a dozen joined the fifty or so women in making daily Communion, a rare practice in those days but an abiding cause of the Curé. Only the very ill were absent from Mass on Sunday. A typical Sunday Mass, described in the diary of a visitor in those early days, "began at eight o'clock and lasted until eleven. There was a procession before Mass and a sermon after the Gospel. The Church was quite full. An extraordinary spirit of recollection prevailed."

Even for people before the age of television, it required a formidable attention span. At the stroke of one in the afternoon, clad in his surplice, he moved to a booth in the tiny nave from which he conducted the catechism. Later came Vespers, Compline, and the Rosary, with another sermon at night with bedtime prayers. The Sunday catechism perhaps intrigued strangers most. To see him surrounded by nearly as many adults as had attended Mass was to learn that the lessons were not only for children. As accounts spread, distinguished intellectuals went to Ars to consider what was being done, and they often had difficulty finding room. Part of the secret, of course, was his way of speaking directly across to the children, not down to them; at such an altitude the adults were able to grasp something, too, about how to approach the Kingdom of God. As much as anyone, he reminds us of his contemporary Saint John Nepomucene Neumann, who was found dead on a Philadelphia street carrying a wrapped chalice and some candy that he kept for the children. On such afternoons in Ars, the language was little different from that of the juvenile catechism he used to make up when he was his own child in the pastures of Dardilly; writers have been fascinated by the ageless intuition, the maturity of the child, and the childhood of the man; or as the Curé said, "How beautiful, how great, to know, to love, to serve God. We have nothing but that to do in this world. Anything whatever that we do apart from that is a waste of time." A child could learn from him all he would need to know about a sacrament when he was no longer a child: "When you go to confession, you must understand what you are about to do; you are about to un-nail Our Lord." The Saint had not entered a second childhood; he had barely left the first. The noble minds who came to listen, and the worthy theologians who came to check, saw that face, the face of Ars and of the world renewed, and that smile as old as creation's first Sabbath. Voltaire would not have lectured this way.

On weekdays the catechism began at six in the morning, held in a schoolroom of La Providence; by 1845, because of the crowds, even this daily exercise was moved into the church. For all his talk of the sky and sea and sheep, this was not a harmless man in a clerical collar talking about friendly animals. High dogma it was, and deliberate. "Worldly people say that it is too difficult to save one's soul. Yet there is nothing easier: keep the Commandments of God and the Church, and avoid the Seven Deadly Sins; or, to put it another way, do good and avoid evil. Here is a good rule of conduct. Do only what one can offer to God." If this was harmless, so was the "hate evil, love good" of the prophet Amos. Little separated the roughshod shepherd of Ars from the battered shepherd of Tekoa. There still are some pedagogues in our own day who would fault Vianney for requiring the young to memorize prayers, lists of virtues, and hymns. But these are the same experts who have given the Church a generation of breathtaking illiteracy. Long after the Curé died, the children grown old and scattered were still saying the prayers on a hundred hills. Anything worth the heart's attention is worth learning by heart.

Not by authority or the privilege of authority did the Curé command such attention. Anyone there was witness to the trust he engendered, and he won the common trust by winning individual hearts. His vehicle was the priesthood; any priest could have done it by being a priest, and it was only when priests failed to be priests that they betrayed the popular confidence. The love of a priest is the unbounded love of the priest for his priesthood, which is what he meant when he called the priesthood the love of the heart of Jesus. By showing the people, even the youngest of the people, himself, he displayed the universal love of which the priest is mediator. In a world of rusty and broken clericalisms, he restored a shining sacerdotalism; if a clericalist is a man who uses the priesthood, a sacerdotalist is a man who is used by the priesthood. And thus the hierarchical constitution of the Church is a bureaucratic artifact to the clericalist, while it is charismatic to the priest. The clericalist pursues a career of which mediocrity is the safeguard, while the sacerdotalist pursues a mission of which ardent love is the token. Consequently, the priestly soul is in the world but not of it, as the clerical caste is of the world but not in it. By being a true priest, the Curé engendered the trust of souls who had come close to losing the very sense of place in the world. One of the great modern English actors has recently told of his conversion to Catholicism, which he formerly had thought a forbidding and obscure thing, and its priests arcane and suspect men. One day, when he was dressed as a priest after shooting a scene for a film about a priest, a child ran up the road alongside him and confidently took his hand, babbling in the language of the land the actor little understood, and then ran off. The trust of the boy in an anonymous figure was a revelation to the grown man, for while he was dressed as a priest, he represented to the boy a universal heart. So it was with Vianney, and all the children who memorized his words entrusted themselves to the confidence that made the world.

The Art of Ars

Few acts were as typically Franciscan as the way the Poor Man of Assisi began the restoration of the Church Universal by repairing little Portiuncula. It was characteristic of the Curé d'Ars that he tried to renew a fractured century by fixing the cracks in his hovel of a church. His schedule of renovation was a systematic fragment of the Passion and Pentecost and Eternity: the cross on the tower was strengthened when he arrived in 1818, the next year he replaced the broken bell, and the year after that he restored the clock. Then in steady order came chapels to the Virgin, John the Baptist, and Philomena. At the climax of his life, the year before his death, he purchased a great marble altar, and plans were in his mind for a whole new edifice.

Questions of taste are another thing. Ars was not artistic. Even Croce or impeccable Ruskin would admit there is no record of anyone getting to heaven on the merits of good taste, and it seems that the world's holiest shrines can be the world's tawdriest. Shrines, after all, are the Church's kitchens, not her dining rooms. The only statue in Chartres not remarked by the guides is Our Lady of the Pillar, before which all the candles are lit. To the shortsighted, painting primeval may look only primitive. André Malraux complained of the early Christian catacomb paintings that their crudeness "answers so poorly to that Voice in all its depths". But there is no evidence that the Voice was offended. Dorian Gray's portrait was more elegant than an icon; but unlike his portrait, an icon improves the longer you look at it. The Curé knew little of great art, but he did want the best that could be had. An innate asceticism was part of the aestheticism: do only what can be offered to God—a far cry from the kind of aestheticism that becomes a substitute for God. By the most admirable instinct, what was beautiful to him was that which was also useful, as Aristotle had held in his sensual rationalism; and was that which was also attractive, as Aquinas held in his rational sensuality. The embellishments of Ars were innocent of frills. Even the gilded statue of the Immaculate Conception, which he lived to celebrate as dogma, had a purpose: the metal heart held a ribbon on which he had written his parishioners' names one by one.

It is hard to imagine how the only 230 residents of Ars could cram into the church. The restrained classicism of Vianney's decorations fit well the intimate scale. The Curé's one hobby, if we can call it that, was his excursions into Lyons to buy vestments and banners; when his time did not allow even this, he considered it a red-letter day when such packages arrived as gifts of the Vicomte d'Ars. On the subject of music the innocence was the same. No one says much about the music in Ars except the suspicious comment that it was hearty. When a marching band surprised him by joining the Corpus Christi procession, Vianney visibly trembled with glee.

Gheon says Vianney had impeccable taste. I think it is truer that he loved beautiful things, though his single tutor was the intuition of spiritual purity. He did exhibit an impeccable contempt for exploitive sentimentalism. There were transgressions, though remote in every way from the folk *kitsch* afflicting modern church architecture and hymnody. Transgression would not be an altogether right word, and he was reaching above himself, not beneath himself. Any hint of gaudiness was not the meretricious vulgarity of weak faith. And by weak faith I mean the sentimental cult of faith in faith itself apart from its higher object. If the limited role of affection in religion exhausts the religion, it distorts true Christianity as does the rationalist's attempt to make cognition a religion of itself. The modern atheist and the religious modernist are equally capable of the self-serving sentimentalism that a vibrant Catholicism refutes. The Curé's aesthetic exploits were really spectacular outrages and not slips at all. For example, there is the saccharine engraving of the Holy Child, as typical of its period as minimalism was of ours; but his decision to hang it over the men's confessional was magnificent and brave.

A depth psychology, which he alone could plumb, was at work there. But no one can deny that it worked. A century from now, critics may dismiss an engraving by Matisse the way they discount the little framed wonders of Ars, but religion has the privilege of insisting that art "work" before it is judged. A connoisseur cannot appreciate the artlessness of Ars until he tries to pray with it. Modern pilgrims complain about the ugliness of the present small basilica there. It encases most of the original church, which was saved from complete destruction by Saint Pius X, the Pope who called Vianney his "companion". But the Curé probably would have liked it and would even have been overwhelmed by it, in his diffident way. He was raising money for its construction at the time of his death, arranging a lottery that was canceled when the government failed to grant a license. In this case, France had become the Curé's ethical guardian. His only objection would have been to calling it his basilica, when he had wanted it in honor of Philomena. His body reposes there now, in the gilded reliquary supported by figures of Saint John the Baptist, Saint Francis of Assisi, Saint Francis Regis, and Saint Benedict Labre.

Then comes the ritual complaint: he was wasting on finery money better spent on the poor. First-class tourists gliding through Latin countries often say that sort of thing with the indignation of the superior man in Bethany who objected to the extravagance of the women with the ointment. Christ disagreed, and the Curé d'Ars disagreed, too; at least he did not think it was a sign of social irresponsibility to agree with Christ. He spent more on the poor than on his statues, and he demanded of no bureaucracy sacrifices he was unwilling to make himself. Generosity is a duty, and it is not generous if it is a favor; it is a duty to God as well as to the children of God. Unlike secular enterprises, Christian works of mercy tend to stimulate an outpouring of beautiful things. But this is an aside. What matters is the hidden philosophy of a holy aesthetic: Vianney, rarely spending anything on himself, knew that his art commissions were sacrifices by which Ars might be freed of that most dreadful of all poverties, banality.

Banality equates poverty only with a lack of things. This is the most insidious kind of materialism. Only the materialist can pretend that the lack of things is the ultimate emptiness. Banality is a coefficient of boredom, and boredom is the dereliction of a limited aestheticism that fails to locate beauty in the virtue of hope. Hungry people are not ugly, but bored people certainly are. Thus the bored cannot understand why the poor should have beautiful things. But conversely, the poor find it difficult to understand why the rich should be bored.

Each time a culture has grown tired of itself, it has been surprised. When a civilization decides that everything explorable has been explored, someone sails home from a new world; and when a social system boasts how best to channel discontent, a flag is waved to start a revolution. Louis XVI's sore mistake and miscalculation was the smugness of his liberalism. Those who make little discoveries find it hard to recognize big ones. It becomes virtually impossible to recognize the greatest one of all, that mysterious discovery of the redeemed human soul called by Saint Paul the weight of glory. So ironies abound. In the Cultural Revolution under Mao, a committee of Party members was commissioned to compose a concerto, and in the same breath Beethoven was declared an enemy of the people.

A most surprising discovery for the bored populist is the heroic populism of the hieratic Church. The papacy has been the most egalitarian government of history. If it has crowned princes, it has also crowned peasants as rulers of princes; many times the Shepherd of Kings really has been a shepherd. The world-weary modern objects to the great weight the Church has pressed down on the world, but the burden consists in bearing the weight of glory, flashing against a million meager imitations of it. To bear the burden means to bear the Christ of Catholicism, and it has been done by surprising people in every corner of the world, and even in lamentable Ars.

The spectacle of Vianney carrying his golden monstrance, under a golden canopy through festooned dirt roads as fireworks exploded, can rattle the mind. Even in dusty Ars the one ritual guide was the Book of the Revelation. The Curé did not believe tyrannical grey to be God's color or that the masses are helped more by massive bureaucracies than by the Mass itself. He would not render the consciousness of his people too weak to bear the weight of this luster. In later years, bathed in perspiration after carrying the Blessed Sacrament for two hours, he was asked if he was tired. "Oh, why should I be tired? He whom I carried likewise carried me."

Chapter 10

GRAPPIN

Satan's One Virtue

The modern age, which has seen the power of evil so gigantically displayed, is also a time of disbelief in the existence of evil. In 1972, Pope Paul VI told nations reeling from hunger, violence, indolence, and nuclear threats that evil is not an absence of good: it is a "living, spiritual being" who is perverted and perverts: "What are the greatest needs of the Church today? Do not let our answer surprise you as being over-simple or even superstitious and unreal: one of the greatest needs is defense from that evil which is called the devil." And he publicly lamented that the smoke of Satan had even entered the Church. The warning redresses what had already become the quandary of Vianney's progressivist culture. Father Ravignan said of the devils in the nineteenth century: "Their masterpiece, Sirs, has been to get themselves denied by the age."

The closer one gets to a thing, the harder it is to see all of it. That which is plain as the nose on your face may be, like the nose, difficult to notice unless you are cross-eyed. A thing very terrible happened when Christ spent forty days in the wilderness, and a thing more terrible happened when he spent three hours on the Cross, and a thing terrible beyond any description happened when he spent the timeless hours between the Cross and the Resurrection. These blanks are absent from the diaries of Buddha or Confucius or Socrates.

But they are the indecipherable pages of the life of the Son of Man. They will impinge on the lives of all those who acknowledge his divinity and accept him as Savior.

In the extraordinary events in Ars, which began in 1824 and lasted until a year before the Saint's death, the terror and wonder of the confrontation between good and evil were palpable. Abbé Sandreau, an authority on exorcism, wrote in his treatise *The Mystical State:* "The devil acts on all men by tempting them; no one can escape those attacks; these are his ordinary operations. In other very much rarer cases, the devils reveal their presence by troublesome vexations, which are more terrifying than painful; they cause a great noise, they move, transport, knock over and at times smash certain objects; this is what is called *infestation.*" Spiritual directors also list *obsession,* by which the individual is affected physically, and *possession,* by which devils act in and through the individual's consciousness. The Saint of Ars was victim of both infestation and obsession and had to deal with souls possessed. He paid the price of holiness, evoking the agony of the spirit of evil who has been vanquished by the Holy One, enduring a procession of explosive confrontations between enormous evil and greater good over a period of years almost identical to the life of Christ on earth.

Good may scorn evil, but Satan and his lesser angels are haunted by any evidence of Christ, and the repeated history of these duels is like the story of a moth that never dies drawn to a candle that never goes out. Virtue becomes the channel of moral reality, since the fulfillment of a design is the degree of the design's approximation to perfection. If evil is substantial, Satan must have one virtue to enable him to exist at all, and it is the virtue of taking Christ seriously. As hatred is the ground of enmity, and fear the ground of guilt, and love the ground of adoration, the secularist denies himself the deadly virtue of being a devil, the vital virtue of being a sinner, and the eternal virtue of being a saint. The secularist denial constitutes the state of alienation, being of the world but not in it. Worldliness is an incapacity for the world, and no amount of sensitivity therapy or assertiveness training can conquer this devastating inability to be either a foe, a penitent, or a friend in the eyes of God. The disintegration of the personality by the misguidance of worldliness is resolved by integration with the life of the virtues; this is fully accomplished when the virtues are resolved in Christ as their chief good. The path follows through four stages: alienation from God, hostility toward God, awe of God, and adoration of God. This final stage is expressed in the seventeenth-century lines of Crossman:

> My song is love unknown,
> My Saviour's love to me,
> Love to the loveless shown,
> That they might lovely be.
> O who am I,
> That for my sake
> My Lord should take
> Frail flesh, and die?

Humanity is recovered by worship, for the soul is made to worship God as its proper end. By corollary, alienation understood temporally as divorce from the self is caused by that wider alienation that is divorce from the Wholly Other. The alternative to monotheism is monomania. Then the social implications of this are enormous and acutely simple: all social relationships, personal and institutional, work well to the degree that God is given permission by the free human will to work through them. Hostility challenges God, as in the case of tyrants; fear misinterprets him, as in the case of neurotics; adoration yields to him, as in the parish of Ars and the communion of saints. But each of these forms, however pathetic or heroic, must be more substantial than the absence of moral consciousness altogether; even a wrong attempt at divine encounter is more human than the denial of human value altogether. Even when we doze into a kind of moral somnolence, the sight on the horizon of leaky vessels bearing refugees from empty workers' paradises reminds us that it is so.

Apathy, more than hate, is the temper of hell; when Ars was ransomed from hell and brought near to heaven, we must expect that it became violent for awhile. The one who can make his bed in hell is naturally a sound sleeper, but Vianney hardly slept at all, for he already had a foot in heaven. He had to be alert, for he detected a malignancy in the very air that wanted him to fall asleep and not wake up. If you will, by showing Ars the road to heaven Vianney was also disclosing the path back to hell. That was not his motive, but it was an inevitable part of the heavenly vision, and it always has been. I have said that there was nothing morbid about the Curé: he did not pursue the mysterious iniquity of evil as a neurotic or hysteric. Because of this alone, because of this incontestable equanimity and soundness of judgment, his confrontations with strange Satan cannot scientifically be dismissed as a weird curiosity of no application to an age that has learned to tranquilize itself, or as a psychotic hallucination, as Thalamas at the Sorbonne once rejected the voices of Jeanne d'Arc.

The infestations of Ars indicate what happens in one form or another when any heroic virtue is attempted. Christ had conversations, or confrontations, with demons. Patristic ascetical theology is fully aware of them and recognizes that temptation can come from diabolical intervention or from human will, as separate causes; and Saint Paul warns against "the prince of the power of the air, . . . the spirit that now works in the sons of disobedience". To impute every temptation to Satan is morally irresponsible; the Manichean dualist was irresponsible that way, but no more than the modern materialist who denies individual culpability. Whether from within or without the soul, temptation is not sinful; as an invitation to sin, it is also an opportunity for grace. By the humble submission of the will to the influences of grace, the tempted soul encounters a love greater than any human love. God looks on the soul struggling against temptation with a love no human can match. Humility is the key to the struggle, then; pride is the ally of weakness, exploited by the dark intelligences. If the devil and his ministering spirits have "lost the good of the intellect", they have not lost the intellect altogether. Their brooding intelligence of the power of grace is their endless torment, and the great intelligence that once was the luster of angelic brightness has trapped them like insects living inside their own skeletons. They exploit the inferior human intelligence by confusing self-estimation through the falseness of pride. Since the Enlightenment, the diabolism has whined into human ears the seductions of an unaided reason that will understand all truth, and of a self-assertiveness that will liberate the conscious.

Christianity has been as solemnly reticent about these operations as it has been definite about their existence. Speculation beyond the evidences of revelation runs the danger of making Satan equal to God in his determinations and effects, a cruel

God over against a good God. Origen declared of the demons that the holy apostles "merely stated the fact that things were so keeping silence as to the manner or origin of their existence, clearly in order that the more zealous of their successors, who should be lovers of wisdom, might have a subject of exercise on which to display the fruit of their talents". Lovers of wisdom at any time can recognize a conundrum and are not reluctant to toss the problem of evil into the lap of the next generation. And it remains for self-styled progressivists, who have abandoned the discretions of orthodox belief, to dabble in occult theorization. Yet there are four certitudes held by the Church against gross naïveté.

The first is an encouragement to the sound intellect: the devil cannot tempt humans beyond their strength, for grace is stronger than evil. The second is a warning to the intellect: the devil deceives. He plots ("Satan" means adversary in Hebrew), he uses great spiritual power (the meaning of the Greek *"daimon"*), and he confuses through syllogisms and other intellectual paraphernalia (*"diabolos"* is the Greek description of a betrayer who faults victims for the very sins he has foisted on them), making the proud intellectual his easiest prey. Third, the devil's method is logical: he camouflages his purposes in excuses suited to the imagination and habits of each personality, a lion for some and a serpent for others, grey and precise for the cerebral, mauve and sensual for the compulsive, tempestuous for the impulsive, ethereal for the aesthetically inclined. Fourth, he operates through human beings and human institutions in a parody of Christ, who uses people as branches to his vine and who establishes the Church as his own body; and as *corruptio optimi pessima est,* the devil first infests, obsesses, and possesses parents, consecrated religious, scholars, and political leaders, who are the essential guardians of the human order. But most commonly, he harms them not through infestation, obsession, or possession but through plain temptation.

Variations of materialist philosophy reject these certitudes, and each modern heresy has neglected them. Consequently, modernism in general has appropriated a Gnostic bias, for Gnosticism is a functional misunderstanding of the relationship between good and evil in the economy of cause and effect. To a notorious and pathetic degree, the modern university has become a Gnostic fief, an institutionalization of the rumbling philosophical disorders of Vianney's own age; and like the *philosophes,* the modern materialists of the academies have encouraged moral and philosophical attitudes most hostile to the life of the intellect. They have, for one thing, replaced the governing love of the good with an unwieldy philanthropy that now is in the process of cannibalizing its own subjects. For much of the modern adventure, higher education has pretended to portray the human epic while ignoring the pathology of evil and the operations of grace. Such a system of education is futile when it ignores the drama that has engaged Satan and the saints since lamps were first lit in the corridors of experience.

The Hauntings

Then the devil is true to himself by being false to others. He displayed this characteristic when he began to attack Ars just when some of the local rancor began to abate, and when construction began on *La Providence.* What is known of these things is a little like the retelling of the great Passion, and the information is a unique literature. The drama of the Passion narratives is all the more powerful for the absence of any striving for effect. The evangelists seem to have hesitated before putting pen to parchment, and that is the only theater they add to the central drama of history. Some have called it "gospel impassibility", and to be impassible about the Passion is either cynical or inspired. Each apparent lacuna is a turbulent lake of grace, rather as a pause in music creates the rhythm and each note is another way of calling attention to the stops between.

In the accounts of Christ's duel with Satan, there is no need to embellish what has been brooding from the start of time when it stunned history into speechlessness. The gospel narrators did little if they tried to make sense of that encounter; it is truer to say that they were trying to recover their sense after it. The gospel is good news because it is traumatic news, and it is shocking by having happened in an unshockable world. The eloquence of divinity is the diction of silence, a full half hour of it in the most momentous revelation of the Revelation. Christ is suffocatingly more silent the closer he gets to Golgotha. The reticence drove Judas to exasperation, and, one by one, the other apostles fled into a huddle. Pilate pleaded from his cobwebby throne for one word from the Man to break the silence. For the rest, the Stations of the Cross are punctuations in a vast unspoken dialogue between uncreated good and created evil. The record extant is only an outline of that, but it says much as an outline: after all, outlines do mean there is something in the lines, and a map of China can tell more about China than a shovelful of China.

From a literary perspective the outlines are guidelines, and from a theological perspective they are headlines. If a dramatist objects to their drama, he is objecting to drama; a headline dramatizes a news item simply by saying in black on white that it is news. All religions began with poetry except one: because Christianity is true, it began with journalism. Then all religions become predictable melodrama, save for Christianity, which is unpredictable drama. The early Christians did not even think they belonged to a religion; they were moving along the Way. Blatant as this is, it should preclude the tendency of literary criticism to treat the gospel narratives primarily as literature: they are indeed high literature, but not typical literature, for they lack a literary motive.

So, too, the hauntings of Ars are bare and blatant. The descriptions are spare, though attested in bold type. The Curé usually was silent on the subject, but an offhand remark, coaxed by subterfuge, could reveal much. Even when he did speak, he tended to tint the events with humor. We report them as circumstances, bound by biographers in leather, but more importantly scarred in the skin of the human animal. They are presented as marks of the struggle that roots the soul in reality and prevents him from being swept away in some meaningless tide of time. In the human experience of evil, there is a fraternity that unites souls through each depredation of time and change: flesh was bought in ancient coagulant Carthage for the same price it brings in Times Square, arrows in Sparta and bullets in the Bronx both aim at hearts, and, in the logic of nature, a widow of the Neanderthal who banged bones on the wall of his cave mourns as deeply as the widow of Mozart. But it took Ars and Vianney to distill the desolation and hurt until the crystals of evil could be seen and smelled.

The two physicians closest to the Curé, Dr. J. B. Saunier

and Dr. Aimé Michel, had no doubts about his veracity and emotional stability. Abbé Chaland said that if these occurrences had been bad jokes, the perpetrators would have been unmasked at once. Efforts to mythologize the diabolical events fly in the face of his solid awareness of them, of his astuteness and his equilibrium. A madman may be mad about just one thing, or about many things, but not about everything: either Vianney was beyond madness or he was totally sane. Certainly there was no evidence even of dysfunctional anxiety. A modern writer volunteered that the manifestations were "the result of his interior conflict" and "were unconsciously caused by him, though in the present state of our knowledge we cannot say how". Possibly most personality derangements attributed to diabolic causes are the result of emotional disintegration, but the Curé's personality was not unhinged. He was in the admittedly suspicious role, but in his case a perfectly true role, of being the only man on parade who is not out of step. To deny that, in view of the natural evidence, requires a whole new science of denial that runs against science itself.

As for delusion, Vianney recognized the happenings for what they were after a long period of denial himself: at first he was as blind as any plain empiricist. The night banging and shouts in the yard were burglars, he said; they must be trying to get at the modest "treasures" from the vicomte that were stored in the attic. He appointed a twenty-eight-year-old wheelwright as night watchman. On his first night, at one o'clock, a banging on the door and a riotous noise like carts rolling through the room began. The house shook violently, and the watchman quit. Vianney was amused that such a burly fellow should be so terrified. He hired others who heard nothing. One winter's night the sound of shouting soldiers tore through the night, but no footprints were in the snow. The Curé grew convinced that these were infestations by the fact that they frightened even him: "God does not do that." His resolution was adept: "I turn to God, I make the sign of the Cross, I address a few contemptuous words to the devil. I have noticed, moreover, that the tumult is greater and the assaults more numerous if, on the following day, some big sinner is due to come." And his "big catch" usually showed up the next day, as predicted, for confession.

The evil one terrorizes no one as much as he is terrified himself by Christ the Victor; a losing foe can still win incidental battles before the war's end, but the outcome for the world is certain even when individual fates are not. A provincial council of Braga, Portugal, declared in 561 against a group called Priscillianists, who did not believe that the devil was a fallen angel created by God; and the Fourth Lateran Council pronounced in 1215: "God by his omnipotent power, from the beginning of time, formed from nothing both types of creature, spiritual and corporal, that is angelic and earthly: and finally the human creature as made up of spirit and body. For the devil and the other demons were indeed created good by God, but by their own devices they became evil." Dualists such as the Manicheans and Lactantius had vigorously held the idea of an uncreated devil engaged as Darkness in an unresolved war against the Light. The secular pessimist and especially the moral relativist come close to this superstition refuted in Saint Anthony's spirited reply to the demons: "If you had any power, one of you would be sufficient. But Christ has hamstrung you, and so you try to frighten me by your numbers." As holiness affirms the unity of being, evil fragments it. Christ makes one Church of us, who are many, and desires that "no fragments be left", but Satan is the anti-Eucharist, who makes his oneness into many. Thus the prologue to the old rite of exorcism: "Evil is Someone, Someone who is multiple and whose name is Legion."

The Curé did not call him Legion. His name for the spirit of division was the diminutive *grappin,* a little rake or grating fork. "The *grappin* is very stupid; he himself tells me of the arrival of big sinners." And thus the timid failure of the Grand Séminaire flung before subtle moralists his guileless truth about the Liar: evil when not seen is very terrible, but when exposed to the higher logic of grace is "very stupid". It seems that he envisioned the ubiquity of Legion as something absolutely unlike the universality of God; if God's center is everywhere and his circumference nowhere, the devil's center is plainly nowhere and his circumference everywhere. Vianney's deft masterstroke of dogmatics, in keeping with his *Roman Ritual,* was to speak interchangeably of the devil and devils while knowing we cannot speak of God as though there were gods. He whose name is Legion, who said, "What have you to do with *us?*" said with one voice, "*I* know who you are"; and though he speaks in many wind-whistling voices in the various ages of man, his singular purpose is to capture the attention of fallen man, to complete in the human race a collective of hollow men leaning together. The aesthetic modern wasteland of T. S. Eliot was already perfectly clear to the Curé d'Ars. For the devil's strategy is clever, but being without imagination or inventiveness, it is predictable once it is deciphered. So as Christ mockingly called the prince of the devils "Beelzebul", Vianney rolled the name *grappin* over his tongue as though he were nicknaming a naughty pet. It was the subtlest and most violent theology of all: ridicule is one affliction that makes the angel of pride feel like hell.

"Vianney! Vianney! potato eater! Ah! You are not yet dead! I shall get you all right!" The sound rattled and overturned furniture. Sometimes it growled like a bear or snarled like a dog; when it did speak it spoke the local dialect. For potato it used the patois *truffe*. The infestations became obsessions. Sometimes the spirit, or spirits, felt like rats running over him, and sometimes they tried to toss him out of bed. On other nights the straw mattress became suddenly soft, and the voice sang a lullaby or seductive tune. In the next morning, the Curé would arrive at Mass pale and shaken. In 1826 as he walked to Saint-Trivier to preach, the atmosphere took on a sinister glare, and the roadside bushes glowed a sickly red color; when he arrived to begin the mission, four witnesses in the presbytery watched his bed get tossed about and deposited in the middle of the room accompanied by shrill squeals. A picture of the Annunciation in his own presbytery had filth flung at it. When his visiting sister heard the noises, he calmed her with words we would not consider a consolation: "It is the *grappin*. He cannot hurt you; as for me he torments me in sundry ways. At times he seizes me by the feet and drags me about the room. It is because I convert souls to the good God." The voices also discomforted a plasterer from Montmerle. In 1838 there was the witness of a philosophy student named Denis Chaland who had been allowed to make his confession in the presbytery: "I knelt on his prie-Dieu. Suddenly, when I was about half through my confession, a general convulsion shook the room; my prie-Dieu trembled like everything else. Full of terror I tried to stand up. Monsieur le Curé kept me down by seizing my arm. 'It is nothing', he said, 'it is only the devil!' At the end of this confession Monsieur Vianney decided my future career: 'You must become a priest.' My excitement was still very great, and I must admit that I never again went to confession to the Curé d'Ars."

In February 1857 his bed went up in flames as he was hearing confession in the church. Possibly, a natural explanation could be had, but the flames burned a clearly defined area around the bed and stopped in front of a small reliquary of Saint Philomena. "The villainous *grappin!* He could not catch the bird, so he burns the cage." On some days shouting matches could be heard from the confessional when the Curé was alone in it. These reports annoyed him when they spread; he loathed hysteria and had spoken out repeatedly against the occult, especially as spiritualism was becoming a fad in the parlors of the *haut-monde.* Things were getting out of hand, hardly as a reaction to rationalism but rather as its logical slide into the deeper cults of egoism. Even Napoleon III himself commended his personal medium to a fascinated Queen Victoria during a state visit at Osborne House in 1857. The nonsense would reach an apogee after the carnage of the First World War and may yet reach fantastic new heights as reincarnationalists, cabalists, channelists, and gurus exploit the vacuum left by modern denials of the Resurrection. When a penitent had been involved in any such thing, Vianney seemed to sense it before the individual confessed, and sometimes he confessed it for him. We know that he did this to a young nobleman and to an army captain.

Rarely did he perform exorcisms, and these he did so unobtrusively that few knew what was happening. This way he calmed a woman who hurled herself at him shouting, "If there were three like you on earth, my kingdom would be destroyed. You have taken more than eighty thousand souls from me." Antoine Gay was an exceptional case, and his life is found in other annals of the period. He was born in Lantenay in 1790 and lived in Lyons, where he appeared to develop a second personality who called himself Iscaron and proclaimed himself a devil. Unlike simple schizophrenia, this other voice could read minds and reveal hidden facts with uncanny fluency: Iscaron became violent at the sound of prayers; replied in his own French to questions posed in Latin, which the subject had not studied; and exhibited varieties of mood unusual in the most distressed personalities. He was examined on two occasions at the behest of Bishop Ginhoulhiac of Grenoble and the archbishop of Lyons, to whom a certain Dr. Pictet wrote in 1843:

We, the undersigned, doctors of medicine, residing at the Croix Rousse, certify that M. Gay was presented to us by the Abbé Collet and by M. Nicod, vicar of the town, in accordance with the instructions of the Cardinal Archbishop of Lyons that he should be put under medical observation. Having therefore observed M. Gay scrupulously every day for four months, at all times and in all situations . . . we have not been able to discover the least sign of moral or physical weakness. . . . We remain convinced that his extraordinary state can only be attributed to possession. This conviction is reinforced by the fact that during our first interview with M. Gay, that extraordinary thing which speaks through his mouth revealed the inmost secrets of our hearts, told us the story of our life since the age of twelve giving details which are known only to God, our confessor and ourselves. And we have seen the same thing happen to others, many of whom have been converted.

Having been placed in a mental asylum at Antiquaille, Gay consented to be taken to Ars by a priest named Chiron and his friends M. Goussard and M. Houzelot in November 1853. On seeing the Saint, Antoine dropped to his knees, shaking his fist violently as the voice of Iscaron called out: "Vianney, you are a thief! You are stealing from us the souls we had such difficulty in winning!" The Curé made the sign of the Cross, and the man shrieked. Vianney became certain that the case was diabolic and wrote to the cardinal of Lyons for permission to perform the rites of exorcism. It is not quite clear why the archbishop was sent the request, since jurisdiction belonged to the local ordinary, who in due course granted it. However, the rites were further delayed for obscure reasons, though Vianney had arranged in this case for a solemn ritual at Fourvière. As it turned out, the exorcism never took place; in the following years, the interior conflict worsened, though Gay died in 1871 in a state of grace with conditional absolution after years of mortification. Until that last release, Iscaron would shout whenever the subject approached a confessor: "No confession, unless I am first freed." He who spoke frequently of such things long ago, to the dismay of later romantics, and who saw Satan as lightning fall from heaven, was careful to teach: "Rejoice not that the spirits are subject to you; but rather rejoice because your names are written in heaven" (Lk 10:20).

Father Faber writes in *Growth in Holiness* of how the devil keeps "overreaching" himself. It is not that he is stupid. Because of ignorance he keeps missing: his pride blinds him to the extent of God's grace, and, in turn, we contract that ignorance and cannot believe or even anticipate the strength of divine love until the soul yields to it.

Thus the devil sometimes tempts us too openly, and we are on our guard; or he sends us the wrong kind of temptation, as one man sometimes gets a letter intended for another; or he sends the right temptation at the wrong time; or, as he cannot always read our thoughts, he puts a wrong interpretation on our outward actions; or he leaves off too soon; or he persists too long; or he under-estimates the effect of penance and our love of God on the old habits of past sin. So it is that from one cause or another he is continually over-reaching himself . . . he is simply our fellow-creature. We have reason to fear him. Yet we are not panic-stricken with the hourly companionship of our own corrupt nature: and we have far more to fear from it than from him.

One thing, perhaps the most important thing, to remark is the power of Vianney to make the overreaching *grappin* panic. On January 23, 1840, in the presence of eight persons, a maniacal woman confronted him in the chapel of Saint John the Baptist:

You ugly black toad, how you make me suffer. . . . We war on one another. . . . But for all that, it does sometimes happen that you work for me. . . . Why do you examine the conscience of your penitents? Isn't what I make them do enough? You were anxious to withdraw into solitude. Why don't you? Why do you rise up so early? You are disobeying the Bishop who has ordered you to take care of yourself. Why do you preach so simply? You pass for an ignorant man. Why don't you preach like a great man, as they do in the towns? Ah! how I delight in those great sermons which do no harm to anyone, but leave the people to live in their own way and do what they like.

Heard carefully, it was a *via negativa* to salvation. And Vianney did listen carefully. The logic of the *grappin* was relentless, prelude to the sinuous pattern by which he now torments the affairs of dissolute individualism: "I delight in those great sermons which do no harm to anyone, but leave the people to live in their own way and do what they like." Surely *grappin* should be subtler than that, to stoop to such blatant inanities. Ridicule dispels him quickly, said Saint Thomas More, and yet Vianney had ridiculed him only to enrage him more. Saint Philip Neri chased him with one slur, Saint Dunstan pinched his nose, and Saint Martin of Tours called his bluff when he came disguised in the trappings of Christ except for the holes. Vianney had tried all that, but *grappin* kept haunting Ars, stuttering like a spoiled child. Is it possible that the evil one, like the good world itself, was growing senile? Lucifer offered the Son of Man the three definitive temptations of satiety, power, and glory, and the Master was only annoyed; was it the same Lucifer now juggling dung and tossing mattresses in Ars? Very well, then, he must have decided that the Curé was too stupid to waste great temptations on; little taunts would whittle the woodenhead into submission. One of the taunts nearly worked and became the single abiding temptation of the Curé's life: when the voice "which was very ugly" prompted him to seek solitude, it was dredging up the longing from the earliest days in Dardilly.

Fleeing Ars

If the devil hates the prayers of cloisters, he is embarrassed by the prayers of parishes. And for the prince of pride himself, as we have seen displayed, the needles of embarrassment are more cutting than the fiery arrows of ardent faith. If the devil cannot corrupt a parish priest with things of this world, he will try to take him out of the world altogether. Tempting a good soul with goodness is a trick sleeker than tempting a sinner with sin. The Achilles' heel of most creatures is their pride: Vianney's was his humility. Satan could not win him by being a devil, so he would present himself as an abbot. He would not demand curses from the Curé; he would receive the Curé's vows. He would ridicule the Saint just as the Saint ridiculed him. It was a backhanded compliment. On a dark day in modern Vienna, the Nazis forced elderly Jewish women to climb into the branches of trees in a park, and made them chirp like birds. Not since God first blessed the birds of the air has bird song sounded so sad, but it is one way the devil would tar and feather creation. And each such mockery is another evidence of that yawning chasm between good and evil: Christ humbles and does not humiliate, while Satan tries to humiliate everyone and humbles no one. Even the scorn he seemed to cast at the Canaanite woman (Mt 15:21–28) was an act to elicit her profession of faith. Only once did Christ humiliate, when he humbled himself to humiliate the humiliator of man. Satan humiliated Vianney by persuading him that he lacked humility; sleepless and increasingly deprived of contemplative prayer by long lines of penitents, Vianney was tormented into the idea of a monastic vocation, the noblest of vocations for those called to it and the very corruption of those meant for another kind of work.

Shortly after the voice grilled him from the throat of that poor maniac in the church, Vianney fled Ars and its adulation. A few moments past two o'clock one morning, he hurried out of the presbytery and out along the road until brought to a halt by the sight of the pilgrimage cross that stood in the field of Les Combes like a flaming sword guarding imagined gates of paradise, though it was hard to tell which side of it was Eden. In dejection he headed back to Ars. The most extraordinary thing about the whole adventure was Vianney's total neglect of himself as the reason for the pilgrimage of Ars. There was a scale to his presence and a measure to his influence so enormous that he certainly could not calculate it; he could not even see it. Vianney actually thought nothing would be changed in the parish if he left.

Another crisis came in 1843. His regimen had not helped his chronic neuralgia and gastritis; then he nearly died from pleuropneumonia. At one point the physician gave him thirty minutes to live. The recovery was sudden, some said miraculously so, and as soon as he could stand he ran out of Ars. This time it was broad daylight and the crowds tagged along, begging him to turn back; but he pressed on the seven-hour hike, his run changing to a walk and then a tortured drag until he reached the family house in Dardilly where his brother now sat at the head of the table. When the Vicomte des Garets arrived the next day to urge his return, Vianney refused to receive him. Even the bishop sent a message. A day later, a Friday, the pilgrims of Ars arrived as a group, and the Curé relented so far as to request local faculties to hear their confessions. On Saturday a delegation of twenty-three young men arrived from Ars with a petition for his return. His curate, Raymond, was not as reluctant as the others to have him gone. He intervened and spirited Vianney off to the seclusion of Beaumont, but after one Mass he shook his head, "God does not want me here." No general in retreat was as dejected as Vianney bouncing in a coach to Amberieux and from there on foot to Ars, leaning on a cane. The sight of the church tower was a tonic and he raised his arms: "I shall not leave you, my children." Then he moved from one to another, repeating his promise to each parishioner, face to face. Going off to weep for his "poor life" had failed, but *grappin* had failed more dismally.

So far as one can tell, the trite threats against the Curé were garish signs of how frustrated Satan is; his own angelic gift of liveliness is gnawed at relentlessly so that it remains like a few scattered bones on a plate, not deadly or lively but an awful deathlessness. The protaganist in *The Man Who Was Thursday* says, "I am more than a devil; I am a man. I can do the one thing which Satan himself cannot do—I can die." The Saint of Ars, who wrote no novels, preached, "The angels sin and are cast into hell. Man sins and God promises him a liberator." Satan's veritable anguish wails against the solid grey stone of the hard Easter tomb. The fumbling Curé's ability to die to himself was another pinch of salt in the gaping lesion of the evil one, who is the festering wound of the world.

In the dark of a night near the end of these tribulations, a cracking and crashing sound rattled the sleeping village. Two galloping horses pulled a coach wildly through the narrow paths and stopped abruptly outside the presbytery. Some men got out and waited silently. At midnight the Curé appeared at the door with his lantern. One of the figures approached, placed a hand on his shoulder, and said in a tender voice, "Monsieur le Curé, if you wish to depart, we have a coach ready." The Saint stared for a moment: "I have not the permission of my bishop." Then removing the figure's hand, he hurried on weighted legs into the church.

Chapter 11

THE PILGRIMAGE OF ARS

The Paragon of Diffidence

One of the strangest things about Ars was its familiarity to foreigners. As early as 1827, an average of twenty outsiders came to the settlement daily; even one visitor to that place would have caused remark. Nothing succeeds like success, but then again, nothing quite fails like failure. Had the Curé failed to touch some responsive chord in the visitors, curiosity would have died out soon enough. But the odd cocoon of Ars changed them from tourists into pilgrims. Numbers of the curious who had neglected the sacraments for years, allured by reports of the "miracle of the wheat" (and by a similar multiplication of bread a while later), left restored to Communion.

Nothing annoys like success, either. The Church's slow resurgence in France was renewing the antipathy of the anticlericalists; the hostility would not abate in the Curé's life, and indeed it would culminate in the expulsion of religious and confiscation of Church properties in 1906. When Archbishop Darbois of Paris blessed the firing squad as it shot him in the Commune of 1871, he was wearing a cross and ring that had belonged to Archbishop Affré, who was killed in the Revolution of 1848, and Archbishop Sibour, who was assassinated two years before Vianney's death. The local clergy of the Ain were trying hard to deal with political realities on their own level and could do without eccentric clerics aggravating the volatile atmosphere. Vianney should make a gentle-man's agreement with bourgeois sensibilities; such a rigid man today might even preach against contraception to suburban congregations. His housekeeper testified that at clerical confer-ences "he always appeared poor and contemptible". This led to reports that he was not hygienic, a virtue among some of the desert hermits but possibly the only sin remaining among the enlightened. Lepers used to be the unclean, while in a more affluent and degenerate society the unclean are the only lepers left. The mendicant of Ars was in fact meticulous about such things, though his cassock was a true disgrace, his hat a shame, and his shoes beyond description. In his first years in Ars, what patching was done was done by himself; when Catherine Lassagne found him sewing some breeches, he said he was a tailor instead of a Curé. Suffice it to say that he did not mind being called shabby, but he turned sullen when those who had never met him called him dirty.

His brother priests had a deeper complaint. One said, "He is no more a wizard than we are." The bishop and the retired priests, who had no vested interests, sided with him. The pilgrimage grew. Some of the clergy forbade their parish-ioners to go to Ars; its Curé, they all remembered, had failed his few motley months at Saint-Irenée. If his education was faulty, his orthodoxy was reproachless; he had a vigorous reputation for urging common sense in the preaching of others. Moreover, an increasing number of theologians sought him out for advice. The wizard of Ars gave no quarter to obsequiousness, nor did he suffer gladly the enthusiasts who claimed private revelations of the Holy Spirit. To a woman who asked with ineffable sweetness how one should go to God, his response was "Quite straight, like a cannonball".

Nevertheless, in 1841 the Abbé Borjon, age thirty-two, sent a letter from his parish, which was a short walk away: "M. le Curé, when a man knows as little theology as you do, he should not go into the confessional." The reply, had it come from anyone else, would have been a masterpiece of caustic irony. To his credit, Borjon realized that his older neighbor lacked enough guile for that. Vianney's letter read:

> Most dear and most venerated confrère, what good reasons I have for loving you! You are the only person who really knows me. Since you are so good and kind as to take an interest in my poor soul, do help me to obtain the favor for which I have been asking for so long a time, that being released from a post which I am not worthy to hold by reason of my ignorance, I may be allowed to retire into a little corner, there to weep over my poor life. What penances there are to be undertaken! how many expiations to be offered! how many tears to be shed!

Borjon folded the letter, walked to Ars, and flung himself at the Curé's feet.

Clerical envy continued. We cannot judge, but it may be that in some of the local clergy there was a spirit of littleness that when it is not virtue is horrible vice; especially among priests, that which is the humility of great hearts can sour as the meanness of small hearts. There are clerics in every generation inclined to private ambition as the recourse of mediocrity: called by a divine vocation but pursuing a human career; obliged to tradition but governed by precedent; commending excellence but condemning the excellent; submissive to authority but enthralled by human respect; conformed to honesty but confounded by candor; consecrated to sacrifice but scandalized by detachment; scornful of the Pharisees but dutiful Pharisees of the Pharisees. A petition was circulated among Vianney's fellow priests accusing him of sensationalism, ignorance, and ostentatious poverty and austerities. As it was addressed to all the clergy, Vianney got hold of it: Vianney read it; Vianney signed it. This paragon of diffidence truly signed it as a man signing his name for the last time. Bishop Devie told the annual priests' retreat that he wished all his clergy had a small grain of Vianney's madness. Typically, the Curé d'Ars, who called himself a sinner, called Devie a saint and preserved one of his rochets as a relic. By 1834 the local priests themselves were going to Ars for confession.

The Servant of God Josemaría Escrivá once compiled an inventory of pride so exhaustive that it is like something written on the shield of a soldier who has learned it all in true combat. Vianney wrote the same thing in shorthand when he signed his name to the clerical petition. The seventeen evidences of a lack of humility are: to think that what one says or does is better than what others say or do; always to want to get your own way; to argue with stubbornness and bad manners whether you are right or wrong; to give your opinion when it has not been requested or when charity does not demand it; to look down on another's point of view; not to look on your gifts and abilities as lent; not to recognize that you are unworthy of all honors and esteem, not even of the earth you walk on and things you possess; to use yourself as an example in conversations; to speak badly of yourself so that others will think well of you or contradict you; to excuse yourself when you are corrected; to hide humiliating faults from your spiritual director, so that he will not change the impression he has of you; to take pleasure in praise and compliments; to be saddened because others are held in higher esteem; to refuse to perform inferior tasks; to seek to stand out; to refer in conversation to your honesty, genius, dexterity, or professional prestige; and to be ashamed because you lack certain goods.

The Local Carnival

There was a report of a Curé in Ars who kept all the precepts of humility and resisted entire each allurement of pride. Monseigneur Devie thought it would be superfluous to give him a title; he was more famous than any canon. The number of pilgrims to the prodigy increased by 1845 to three to four hundred arrivals daily. A special office was set up in the principal train station of Lyons to book tickets for eight-day tours: that had become the usual waiting period for the confessional. Special omnibuses met the trains from Paris. By the year of the Curé's death they were coming by the tens of thousands. Bishop Ullathorne of Birmingham saw many pilgrims sleeping in the meadows; to him the Curé described the day when England would return to its ancient Catholic splendor. Hotels could not be built fast enough. Even with the sound of their construction and the clatter of new traffic, Ars was padded with a pregnant silence. France had a saint.

Of course the Curé complained, and loudly: Ars had become a carnival. And he was the fool at its center. As he was to blame for refusing to sit for a proper portrait, he had to stop objecting to the poor likenesses hanging in the shop windows along the main street. When the sculptor Cabuchet surreptitiously tried to capture his features in a ball of wax during the catechism, Vianney sternly bounced him out of the church.

The Saint had another simple idea: he would pretend to be a simpleton. That would get rid of the pious fans. There was a genuine village idiot, and Vianney carefully studied him; soon the Curé was standing in the square juggling coins and mimicking the gawkers. In exasperation he gave up: his dunce's cap had increased the public wonderment. Vianney could be only Vianney; and that was the whole point of Ars, for as only a saint can be himself, so a saint can only be himself.

His schedule was a marvel of its own, and possibly a sensible miracle of sanctifying grace; if not absolutely supernatural in its very essence, *quoad substantiam,* then certainly preternatural as beyond human wants and capacities. It is a simple fact that he hardly ever slept. He began the day by taking his lantern through the sleepy crowd to begin his prayers at one o'clock in the morning; the Curé was punctual about this. From then until six, when he celebrated Mass, he heard the women's confessions. From six to eight, following private acts of thanksgiving, he mingled with the knots of pilgrims, blessing medals and chatting freely. Then he crossed the square to La Providence for half a cup of milk. Nuns were living in community in Ars in the later years, and he was able to use this time to talk with them. The men's confessions began at half past eight in another confessional, a rather crude wooden affair set up in the sacristy.

He heard the men's and women's confessions separately because the animated universe is sexual, and not unisexual or bisexual, which are forms of hostility to the charisms of femininity and masculinity. Difference is a necessary condition for equality, and as I have noted in an earlier chapter, to deny that is blatant sorcery; and with high irony modernism, having tossed aside true priestcraft, has dipped into the dark regions of nature and drawn out witchcraft. Sexual dignity is not sexist for the same reason that natural law is not sexist; a woman being a woman and a man being a man do not play roles unless the roles are part of the divine drama of creation. The creation of man and woman was God's greatest outpouring of perfection; we cannot pretend it was his one mistake. And to think sexuality is mere costuming, as if it hides some authentic asexual nature, is an anthropological heresy as miswrought as the christological heresy of the Monophysites. By respecting the delicacies of sexual order, Vianney used an astute psychology based on created reality and sanctified by the sacramental distinctions that God has made in the order of grace and ministry, contrary to the Gnostics. The women of Ars became more heroic in their womanhood, and men were restored to the Faith who had been lost to it for many years. And all because Vianney knew his Church is a mother, and so fecund a mother that she would make him father of a large family.

There was a break in the daily schedule at ten for prayers and then more confessions, until eleven when he returned to *La Providence* for the catechism, which ended with the noonday Angelus. It took fifteen minutes to get through the crowded square back to the presbytery to eat what he called lunch, standing all the while and talking to visitors. Abbé Monnin says he never sat down before anyone else and never let anyone stand out of respect to him except during liturgical ceremonies. The conversation during lunch was usually well animated, with the Curé telling most of the jokes. Then at half past twelve a large group escorted him to sick calls. This was a trying time, as more than a few took the opportunity to snatch pieces of his clothing; when someone produced a pair of scissors to snip some of his hair for a souvenir, he stared meekly but afterward confessed that he "nearly boxed his ears". After Vespers and Compline he heard women in the confessional until five and the men until eight. Then he climbed the pulpit to lead evening prayers and the Rosary. Sometimes more confessions and special conferences followed. He had no time for committees and never took a day off. The bishop would not permit the Curé to go on retreat despite his pleadings; the bishop, possibly with imprudence, insisted that a retreat would be superfluous. The Curé never left the church before ten and sometimes remained until midnight. He was back at the stroke of one. This means he slept two hours at most before beginning a new day. And he did this seven days a week for thirty years.

Monsieur Toccanier asked him, "Father, if the good God gave you the choice, either to go up to heaven at once or to go on working as you are at present doing for the conversion of sinners, what would be your decision?" "I should stay on." "But the saints are so happy in heaven! No more sufferings, no more temptations!" "Yes, in heaven the saints are happy indeed, but they are like men who live on their income. But they have labored well, for God punishes laziness and only rewards work; however, unlike ourselves, they cannot, by their labors and sufferings, win souls for God." "If God left you here below until the end of the world, you would have plenty of time in front of you; surely, you would not then get up so early in the morning?" "Oh my friend," the Curé replied with tears, "I should certainly always get up at midnight; fatigue has no terrors for me: I should be the happiest of priests, were it not for the thought that I must appear before the tribunal of God in the capacity of Curé!"

Cardinals, doctors of divinity, merchants, aristocrats, the

military—all waited their turn in the aisle. Some of the richer
tried to buy the places of the poorer. An indignant woman
pushed ahead, muttering that she did not have to wait even in
the Vatican; Vianney raised his head and said that if the
empress herself arrived, she would have to wait in line. A tale
was told in which the empress disguised was said to have
made the pilgrimage; there is no evidence, but many other
prominent figures arrived incognito to avoid journalists and
gossip. No one was concealed to Vianney. A disheveled woman
in the throng was surprised when he sprang out of the confessional and stared at her: "You, Madame, you are in a hurry.
Come at once." A bewildered sacristan got used to being sent
into the square in search of individuals described as wearing
such-and-such by the Saint, who could not have seen them. A
stranger confessed that he had not been to confession for
thirty years; the Curé corrected him: "Thirty-three". The man
took out a pencil, did the subtraction on the wall, and admitted that the Curé was a better mathematician than he.

For every distressed soul reconciled by his encouragements,
a self-satisfied soul became distressed. The Curé might say
after a quick glance, "My friend, you are damned." Except for
the still hours between ten or so and midnight when the
church was shut, it was crammed with bonnets, birettas,
uniforms, farmers' smocks, and no sound save the whisper of
petitions, boots on stones, beads rattling, and the occasional
cry of a baby. Heavy with the scent of incense and burning
wax, it could be miserably hot in summer, frigid in winter;
sometimes it had to be fumigated with vinegar. From the
small aperture in the confessional day and night at each season
he seemed to be singing more than speaking when his voice
carried: "Love! Love! Love the good God!" "Love your priests!"

"What a sin! What a pity!" Most times the counsel was little more than a word or two. The Curé did not confuse the confessional with the psychiatrist's office; even in pre-Freudian days he could distinguish between sacramental acts and analysis. And so when that one man asked him why he wept so much, he replied it was because his penitent wept so little.

He refused to make a little trip to have a look at the railway that was bringing so many to Ars, but not because he thought like Baudelaire that the steam engine is a denial of God. Such silly romanticism would have made authentically romantic Vianney laugh. He did not visit the railway simply because he did not have to use it. This was romanticism at its highest level, pragmatism. Not the capitalized Pragmatism of philosophy, yet clearly a pragmatic efficiency typical of the daily lives of inventors and laborers, and of the one young Carpenter of Nazareth. Lyons and Grenoble were the only cities he ever glimpsed. Rather than saying he overcame these limitations, it would be truer to say he took advantage of them; to be so limited as that is tantamount to being limitless. Although he made it a practice to read the newspaper as little as possible, he predicted that the infant prince Napoleon, of whom he had not seen a picture, would do well because he had a "well-shaped head". Napoleon III, on the other hand, would "one day be an enemy of the Church".

This was a time when liberals and ultramontanists in the Church were closing their ranks, but the abstruse concerns of both signified little to him. He was, or seemed, oblivious to the cause of Dupanloup; and neither Lammenais' *Avenir* or Veuillot's *Univers* figured in his discussions. In retrospect, it might be tempting to pin a party label on him, but such would have been implausible: his one party was Catholicism.

One day in 1849 an exiled Carlist officer fulminated far out of Vianney's hearing about the "liberal Pope". That afternoon the Curé challenged him: "Pius IX will be one of the greatest Popes that ever ruled the Church." He would have been of a mind with John XXIII, who is said to have wanted to beatify Pius IX and Newman together. But any party identity that is more of a habit than a philosophy was out of his consideration.

Far removed from the world of abstract speculations, Vianney nonetheless lived the same verity that Pius IX and Newman, according to their different styles, rained down on the aridities of nineteenth-century liberalism. The Pope perceived a shadow cast by the democratic enthusiasms he had favored until 1848: and it was the denial of Christ as the point of reference for all history. According to the liberalism of the age, humans are victims of history. It was a relatively inchoate socialization of naturalism, according to which truth itself is only a natural evidence conditioned by events, and conditioned even more by subjective response to those events. To this way of thinking, God must be a projection of the self; in the modernist idiom God did indeed come to be an allegory of the higher human will. Twentieth-century modernism is the residue of that nineteenth-century idea; Newman had consecrated all his life's endeavors to expose and defeat it. His predictions of what it could lead to were as severe as those of the Pope, for whom he penned more than one fervent and affectionate prayer. He said outright in his *Discourses and Arguments on Various Subjects:* "Surely, there is at this day a confederacy of evil, marshalling its hosts from all parts of the world, organizing itself, taking its measures, enclosing the Church of Christ as in a net, and preparing the way for a general Apostasy from it."

The disillusionment of Pius IX, expressed in the *Syllabus of Errors* five years after the death of the Curé d'Ars, was stamped with the same realism of Newman, and for that reason it was a specimen of hope. I say that because disillusion employs reality to subvert those illusions that, when mistaken for the way things really are, sow the seeds of a thousand pessimisms. The courage to be objectively disillusioned requires hope in objective truth, and hopeful the Pope was. Indeed, he was so animated by the virtue that he braved wide ridicule in order to deny "that the Roman Pontiff can and ought to reconcile himself and reach agreement with progress, liberalism, and modern civilization". The phrase was laughed to scorn; but the laughter is now being drowned out by the disappointed howls of those who trusted progress, liberalism, and modern civilization. The Pope did not deny the vernacular facts and goods of cultural advancement, or equality of social initiatives, or the scientific future; but he refused to impute to those things the naturalistic definitions of atheism. He dignified his opponents by using their terms exactly as they meant them, and his categories sound arcane only if they are not understood in that sense. So he was not Canute holding back the sea; but he was the fisherman who knows much about the sea, who knows that the sea rolls back and forth and that Christ has walked steadily upon it. Canute was the progressivist, the liberal, the modernist, who thought he could command the sea of time and events by reciting the molecular formula for water.

Newman and Pius IX have been done disservices by the modernists. They called Newman a modernist because he spoke of the development of doctrine, and they called the Pope a reactionary because he spoke against the doctrine of development. But in fact it was the modernists' misfortune to neglect their common voice: both taught an objective truth, ultimately revealed by a transcendent source to which culture must subscribe if it is to survive as culture. The modernists picture Newman as the herald of the twentieth century and the Pope as the retainer of the nineteenth. Both actually had more of the twenty-first century in their bones. They had every expectation of the twentieth century being a cacophonous interlude between harmonies of faith.

Modernism is now a defunct artifact without quite yet seeming so, like an elephant that has died standing up. It stands indicted by the events it sought to shape, disproved by the philosophical structures it appropriated, and propped up by ideology. The modern dialectician is an oracle who waves his scrolls long after the words have faded, a philosopher who keeps on talking after he has lost his argument, a man of ideas who has forgotten his idea of man. Pius IX's stern words were classical in their due proportion; they calculated the difference between philosophy and ideology and chose philosophy. His *Syllabus* was just what mere reaction is not: it was a contradiction of those views that isolate the intellect from the true future. If you will, it was a reaction against reaction, and in this it was immensely prophetic, one of the first inklings of postmodernism. If the twenty-first century corrects the mistaken confidences of the recent past, it will hold Pius IX and Newman in mutual honor. What the Pope solemnly taught and what Newman preached and set to rhyme, the poor Curé in poorer Ars whispered in more limited lines to the poorest sinners. As is the case of the Pope and the Cardinal, if Vianney annoyed the nineteenth century and was ignored by the twentieth, he may be uncovered anew in the century to come.

The Old Wizard

Vianney's intuition was free of conditional clauses. His was an ecology of thought, trim rather than meager, spicey with regionalisms and clear with the Cartesian perfunctoriness of the national tradition. Gheon says, "Freud, who explains everything by 'repression' would have to say that M. Vianney gave back to his environment immeasurably more life than he received from it." Now, Eric Hoffer has said that the scientist reads the equation "human nature = nature" from left to right, while the savage reads it from right to left. But since a part of something cannot be the whole thing, only magic according to Hoffer could make this equation work. And in one degree he was correct. We might say, for instance, that modern behaviorists were magicians who turned man into a rat in a maze, and the nihilists were magicians who turned man into a superman. Science without God is magic, and when science is magic it is also savagery. We can go back to our old axiom: the alternative to orthodoxy is superstition. There is some of this superstitiousness in attempts to demythologize Christianity, but that just remythologizes with myths that are not valid. Sanctifying grace is literally the saving grace by being the violation of magic. It works by an efficient equation that is true, the equation formulated by the mathematician of Psalm 82, who wrote "You = gods", and by the mathematician of Aquino, who wrote "nature + grace = NATURE".

For Vianney, to confuse a priest with a magician was such an elementary contradiction that he treated it as a jest: he mocked himself as "the old wizard". So wild and rare was his flair for the symmetry of nature and grace that he examined the very days of the week according to a redemptive scheme:

Sundays were dedicated to meditations on the Blessed Trinity ("Whenever we pray or enter the church to pray, we please the Three Persons of the Holy Trinity"); Mondays were for the mystery of the Holy Spirit ("In heaven you will be nourished on God's breath"); Tuesday was the day of the angels ("Goodnight, my guardian angel, I thank you for protecting me this day; offer to God my heartbeats while I sleep"); Wednesday was the court of heaven ("The fish swimming in the little stream is content because he is in his element, but he is even better in the sea"); Thursday the Holy Eucharist ("There is nothing so great as the Eucharist ... if God had something more precious he would have given it to us"); Friday the Passion ("To understand that we are the work of God is easy, but that the crucifixion of God should be our work is incomprehensible"); Saturday the Immaculate Virgin ("If the sinner invokes this good Mother, she'll find some way to get him in through the window").

Here is a curiosity we cannot pass off, a glimpse of a great science of soul behind smaller sciences of time and space: within the limited horizon of Les Dombes he acted as though he could see beyond the peripheral vision of human imagination and memory. A considerable part of the world came to find all the parts of the world put together in Ars, as if all the paradoxes of nature were becoming splendid platitudes. For example, a woman he had not met went to Ars privately mourning her husband, who had drowned himself; Vianney singled her out in the church, and before she could say a word he told her, "Do not worry. Between the bridge and the water your husband repented and made an act of contrition. Pray for him." It was an ability produced by the union of moral and physical reality. That is, Vianney had not only anticipated the modern "conquest" of nature; he had positively conquered the illusion of conquest. If nature is totally understood by human reason, then it is not totally natural. It is only the rational part of it.

What once were thought to be scientific challenges to God are now more clearly clues to the complex order of his creativity, and the supernatural intuition of Vianney remains part of that stunning network. A considerable theological significance lies in the words of the Berkeley physicist Henry Pierce Stapp: "Everything we know about nature is in accord with the idea that the fundamental processes of nature lie outside space-time but generate events that can be located in space-time." When Copernicus flung the gauntlet down before Ptolemy, he also flung a red carpet before the mystery of divine particularity. Einstein's chalk marks on his blackboard intimated something deep about time and space, in which "I AM" is a name, and Alpha is Omega. If earth is not the center of the universe, then God's moral regard for his human creatures is more miraculous than the Ptolemaists and flatlanders thought. In the confluence of physical and moral reality, which modern scepticism has tried to divorce, sin and virtue are intrinsic to physical meaning. And the ability Vianney shared with some other saints to converse with figures long dead, to perceive thoughts and anticipate events, is a graceful conformity to the deep facts of life: facts that are obscured by limited intelligence in the physical degree and by limited virtue in the moral degree. Brilliant without benefit of academic rank, elegant without benefit of social rank, and worldly wise without benefit of political rank, the Curé was one of the rare mortals who could command nature to be more real. Natural physics has reached a frontier so wide that the physicists can hardly open their mouths without sounding meta-physical. When the frontier is crossed, we will find that there really are giants in the land, and the giants will be what they have always been, what for want of a better name we call saints. Long before the fruition of subatomic physics, the saints knew what they did not know, and this holy and mystical lacuna was the secret of their powers.

A casual anecdote here, an elaborate account there, make it difficult to choose what incidents to single out: there are so many. Vianney was merely perplexed by people who were astonished by them, when the greatest wonder often went unnoticed on the altar. Long after he had ended his day, and all night on Holy Thursday, he knelt singing to the Blessed Sacrament. It was intolerable that anyone should receive the Sacrament lightly, and he had the unsettling habit as he passed along the Communion rail of denying the Sacrament to those who had not fasted; how he discerned was a mystery, but he was invariably correct.

Walking along the road to Ars from the general region of Saône-et-Loire on a rainy Ash Wednesday in 1857, one could have noticed a working woman named Anne Devoulet push-ing her eight-year-old crippled son in a broken-down handcart. In Ars she made her confession and then brought the boy in for a blessing. "The boy is too big to be carried. Get up, my good woman, and set the little one down." "But he is unable to stand!" The Curé kissed the child on the forehead and ordered him to walk. The boy first crawled, then walked, and then ran outside where he skipped in the mud.

A girl who had been mute for three years after a paralytic stroke recovered her speech when he gave her Communion. Walking through the square on February 1, 1850, he singled out the deaf-and-blind Claudine Venet and led her into the confessional; she came out with hearing and sight fully restored. The Apostolic Process details more than thirty such happenings.

Of greater importance to the Curé were the miracles of souls, and these had fewer witnesses. There was the time a woman of fashion stopped by. Bored on her return to Paris from her villa in the south, she made a detour to see the spectacle of Ars. Vianney confronted her outside the front door of the church: "You, Madame, follow me." Proceeding to relate the sins of her life in his disconcerting way, he told the struck woman that confession was useless in her case. "I can read your soul, and there I see two devils that enslave it, the devil of pride and the devil of impurity. I can only absolve you on condition that you do not go back to Paris and, seeing your dispositions, I know that you will return there." As she was honest enough to admit he was right, he agreed to see her again that next morning; when the appointed hour arrived, he denied her absolution again. Then he told her she would quit Paris eventually for her villa, which he described in detail, and there would receive grace for repentance. Obdurately, she returned to Paris, soon found herself back in the south, and after no little time confessed her conversion.

In 1852 François Dorel, of Villefranche-sur-Saône nearby, accompanied a friend to see what was going on. In his early thirties and not wanting to look pious, he brought his shotgun and dog along for some duck shooting after Mass. The Saint was passing through a bevy of petitioners outside as the two arrived, and he walked up to Dorel: "Monsieur, it is greatly to be wished that your soul were as beautiful as your dog." Dorel put his gun down, went in to confession, and died in 1888 in the habit of a Trappist. Others, as ardent as the young hunter was cool, came to Vianney to say they had vocations to the religious life and so on, only to be discouraged. One young woman cooed, "Father, tell me where I should enter the novitiate: at the Madames of the Nativity or the Madames of the Sacred Heart; I should prefer the Madames of the Nativity because they know me." "I fear", was the holy man's reply, "that is not saying much." Some who went to him, such as Caroline Lioger, went on to found congregations. The panoply of the people of God lined up outside the confessionals like peacocks in display: Dominicans, plasterers, Jesuits, housemaids, barons, silk dyers, bankers, in ever-increasing numbers. Agitated personalities who found no complete resolution of their disbelief were changed in some immeasurable way and gave the little Father in Ars their own halting blessing.

The clarion message of Ars to all was this: there is a more perilous impediment to holiness than misdeeds, and it is tepidity. The human soul can share, above even angelic knowledge and love, in the intelligence and nature of God himself, but only through divine union. Goodness is a fruit of the Christian life; it is not the tree itself. Thus the symbol of salvation is the Cross and not the holy Commandments, for holiness as a state more profound than conformity to moral precept requires identity with the salvific sacrifice of Christ: "Father, I desire that they also, whom thou hast given me, may be with me where I am . . . " (Jn 17:24). The Calvinist moral tradition had been uprooted from the unitive vision of the natural law; consequently, the common environment of much Western culture has a deontological morality, aware of legal precepts but unaware of holiness as their end. It festers even among nominal Catholics, who become indigenized to its cultural matrix. People then can ask in perfect seriousness, "Is such-and-such still a sin?" and they can think that if a mortal sin is legalized by the civil courts, then it is not a sin at all. The lukewarm spirit lacks the resolve to investigate the inconsistencies of these errors; certainly it lacks the courage for sacrificial worship. A veritable hallmark of the tendency, in fact, is the decline of the high concept of the Eucharist as a sacrifice; it is easier for tepidity to find expression in ritual fellowship meals and the like when it has not yet slid out of religious customs altogether. The Saint of Ars stands as a refutation of the mediocrity of both the old deists and their new counterparts, who have celebrated life in ways that have forgotten how to celebrate death and Resurrection. By a dreadful amnesia of all that makes the soul breathe, the blood of Calvary and the white of Easter have been blended through the alchemy of reductionism into a sentimental pink.

More than Socrates

Generally speaking, there are two kinds of reactions to the penances Vianney gave. Either they seem too severe or too lax. On careful examination, it seems that he measured them carefully; even after hearing thousands of confessions, he did not fall into a machined uniformity. Each who went to him got, as they say, a custom fit; he was not exaggerating when he told Catherine her priest was a tailor. The penances, most of which he took on himself, had the purpose of what the spiritual directors name *metanoia,* a complete change of spirit. The idea of a priest as a "change agent", who does little more than help a soul adjust to the environment, never entered his head. For all his humility, he was a triumphalist, if in its better sense it means jousting with dragons instead of petting kittens. The beast alive in the form of selfishness forces the soul to fight instead of to adjust; that alone, not counting his uncongenial tooth and hide, is what makes him beastly. The Curé might assign a blasphemer or a cheat three Hail Marys and might excommunicate for a dozen years a woman who went to a modest party. It sounds ridiculous, and many still consider this side of him even offensive, since we do not see the real beast as he did. People on television can look ridiculous, too, when watched with the sound turned off. Vianney saw sin, but he could also hear and smell and touch it, and that is why his response often seemed out of proportion to those who could only think abstractly about abstractions. The penitents were hardly the dragon; they were more accurately the victims being rescued from the dragon in this extraordinary and, to us, baffling romance. Yet with outrageous fire of will, he determined to let the sinner be well instead of merely being good. As a man, he was no different from any of his parishioners, save that he enjoyed the grace of supernatural concentration through spiritual union with the good God who is the font of particularity. He had what would seem an impossible intensity and capacity for uninterrupted observation of the drama in souls, and at the same time his life was a total lack of self-regard and human respect. Perhaps the greatest battles since the Passion were not at Crécy or Verdun; they took place in a wooden confessional box in plaintive Ars; at least those who fought there thought it so. As masters of the confessional, possibly his only peers to any plausible degree have been Saint Leopold Mandic and, in these late times, Padre Pio and the Jesuit of Rome, Don Capello. Sin and death are part of the same battle because they are the same dragon; were that not the case, a simple course in euthanasia could substitute for the Viaticum.

William Blake was one of many to say this flat out: if Christianity is purely a matter of morality, then Socrates was the Savior. The dying Socrates delivered no panegyric on the city-state and no valediction to the sun and sea; he said, "I forgot to buy a rooster." By this he meant the rooster traditionally sacrificed to the god of healing in petition for a gentle death. The contemporary equivalent, we could say, is to die that way, as the great and good Socrates, nobly and simply. The moralist's "great man" theory of Jesus the Sage of Galilee is uncomfortable with his different kind of death. There was a rooster in his passion, too; but it was a tocsin of the denial of God. He drank from a cup, but his own blood of life and not poison. So Vianney's Savior did not whisper of death with dignity, for his Savior was a young castaway, deserted by those in whom he had trusted, afflicted sorely on the Cross as he was pierced by the temptations of meaninglessness, alienation, and despair. Vianney's counsel to most of his penitents is lost to history; but history does keep a huge record of those thousands of saints, cynics, and the indifferent who left the confessional of Ars with the veils on their hearts torn open. Their Savior was more than Socrates; their priest was more than a philosopher.

When Vianney laughed it sometimes was, as the phrase goes, *de peur d'être obligé d'en pleurer* (for fear of having to cry). More than ever the quick slight figure was impish in the face of pathos, his palsied hand shaking, coyly opening one confessional door to attract a swarm of impatient ones, and then, when they had rushed to the decoy, scurrying to the other box to hear first the ones who had been waiting. Other times his mordant wit burst into the full hilarity of Saint Philip Neri, whose two most prized books were the New Testament and a collection of riddles. To some he resembled the transparency of Saint John of Vercelli, who could not frown. After all, Christ of the saints came that joy might be full; there is room in joy for some happiness. If Saint Ignatius could do a Basque dance to amuse his friends, the clumsy clod of Dardilly had it in him to be a minstrel, at least figuratively, when his old friend the young Lady of Grace appeared.

Visions

It may be that he also had visions of Christ himself; with his customary reserve he only implied such, once remarking that he had not seen the good God since Sunday. By one tradition, he had seen the cousin of the Lord, since he said from the pulpit, "My brothers, if you knew what had taken place in the Chapel of Saint John the Baptist, you would not dare place your feet there." But surely the wide smile and open eyes that Cabuchet finally captured in his statue are what he looked like when he was with the Lady.

Saint John of the Cross, as fervently as any of the true mystics, had warned against illusion. Vianney warned others: when spiritual visions are exterior and physical, "the less is the likelihood of their being from God". Regarding the apparition at La Salette, for instance, he was dubious, especially after interviewing one of the young visionaries; in fact, he refused to believe except under obedience. Yet he had visions and auditions that put him into a state of conscious ecstasy; Richard of Saint Victor called it the "Third Stage of Ardent Love". Saint Teresa says in *The Interior Castle,* speaking of apparitions of Christ:

> The vision passes as quickly as a flash of lightning, yet this most glorious picture makes an impression on the imagination that I believe can never be effaced until the soul at last sees Christ to enjoy Him for ever. Although I call it a "picture", you must not imagine that it looks like a painting; Christ appears as a living Person, Who sometimes speaks and reveals deep mysteries.

In the case of the Marian apparitions, the Lady seems to have tarried with the Curé longer.

In spite of a chronic illness, a certain Madame Durié helped the parish by collecting door to door in different villages. On his birthday of May 8, 1840, she arrived at Vianney's house to drop off her offering. The Curé had abandoned his privacy long before, and Catherine, who was now in charge of the presbytery, directed her upstairs. From the staircase she could hear a woman's quiet voice saying, "What do you ask?" It was easy to recognize the far less musical voice of the Curé: "Ah, most loving Mother, I ask for the conversion of sinners, the consolation of the afflicted, the relief of the sick, and more particularly of a person suffering for a long time and now praying for death if she cannot be cured." Madame Durié felt certain he was speaking about her; the other voice answered: "She will be cured but not yet." According to her testimony, Durié slowly opened the door, which was already slightly ajar:

> What was my surprise to see standing by the fireplace a lady of middle height, clad in a robe of dazzling white, sewn

with golden roses. Her shoes seemed to be white as snow. Her hands gleamed with the richest diamonds. Her brow was circled with a crown of stars shining like the sun. I was dazzled. When I could lift my eyes to hers, I saw her smile sweetly. "My good Mother", I cried out, "take me to heaven." "Later." "Ah, my Mother, my time is now." "You will always be my child and I shall always be your mother."

The figure vanished, leaving the Curé standing with his hands pressed against his chest, staring straight ahead. He remained like this long after Durié had calmed a little; she tugged at his cassock. "My God, is it you?" "No Father, it is I." Vianney looked at her. She asked, "What did you see?" "A lady." "I too. Who is she?" "If you speak of it, you will never set foot here again." "May I tell you, Father, what I thought? I thought it was the Blessed Virgin." The Curé grinned a little: "And you were not wrong."

The Comte de Tourdonnet said, "The eyes of the Curé d'Ars are not made like those of other people." Although a lapsed Catholic, on September 3, 1856, he had brought his deaf maidservant to Ars, evidently at her request. He pressed his way through the crowd and into the sacristy; one can sense his elegant discomfort. "Monsieur le Curé, could you cure my servant?" The Saint of course had not met him or the girl before; the comte had left her in the rear of the church, and she had gone on her own to pray behind the main altar, where no one could see her. "Ah yes, you mean Marie? I can see her in the chancel." Then he cured her. In the normal run of things, the Curé's gift did shock some and perplex others; penitents made better confessions when he told them the where, when, and what of their trespasses. And being the paramount pastor, he performed his miracles quickly and spent much more time calming the people down. When caught in the act, he passed it off with a shrug: "Bah! I am like the almanacs: when I hit on it, I hit on it."

That did not satisfy the police. When a rumor circulated through Lyons in 1851 that Vianney had predicted the assassination of the prince-president, a police inspector was dispatched to the parish. The poor mayor found the Curé in the confessional and left the two together. Vianney shut the sacristy door and in ten minutes reappeared with the inspector, who sobbed out loud: "Your Curé is wonderful: he is a saint." The police dropped the case.

After celebrating the Mass on June 24, 1859, as the bloody battle of Solferino raged, he was approached by a woman who asked if her soldier son was still alive. "Yes," he answered with a tired voice, "but there are many dead." Not infrequently did he single out individuals waiting in line and address them as though he had been in the habit of conversing with them all their lives. Names are important to our God; in the Apocalypse the victorious are promised a new name on a white stone known only to him who receives it. And names were important to God's Curé; he does not seem to have forgotten any. I do not know how the child felt who held up a stolen medal to be blessed, one among many others, to hear him say, "I cannot bless this one." Nor do I know what it was like to feel healthy and be told that I would be dead in six months.

I do know that had I been the younger son of the Baronne de Lacomble I should have appreciated him very much; his widowed mother made her visit to the Curé, distressed by her eighteen-year-old son's decision to marry. She had heard of the holy man of Ars, but the village seemed so far away. She prayed and set out with determination. After a rigorous three-day journey, there were only a few hours left before she had to return. Crowds were milling about outside the humble church, and the woman was crestfallen when she entered the front door: every seat was taken. She would never get to speak. Finding a place near the holy water basin at the far rear, she began to say a few prayers. At least she had made the effort; soon she would have to leave. Fervently she prayed, looking intently at the chapel of Saint John Baptist, where the Curé was hearing confessions. Suddenly a white-haired figure came out of the confessional, stood for a moment at the entrance to the chapel, and then walked down the nave directly to the woman. Her heart sank, and she felt more dead than alive. He was moving straight for her. He stopped, bent down, and whispered into her ear: "Let them marry; they will be very happy!" Then he stood up and immediately returned to the confessional.

Sobornost

There are striking parallels between the Saint of Ars and his Russian contemporary, Father John of Kronstadt, to whom the French freethinkers were "learned men, yet did they not vividly personify the furies of hell!" His lifetime lasted from 1829 to 1908, during which he lived a life of great austerity, preaching the Risen Christ over against the residue myopia of rationalism. He lived on little more than almond milk, loved red vestments, absolved upward of three hundred penitents daily, instituted schools for technical job training, and lived the divine liturgy as heaven on earth: "Oh my Lord Jesus Christ! Thou art all present! We see, touch, perceive, and feel thee here!

The highest recompense for a Christian, especially a priest, is the presence of God in his heart. He is our life, our glory."

But the sheer cataract of supernatural phenomena and godly counsel in Ars had an even closer parallel in a slightly earlier Russian, Seraphim of Sarov, who lived from 1759 to 1833. Growing up in the wake of Tsar Peter's anticlerical statutes, he so reformed the channels of scepticism that another tsar helped carry his coffin. Most of his life was spent in a forest hut, and his diet, which consisted for a few years of nothing but ground elder, might have famished the Saint of Ars. He shared Vianney's gifts of intuition and predilection and experienced almost identical infestations and obsessions: "The hermit, tempted by the spirit of darkness, is like dead leaves chased by the wind." In 1792 he witnessed a miracle of grain something like that of La Providence; and his visions of the Mother of God, "the beautiful Lady", were witnessed by Helen Manturoc and Mother Eudoxia, as Vianney had shared his with Madame Durié. A child in one of his classes said, "Father Seraphim only looks like an old man, but he's really a child like us." With Vianney he had mastered the art of perpetual youth, which in the instance of those not yet sanctified is only arrested development. He wept and laughed with Vianney's transport and at times, to use Donne's term, was nearly ravished by joy. Like Vianney, he was not in the least annoyed by little annoyances such as the "poor flies" on his face; and, as in the etiquette of Ars, whenever he healed the blind or lame he ordered a hymn to be sung and shrank away.

In 1831 a young man named Motovilov met with him in a glade to discuss the goal of the Christian life, the sort of conversation more familiar to the Slav than to Westerners.

During the talk, dare we say it, Father Seraphim glowed. It was an almost shattering brightness, the atmosphere smelled like something sweeter than the heavy oriental incense, and the snow felt warm. We may discount these as subjective, but the monk said:

> I'm quite sure that God will help you to remember these moments for ever; otherwise in his goodness he would not have been so swift to answer poor Seraphim's prayer. Besides, this revelation hasn't been given you just for your own sake but, through you, to the whole world, so that, confirmed by the action of grace, you may use it in serving your neighbor. The fact that I am a monk and you a layman doesn't make any difference. What counts in God's eyes is true faith in him and in his only Son. It is for this that the grace of the Holy Spirit is given us; the Lord seeks hearts overflowing with love for him and their neighbor, and this is the throne where he would sit and reveal himself in the fullness of his glory. "My Son, give me your heart", he says, for in the heart he builds the kingdom of God.

The Russians speak of a *sobornost,* of a bond of fellowship in communion with Christ; it existed spiritually between places such as Ars and Sarov and Kronstadt, no matter what their differences ethnically and culturally and ecclesiologically. Nothing less than sanctity can be the ground of unity; it cannot come about just by the sustained regard of ecumenical commissions. These holy men in their various places died receiving the sacraments and kissing the book of the Gospels. Through their intercessions there may come a time when saints of the East are honored with Latin hymns and Vianney's face is painted on an icon.

Monsieur Raymond

One more thought before moving on. As Job was given boils, so some pastors may think they are given curates. It is not an inflexible maxim, but it is a considerable one, and Vianney gave it substance. His poor curate, Antoine Raymond, has been fated to be in the biographies of Ars what Pontius Pilate is in the Creed. Life had started out well. As a boy in the schoolyard at Meximieux in 1822 he called to his friends as the figure passed: "It is the holy Curé d'Ars!" A few years after his ordination he made the mistake of wanting to be like the Curé instead of like Christ: anyone can be Christ by grace, but no one can be anyone else, not even by imitation. According to Vianney, the pilgrims were coming to Ars and to Philomena; so, Raymond freely thought, any Curé would do. He did not want Vianney; he very much wanted Ars. The Saint cooperated by appointing him as his replacement when he fled to Dardilly in 1843, and Raymond was abashed when he decided to return. Even then, Raymond, who was twenty years younger, continued to sign himself "Curé" and slept in Vianney's room while the real Curé used a damp room on the ground floor without complaint. Vianney had paid Raymond's tuition through the seminary, where he had done well; he did so well that he dominated the Ars pulpit, sometimes using it to obliquely ridicule his pastor, as though Vianney were some dotty uncle in his care.

With a thoroughly modern prejudice, Raymond even reached the point of thinking Vianney must be mentally incompetent. And once again the Curé did not help his defense when he agreed. When grace is denied, the only explanation for it is insanity. One of the Soviet dissidents of our time, Pyotr Grigorenko, was twice committed to mental institutions that way. Later released and examined in a cooperative series of tests at the New York State Psychiatric Institute and Harvard University, his condition was reported to the 1979 convention of the American Psychiatric Association: "where (the Soviet psychiatric analysis) claimed obsessions, we found perseverance; where they cited delusions, we found rationality; where they identified psychotic recklessness, we found committed devotion, and where they diagnosed pathology, we found health." In different language, Vianney's bishop made the same review of Raymond's diagnosis.

When the bishop's vicar wanted to remove Raymond, Vianney protested, "Let me keep him; he is not afraid to tell me the truth about myself." If little else, Raymond served his Curé well as a *memento mori,* however depressing that talent might be in a curate. Raymond was assigned to another parish six years before Vianney's death, but by that time he had grown in wisdom and grace and even came to believe that holiness can make a man whole; up to then he had the disadvantage of seeing holiness so vividly face to face that he had supposed it to be two-faced. Later he tried to write a *Life of the Curé d'Ars,* but if we have proved nothing else, we have triumphantly shown that any such attempt must be a failure. The remaining melancholy fragments were his atonement. In the canonization process Monsieur Raymond made several testimonies. There is no greater or rarer tribute on earth than that a pastor should be called a saint by his curate.

Chapter 12

A PITIFUL DISTURBANCE

The Greatest Cross

The tanned young priest who brought his cart of books to Ars and knelt crisply on its misty border was now a white-haired man who looked more like 607 than sixty-seven. His eyes, though, remained youthful, and his movements were quick, except when he made the sign of the Cross, which he did slowly and with great reverence each time he entered the church. As he sprinted across the square, the veins in his fleshless hands stood out like tight cords as he clenched a small can of buttermilk. He had cropped his hair short from the front in an attempt to relieve his chronic headaches, and arthritis plus a double hernia made him severely stooped. The face, emaciated as it was, seemed now constantly to radiate. His color, if there is such a color, was a deep white—not a bright white, but a deep and dark white. It is not a color at all, certainly not one found anywhere but on some holy faces, and so unlike the pink and bronze people of the land. When the astute Abbé Toccanier, age thirty-two, replaced Raymond in 1853, his florid and affable face was a study in contrasts; rather, it was a complement, for his modesty and directness made him kin to his Curé.

In 1852 a house of perpetual adoration had been established at Saint-Symphorien-sur-Coise, forty-five kilometers from Lyons. Bishop Devié died two months later. He had forbidden

Vianney to leave Ars, but under the new bishop, Chalandon, the Saint revived his fitful dream of going off to a modified Trappist life at the new house of La Neylière. The arrival of Toccanier satisfied any scruples about neglecting the parish, so in September of 1853 word leaked out that Vianney was plotting another "flight". As one can predict the result by now, the anecdote has about it the aura of a cat-and-mouse game.

One midnight, Monsieur Toccanier and a group of companions stood in the garden of the presbytery and watched the agitated shadows in the candlelight of the Curé's room. Soon enough the front door opened and the Saint stood in the souvenirs of his arrival in Ars: his old-fashioned tricorner hat, the cassock, the Breviary, and Monsieur Balley's old umbrella. "Let me pass, let me pass." Toccanier did all he could to stop him, finally grabbing the Breviary, which was the Curé's only anchor, rudder, and sail. Now the village fire alarm added to the confusion. With all the village running toward him, the poor Curé fell to his knees saying the Rosary. He jumped up, scurried back into the house, and grabbed another Breviary, green-morocco bound; as he did, his eyes in the dim light saw the picture of Bishop Devié. "Monseigneur will not reproach me: he knows very well that I have to go and weep for my poor life." The crowd was massive now, the pilgrims having joined in. He pushed his way through them with a magnificent strength probably surprising even to himself, smiling and crying at the same time; witnesses later compared the confused shouting in the lantern light to the capture of our Lord in the Garden. The Comte des Garets persuaded him to stop for a moment to discuss the matter in the sacristy. In a matter of moments, a tide of local humanity picked him up like a helpless piece of flotsam and carried him to the confessional. A few hours later he confessed, "I behaved like a baby."

It was settled. The Curé would work until he died, and he would die in Ars. He had fancied for himself the hardest labor of contemplative prayer at La Neylière, but he was fated to the prayer of labor, and no rest. His own words had returned to him: "The greatest cross is to have no cross." His world had been a catalogue of the many ways those who think there is nothing beyond life seek respites from life with a passion that he had for passion itself. When he stretched out his arms at the altar, he had become his own crucifix. In 1855 he was too weak to make the short trip to his elder brother's deathbed; he tried, walking part of the way and then using a carriage, but he was far too ill and gave up, turning his back on Dardilly for the last time. Even then the crowds followed him along the road back to the confessional. His brother François died on Good Friday, and the Curé wept alone while he heard the Holy Saturday confessions for eighteen hours without interruption.

Honors

We can see him in those last years cutting a path through the square, going about his work much the way he always had, though even thinner, bent over another degree like a tower not quite on the verge of toppling; the cane indispensable now; and, if it is possible, more intense, more blatant, and more gentle. "Good gracious! I have spent thirty-six years at Ars; I have never yet been cross, and now I am too old to begin." A great love from the people swept back on him, transporting him like a feeble feather in a breeze; the animosities of the first years were of a vague and prehistoric world. His earliest foes were among his loyalest friends. He had sent some to heaven, and the youth who had been denied their old carnivals were now mature celebrants of a huge and whirling fact. "When you are with me, things are not so bad, but when I am alone, I am worth nothing. . . . I am like the zeros that have no value except alongside some other figures."

A casual episode here, a chance encounter in passing, shows his realism more flinty by the day. To a foppish undergraduate, who arrived to "discuss religion", he advised: "You are an ignoramus, my friend." He told a woman that she gossiped least in February because it is three days shorter than other months. At least from those who gave depositions in the canonical investigations, the remarks were accepted as revelations; his tone was above mere insult, and his prudence wilder by the moment. A boy who would not do his homework was sent by his mother to the Curé for a warning. "Monsieur, le Curé, must I learn or shall I play?" "Play, my child, it is the privilege of your age." Among the vignettes of those closing years, an especially pleasing one is a meeting with a daughter of his old patroness, Mademoiselle d'Ars. He proffered the requested spiritual attentions and must have indulged some reverie. Then the tattered Curé made a rare move: he handed the attractive woman the gift of a silk parasol in the latest style.

A disciple of the premodernist Lammenais came out of the confessional shaken. "My God," he exclaimed to Toccanier, "is it possible that I should have allowed my head to turn white before coming to see him!" More leading intellectuals took pride in the association; their consultations no longer were surreptitious or patronizing. If a visiting preacher made the mistake of lauding him, he still curled up in the choir stall and kicked. To ward off relic seekers, he had to burn the cuttings after his infrequent visits to the barber. "Humility is to the various virtues what the chain is to a rosary: take away the chain and the beads are scattered; remove humility, and all virtues vanish." Virtue itself had lodged in one parish of France, and any virtuosity in that precocious age was commentary.

Bishop Chalandon, with his vicar-general and Comte Prosper des Garets, made an unannounced visit in 1854 to the horror of the Curé, for he placed on his shoulders the scarlet-and-ermine mozetta of a canon. As the bishop intoned the *Veni Creator,* the pained Vianney stood with the fur hanging lopsidedly; Mademoiselle d'Ars said he looked for all the world like a condemned man with the noose around his neck. When the officials left, he straightway sold the garment for fifty francs. Juridical honor, though, is of a different order from honors due the liturgy. On December 8 the new canon stood at the altar to celebrate Pius IX's definition of the Immaculate Conception, nearly bursting with appropriate pride in the fourteen-hundred-franc blue-and-gold cope designed by the architect Bossan.

With an eye not distracted from the public benefits of the Ars pilgrimages, the sub-prefect of Trévoux, the Marquis de Castellane, nominated Vianney for another honor some six months later:

In a small commune of my arrondissement, the population of which numbers 510 souls, there is a clergyman whose evangelical holiness and lofty piety have gained him a European reputation.

This description, however vague it may be, can only apply to M. Vianney, Curé d'Ars.

The commune of Ars, formerly the most obscure in my

arrondissement, witnesses a daily influx of a prodigious number of pilgrims.

Transport facilities have had to be organized; these have been functioning for a considerable time.

This concourse, now of long standing and wholly due to the reputation for sanctity of a humble priest, constitutes a truly marvelous event in a century which had inherited so many doctrines that are antireligious and hostile to the Christian faith.

The confidence of the people in M. le Desservant (Curé) of Ars is unlimited; it is the faith that transports mountains, spoken of in the Gospel.

Hence more than one occurrence is mentioned which it would be difficult to explain by purely natural causes.

The limited space at my disposal does not permit of an enumeration of them; but it is enough to state that in the procedure of the venerable Curé d'Ars there is nothing that savours of charlatanism.

M. Vianney is another Saint Vincent de Paul, whose charity works wonders. . . .

Wherefore, even from a purely material point of view, he is a most valuable man.

So in August of 1855 the mayor of Ars informed his most valuable Curé that he was a Knight of the Imperial Order of the Legion of Honor. Well, the Curé expressed appreciation of those who had been so courteous, and then: "Since the poor have nothing to gain by it, tell the emperor, please, that I do not want it." When the decoration and certificate arrived, the newest imperial knight refused to pay the twelve francs for the postage.

A year before, Doctor Saunier had ordered him to improve his diet. Still declining a chair during meals as a waste of time, since he liked to go through his mail while eating, he stood at a bare table in his bedroom. On it daily, according to the doctor's prescription, were a few vegetables, a couple of eggs, and a bottle of wine along with an occasional piece of meat and some bread. Most of the food was left untouched: he took only the bread and a little wine diluted with water. He was fascinated with his increasing debilitations, as a botanist discovering some new peculiarity in fauna. He thought it fun when his legs collapsed, chuckling that he was like a drunkard.

The Poor End

With close to a hundred thousand pilgrims filling Ars in his last year, missionaries had to be delegated to help with the confessions. The old shepherd's speech was becoming less intelligible; he had frequent coughing fits now, and sometimes passed out. "My head gets confused." Finally he was obliged to give up kneeling during the Divine Office and allowed himself an afternoon nap. The sermons of these last days had become almost entirely public conversation with the Blessed Sacrament; a soul estranged from the saga of Ars would have been bewildered at the rapt silence of the packed church as the wrinkled and toothless Curé kept shaking his bony finger toward the gilded tabernacle, calling out words that sounded like Love and God, and little other. One noon he sat down in his housekeeper's home: "Ah! my poor Catherine, I can do no more!" He returned to the presbytery for his nap but chose instead to head back to the church, surrounded as always by the indeterminable number of staring folk. Nothing was unusual about this, though he had taken an extra cup of milk from Catherine and it seemed to her he needed it to live.

On Easter Day, April 24, 1858, he noted that a half dozen parishioners had not made their Communion. In his customary way Vianney did not count the swarms of visitors around the altar. He was first and last a parish priest and would have to answer for the souls of his "own people". Rod and staff both were instruments of the shepherd, and so long as he could move he prodded and pulled. The priesthood is the sacrament of spiritual fatherhood. Having gathered the men and boys of Ars together, he spoke as a patriarch in valediction to the fathers and future fathers of the house of Israel: "Oh my children, what a beautiful deed you have just performed. By fulfilling your Easter duties you have prepared, in your hearts, an abode for the good God, and you are about to prepare another for him by building a beautiful church. On other occasions, my brethren, it was I who came to you; you have never refused me anything. I thank you for it. . . . Today, it is the missionary who calls on you, but that is as if it were myself: my heart goes with him. . . . Ah! there are still some sinners in the parish. It is necessary that I should go so that another may convert them."

The speciality of Ars, the Corpus Christi feast, fell on June 23 in 1859 and Vianney was too weak to carry the monstrance either in procession or even within the church; assistants placed it in his hands at the moment of the Benediction itself. In July Madame Pauze of Saint-Etienne was puzzled in confession when the Curé told her that she would return to Ars in three weeks; and he told Etiennette Durié that he would live no more than a few days, instructing her at the same time to avoid telling anyone, lest there be a deluge of pilgrims and the curious.

An unusually severe heat wave, something of a meteoro-
logical phenomenon well noted in the records, spread east-
ward from the far western parts of the United States and
reached France by the end of July. The miasmal earth of Ars
was never agreeable in any summer, but now the sun hung
like a huge deadweight, and the church interior became more
insufferable with the stifling heat of the jammed crowds and
ranks of burning candles. In the center of the torrid spectacle
the Curé shivered with a fever. At one o'clock in the morning
of July 29 the Curé weakly grasped his lantern and crossed
from the presbytery to the church for confessions. The hours
wound on slowly, and he made several painful exits for a
breath of air. The lines looked endless. By eleven in the
morning he was glad for a little wine. During the catechism
his lips moved, but there was no sound; the faces inside and
the leaves on the trees outside were still. The sacristan helped
him back to the presbytery in the evening as the red sky
melted; by some providence the whole family of Mademoiselle d'Ars was passing by, and knelt for a blessing. The cycle
was complete as they said farewell, the way the lady of the
château had said welcome in that long-ago moment. The
family knew that time was short but said nothing, and neither
did the Curé. At one o'clock in the morning no lantern
appeared. He called to Catherine: "It is my poor end. You
must send for Monsieur le Curé de Jassana." The Abbé Toccanier
received word and rushed in to assure him that Saint Philomena
would repeat her grace of sixteen years before. "Oh! Saint
Philomena can do nothing now."

This time he made no resistance like the stubbornness of his
first illness. He accepted a mattress and asked that the window
not be screened: "Leave me with my poor flies. . . . The only

vexatious thing is sin." The teenagers, feeling helpless, tried stretching wet canvas over the roof to relieve the heat; the room grew more stifling as more dignitaries arrived. Vianney continued to bless medals, which were being sent up by now in large baskets. Priests were received at the bedside and he heard confessions, though it was difficult for him to raise his head as he gave the absolutions. For those who jammed the garden and streets, a small bell was rung each time he made the sign of the Cross. It was the one audible sound in the village.

He used to speak of his "shuttle pocket": money went out of it as fast as it went in. Asking for the pocket, he reached in and dismissed the physician with his last thirty-three francs. Then he motioned to Toccanier and whispered that money would be received within three years for a new church, even without a lottery.

He made his confession, and in the afternoon a procession of twenty priests carried the Blessed Sacrament from the old church to his room. The church bell tolled as they processed along the square, and he wept at its sound: "How kind the good God is! When we are no longer able to go to him, he himself comes to us." As the priests crammed around the bed, he watched them extinguish their candles dripping in the dreadful heat. "It is sad to receive Holy Communion for the last time."

He was still the pastor, and parochial details had to be taken care of. The mayor and a select committee of the parish asked him to designate where he would be buried. "At Ars ... but my body is not much." He could not sign the affidavit when it was handed to him. The bishop of Belley arrived breathless on the evening of August 3 and knelt at the bedside. This brought a smile to the drawn face. He had loved his bishops, all of them, even those who had given little thought to him: grand Fesch in his wobbly carriage, the silent Simon at Grenoble who placed the chalice in his hands, wise Devié still staring from his picture on the wall, and now Chalandon on his knees. The bishop embraced the Curé.

On August 4, nature did the sort of thing that would be vulgar in an amateur stage play; it would be vulgar in nature were it not nature's prerogative: she unleashed a violent thunderstorm, and the sheep scattered on the hills. In the thunder, a young priest named Monnin was instructed to begin the final prayers for the dying. Jean-Marie-Baptiste Vianney, shepherd of sheep in Dardilly, had been shepherd of souls in Ars for forty-one years, five months, and twenty-three days. Beyond the garden every candle that could be found was burning in the church; in the reflected lightning flashed the gilt-metal heart of the Immaculate Conception with the names of the first parishioners on a ribbon inside. Across the way in the upper bedroom Monnin shouted over the thunder, "May the holy angels of God come to meet him and conduct him into the holy city Jerusalem." Without a motion at these words, the priest Vianney died. *Veniant illi obviam sancti Angeli Dei et perducant eam in civitatem coelestem Ierusalem.*

Jerusalem and Ars. Ars was no longer Ars. As the sacristan laid out a black chasuble for the first Mass of the Dead, he paused and wanted to bring out a white one.

The body had changed so much, furrowed with the secrets of those he reconciled to the good God. The face's radiance of the last years vanished to the high noon and shadowless land, and the bones with skin were lifeless, as lifeless as the young Curé had been lively when he first arrived at the border of Ars, the same age as Christ when he looked at the city. A long list of names had watched him grow white. Their names were in the little heart. Some were wise; some were buried; some had shaken off the dust of Ars. Wherever they were, there was Ars.

The red mozetta had been sold. They carried the body down the stairs and placed it on a board, dressed as it had been on the day he was installed: cassock, surplice, and stole. Vianney had promised on that youthful day to be a good priest; he promised as the stole was placed on his shoulders. The stole is light on the shoulders of a young priest. How heavy is a stole on a dead priest? For that matter, what is the weight of a priest? Is he weighty when he is ordained and the days are yet to rise up? And does he weigh nothing when his body faces west and all his past is prologue? How much does he weigh when the good God weighs in the balance? If he is a priest, and means to be a priest, then the stole and the priest weigh the same.

Beginning at five in the morning on August 4 and continuing for two days, a constant stream passed through the old house. Some touched the stole; some touched the hands. There was one interruption. In the high heat of the first afternoon the body was carried into the garden, and under the shadow of an umbrella the Curé was made to pose for his first photograph. The medal of the Legion of Honor was placed on him for the first time.

A procession of three hundred priests and religious and six thousand pilgrims escorted the coffin to the church for the Requiem on Sunday. Directly behind the body walked Antoine Givre. An eternity and a day before, when he guided the Curé and his cart to the village, he had been the first of the people to hear the voice: "My young friend, you have shown me the way to Ars; I shall show you the way to heaven."

On August 14, 1859, the remains of the Curé d'Ars were lowered into a vault in the middle of the church.

A freethinker in nearby Villefranche said it was a pity that Vianney had come to disturb the nineteenth century.

Appendix I

CHURCH AND STATE IN VIANNEY'S YOUTH

The "underground Church" in the time of the childhood of Jean Marie Vianney is one element in a very complicated picture; few periods of Church history are so replete with contradictory factions and ambiguous interests. The witness of loyal Catholics throughout those years, not to mention the countless martyrdoms and massacres, such as that which makes Poulenc's music in the "Dialogues of the Carmelites" so haunting, is like the stark scene of Elijah being fed by ravens in the wilderness. It is edifying, if melancholy; but for it to make sense one must also try to understand Ahab. In Israel, "the stream dried up, for the country had no rain".[1] The question of interest today is, What caused the drought?

"A state", wrote Montesquieu, "cannot change its religion, manners and customs in an instant, and with the same rapidity as the prince publishes the ordinance which establishes a new religion."[2] Napoleon understood that; it was only a half-hearted bluff when he told Cardinal Consalvi, "If Henry VIII who did not have one twentieth of my power tried to change the religion of his country and succeeded, I could do it much more easily and succeed!"[3] His genius understood the weight

[1] 1 Kings 17:7.
[2] Montesquieu, *The Spirit of the Laws* (New York: Colonial Press, 1899), 52.
[3] G. Constant, *L'Eglise de France sous le Consulat et l'Empire* (Paris: J. Gabalda, 1928), 46.

of the cardinal's reply, that the emperor could not ruin a Church which even a millennium of bishops had not been able to destroy. And Napoleon's prudence was too informed to ask like Stalin how many divisions the Pope has. The emperor of the French, rationalist though he was, was more philosophical than the *philosophes* untinged by common sense; he knew that reason was better displayed in diplomacy than bedecked on the altar of the Cathedral of Notre Dame.

France learned this the hard way. The First Directory had seen a flurry of fanciful attempts to change the old religion. Few were as pompous as the *Panthéonisme* of Félix le Pelletier, Benoist-Lamothe's social cult with its bread of fraternity and regard for the "Sage of Galilee", and Daubermesnil's "Cult of Adorers". It has been left to our most recent generation, having neglected its history, to make similar depredations on the liturgy. One thinks of a convent chapel in the American Midwest where the altar has been replaced with a potted tree. Recently an official communication of the United States bishops had to remind the faithful that clowns are not liturgical ministers. Anyone today who would worship with mimes and balloons, with instant folk music composed by commercial interests, is capable of singing the *"Ronde de la Décade"* about the elimination of the sabbatarian calendar:

> Oublions saint Roche et son chien
> Saint Crépin et saint Crépinien
> Et Monsieur le Cochon
> Du saint en capuchon
> Celébrons la Décade.[4]

[4] Albert Mathiez, *La Theophilanthropie et le Culte Decadaire 1796–1801* (Paris: Félix Alcan, 1904), 64.

A work written possibly by Goupil de Prefelne, *Les Réflex-ions d'un pauvre diable,* although anti-Christian, appeared a few days after Babeuf's conspiracy and recommended reform of the cults. There was a significant theist reaction. Le Gaigneur grew concerned about the political threat of the more extravagant fraternities, citing the Quakers as the only sect that did not become intolerant in its demand for toler-ance.[5] Rallier, as member of the *Conseil des Anciens,* pro-posed a vague united deist rehabilitation, issuing in the curiosity known as the *société Théophilanthropique,* which held its first public ceremony on January 15, 1797, in the Church of Saint Catherine in Paris. Its basic theme was the immortality of the soul as a civilized antidote to the resurrection of the dead. Nurtured by Goupil de Prefelne, Dupont de Nemoins, Creuze-Latouche, and Rallier himself, it even attracted a small following in England under a Methodist minister named Daniel Williams.

In most cases products of fuzzy local sympathies, the cults were fueled by the hostility of the Catholic Church to the Revolution. They did not flourish until the uprising of the Vendée provoked the Church's censure. Gallicanism, the asser-tion of national autonomy for the Church, was a convenient theme for the cultists, but only cynically so; they had gone far beyond concern with the government of a Church whose very doctrines they had abandoned. The Gallican Declarations, as they had been drawn up by Bossuet in 1682, denied the Pope's authority in temporal affairs, asserted the authority of ecumenical councils over the Pope, gave permanency to vari-ous independent privileges enjoyed over the years by the

[5] Ibid., 66.

Church in France, and professed that the ordinary teaching of the Pope does not command assent of the faithful until it is ratified by an ecumenical council. In the experience of the Revolution, the meaning of the Gallican liberties, familiar as they are in some ways to theories proposed in recent years as means of renewal and modernization by restless elements who would misrepresent the authentic Vatican II in their rush for a Vatican III, varied from the Civil Constitution to the Concordat but was almost totally political; any ecclesiological tone was imputed by a small group of the constitutional clergy headed by Grégoire.

Under Louis XV and Louis XVI, between 1768 and 1780 nine religious orders had been suppressed by the state with no formal Vatican opposition. Louis XVI had returned the Protestants to civil life in 1787 without consulting Rome, rather as the regulations of Emperor Joseph II had proceeded relatively unchecked in Austria. But then the spirit of ecclesiastical decentralization became a symbol of the Revolution. The appearance of the Civil Constitution of the Clergy in March of 1790 is commonly cited as the efficient cause of the Holy See's opposition to the Revolution as a social theory; but the Pope had already spoken against the unrest in the provinces of Avignon and Le Comtat in terms that showed no approval for the republican assertions.

Le Comtat (Comté Venaissin) had been ceded to the Pope in 1228 by Louis IX in return for support against the Albigensians in Languedoc. The Holy See confided it to the trust of the Count de Toulouse, Raymond VII, who protected it from 1233 to 1243, when it was returned to France. In 1273 Phillipe le Hardi abandoned it to Pope Gregory X. Avignon was given to the Pope by Queen Joan in 1348. On November 12,

1789, the lawyer Bouché petitioned the Constituent Assembly
to annex Avignon and Comtat to France, in retaliation for the
Holy See's attempts to reform restrictions of grain exports,
price fixing, and nepotism.[6] Two days before this, Montmorin had written to the apostolic nuncio, Bernis, urging that
the Pope would win sympathy by permitting the annexation.
The Pope adamantly refused.

There was not a single ruler, so it seemed, on whom Rome
could count. The Pope was at open war with Joseph II and
was in difficult straits with the Bourbons of Naples. The kings
of France and Spain had been treating him with negligible
respect; any slight was not likely to be ignored by a pontiff
who, regardless of high principles and rectitude, had difficulty distinguishing his own person from the dignity of the
Holy See and, unduly sensitive to opinion, was not above
taking pleasure in what the public thought of his profile and
the turn of his ankle. Louis XVI was in fact peculiar among
his peers for his attentiveness to the papal messages but remained
feckless in carrying them out. Pius VI proceeded, nonetheless,
as a man with competent alliances; he does not seem to have
fully understood the degree of his isolation. On top of that,
he was occupied with many civil, cultural, and sanitary
improvements that worsened the financial situation; his reaction to the suppression of his tax privileges, the annates, was a
practical one, not a simple jealousy for prerogative.[7] The
suppression of the annates had been debated by the National
Assembly on August 4, 1789; four days later the nuncio
delivered a warning. The Pope's own comment was swift,

[6] Albert Mathiez, *Rome et le Clergé Français sous la Constituante* (Paris:
Librairie Armand Colin, 1911), 65.

[7] Ibid., 45.

being received by the king on September 13 (it took at least two weeks to travel from Paris to Rome), but in fact said little specifically about the annates. Rather, the Holy Father used the opportunity to speak more generally about the king's duty to "unite France to the center of Unity". The Pope's confidence in Louis was not increasing: "We will never be persuaded, in spite of the public rumours, that Your Majesty wishes to cease being the Eldest Son of the Church and her Defender."[8]

Nonetheless, there was a sense of resignation in the Pope's expression, and he was content to secure a promise that his nuncio would not be dismissed. But this was some months before the actual Avignon-Comtat rebellions; the change of attitude in those weeks was dramatic. Conciliatory diplomacy had not worked. Not only had the annates been proscribed, but the provinces appeared to be in full rebellion. An even worse affront in the eyes of Rome was the deliberate appointment of nonbelievers to every kind of municipal office.[9] The Pope decided his new course. In a secret consistory on March 7, 1790, he vehemently condemned all proceedings beginning with the opening of the estates-general. Then he attacked the decrees of September 27, which had suspended the right of Rome to nominate all benefices other than local parishes. For the first time the canons were invoked without consultations with the national assembly. On the third of March the Pope replied indignantly to a message from Montmorin that had urged acquiescence to the abolition of religious orders. But seeing the inevitable, and still endeavoring to reserve formal initiative for Rome, the Pope delegated

[8] Ibid., 29.
[9] *Arch. Vatic. Francia* 911.

authority to the French bishops to dissolve the monasteries before the government did.

On March 29, the Holy See denounced the subordination of religion to politics in the course of the Revolution.[10] Objectionable and unfounded as the Gallican Liberties of 1682 had been, they were even worse when appropriated by atheists in their own interests. It was like muddling the establishment clause of the First Amendment of the U.S. Constitution to create a wall of separation between church and state.

The subordination took the form of the Civil Constitution of the Clergy, though it was not the instrument of outrage one might imagine, nor was it the first occasion of rupture between Rome and the French government. Its chief offense, and a totally unnecessary one, was to allow popular election of bishops by Catholics and non-Catholics alike, and to deny the papacy any control; the Pope was merely to be notified. It may be that few of the clergy understood its significance; it is certain that villages such as Dardilly, where Vianney grew up, were unaware of it at first. The papal secretary of state, Cardinal Zelada, wrote to the Nuncio Bernis on May 26, 1790: "The Holy Father is not persuaded that the zeal of his bishops is suitably stirred up in reaction to this enormity."[11] Given the state of the French bishops, it is hard to imagine them being stirred up by any attack on religion. And on June 16 he complained that the "discouragement of the bishops and the inactivity of the Court serves only to help the ene-

[10] Cf. E. Pressensé, *The Church and the French Revolution* (London: Hodder & Stoughton, 1869), 145–46.

[11] *Arch. Vatic. Francia* 463.

mies of Religion and the Church".[12] If the Pope saw an ominous creature stirring in the shape of what we today might call a "People's Church", soon to become a means of confusing the people about the government's real intentions and a means of promoting atheism in the guise of an indigenous religious idiom, he was alone. King Louis and even the nuncio, admittedly against their better inclinations, urged the Pope to sanction the constitution to keep some peace. The only real formal support for the Pope and the integrity of the Faith was the archbishop of Arles' moderate and eloquent *Statement of Principles on the Civil Constitution of the Clergy by the Bishops Deputed to the National Assembly*.[13] The assembly received it badly, and Mirabeau's denunciation surprised even the leftists.

At best the assembly's reaction was impetuous, goaded by an unforgiving Jansenist minority that included Martineau, who had submitted the bill. The fifth article of the constitution nearly overturned the right of papal initiatives: "It is forbidden . . . to acknowledge in any case and under any pretext whatsoever, the authority of bishops or metropolitans whose sees shall be established under the rule of a foreign power, or that of its delegates residing in France or elsewhere." With increased pressure from the emigrés, the Pope was forced to a showdown. The *Moniteur* of June 6, 1790, claimed that Austria and Spain were encouraging Rome to lead military resistance to the Revolution. Though not more than rumor, the Pope had made the equivalent of a declaration of war against Avignon in his brief of April 30; an apostolic delegate, Jean Celestini, had been sent to the province with full authority to restore

12 Mathiez, *Rome*, 190.
13 Pressensé, 148.

the old order. Several days later a new brief invested him with the same mission in the Comtat. On June 11 Avignon voted for union with France.

With the assistance of the Spanish ambassador, d'Azara, who took the informal position of head of the counterrevolution, Pius VI promulgated the formal rejection and condemnation of the civil constitution on March 10, 1791, likening the enterprise of the assembly to the schemes of Henry II Plantagenet and Henry VIII; on April 13 he declared the constitution to be established on heretical principles. When the news reached Paris, the Pope was burned in effigy at the Palais-Royal. Dismayed at the tardiness of the assembly's apology, the nuncio left for Aix-en-Savoie on May 24, completing the diplomatic break. A brief of July 10 declared the civil constitution schismatic. On July 28 the anguished king sent the Holy Father a personal message from Saint Cloud announcing his forthcoming execution of the decrees.

The revolutionaries of Avignon marched on Comtat on January 9, throwing the local inhabitants into a frenzied rally in the Cathedral of Saint-Siffrein, where they voted for union with France. The predictions of the *Moniteur* were realized to the extent that Spain threatened an invasion. The assembly withdrew its troops from Avignon, giving the Pope a brief moral victory, but it meant little when sad Louis met his end.

The Civil Constitution was a failure, provoking loyal Catholics' last limits of patience and causing more domestic problems than it meant to solve. The Vendean reaction opened the eyes of the assembly to their foolhardiness. The Thermidoreans, most of whom were regicides, made some grudging attempt to restore religious toleration by the decree of February 21, 1795; their motive was purely utilitarian, as Boissy d'Anglais said in defense of the decree, "Religion thrives on martyrs as love thrives on obstacles."[14]

By 1796 the sacraments were being celebrated in more than thirty-two thousand parishes. The constitution, though, was not the dead letter some historians would have us believe. Its manipulations were still felt even in remote places such as Vianney's Dardilly. Following Napoleon's victory at Bologne, the directory sent to the Pope, through his delegate at Paris, Count Pierucchi, with demands that he withdraw his earlier briefs against the constitution. The purpose was clear. Napoleon wanted war. Possibly he had decided on a course that would establish a servile Vatican in Paris.[15] Cardinal Mattei accused him of an "intolerable abuse of prosperity". Other opposition came from the directory itself, in a dispatch on February 1797:

> You are too accustomed to politics not to have felt as well as we, that the Roman religion will always be the irreconcilable enemy of the Republic: first by its essence, and then because its servants and ministers will never forgive the blows which it had inflicted on the fortune and credit of some and on the prejudices and habits of others.[16]

In the Treaty of Tolentino, Napoleon was able to secure papal abandonment of the legations and the renunciation of all claims to Avignon, as well as a large war contribution and the surrender of many precious works of art (February 17, 1797). But most importantly, he defied the directory by not insisting

[14] Crane Brinton, *A Decade of Revolution* (New York: Harper & Row, 1963), 201.

[15] Cf. Victor Bindel, *Le Vatican à Paris* (Paris: Editions Alsatia, 1942).

[16] Pressensé, 369.

that the Pope withdraw his condemnations of the civil constitution.

Freed from all inhibitions after the coup of Fructidor, the directory pursued its plan to abolish the papacy altogether by openly favoring the revolutionary party in Rome. The decisive event in the progress of the directory's fortunes was the murder in a Roman riot of General Duphot, the intended brother-in-law of Joseph Bonaparte, plenipotentiary of the republic to the Holy See. Pius VI, old and hardly able to walk, his face pale and his fine ankles failed, was carried off from Rome, transferred to Tuscany and then to France, where he died at Valence.

Judging from figures at the start of the Revolution, the church in France had lost about 135 bishops by the end of the eighteenth century. Forty-two had died, and ten more followed by 1802. Eighty-three survived, many by neglecting every activity save compromise, three had abandoned their offices, and only seven had not left the country altogether. The others emigrated to Italy, Spain, Portugal, Germany, Austria, Switzerland, Russia, and England.[17] We can begin to appreciate the desolation of the Lyonnais churches during Vianney's youth. Nevertheless, full advantage had been taken of the concessions granted after the Vendean uprisings. At a National Gallican Council in Paris during August 1797, a definite overture was made toward the Holy See and the nonjurors. Retaining the Gallican Declarations, the constitutionalists recognized the Pope as head of the universal Church, and suggested that where there were two bishops, constitutional and nonjuring,

---

[17] Simon Delacroix, *La Réorganisation de L'Eglise de France après la Révolution* (Paris: Editions du Vitrail, 1962), 1.

claiming the same diocese, or two priests for one parish, the senior should be recognized. The situation might be compared to the problem of the "Patriotic Church" in China today. Although Rome's agreement could not be expected, there was a sense of hopefulness about future arrangements. To the degree that the move was promoted by Napoleon, it signaled an inevitable tide toward some accommodation with Rome. Napoleon was only responding to what seemed an inevitable recovery of Catholic loyalty; he certainly had not instigated it.

As Napoleon assumed responsibility for France, a remarkable man was elected universal pastor. Pope Pius VII had taken the Benedictine habit at the age of sixteen, and his intellectual and spiritual gifts fitted him suitably for the world at large. While the future was uncertain, the world of Pius VI was surely dead. Pius VII had not been rigorously opposed to the Revolution, and he was scarcely even a royalist. As bishop of Imola, he had been called a Jacobin for saying that the new democracy required of citizens virtues that, if practiced, would make them better disciples of Christ.

The French victory at Marengo had shaken the ability of Austria to continue her protection of the Holy See; besides, the first consul called out in the Cathedral of Milan, "I have spoken to the patriots, let your priests say the Mass." The moment was opportune for some formal understanding.[18]

Napoleon's instrument of reconciliation was the Concordat, which in its original form understated the Gallican claims. Eager to have a legate *a latere* in Paris, the Pope agreed to

---

[18] Henry H. Walsh, *The Concordat of* 1801 (New York: Columbia University Press, 1933), 32.

Napoleon's request that the obsequious Cardinal Caprara be appointed. Napoleon appointed J. M. E. Portalis as regulator of all religious affairs. The nephew of Portalis was Cardinal d'Astros, a staunch papalist, and Portalis was a Catholic himself, though by no means a clericalist in matters touching on civil interest. Apparently enjoying Napoleon's full confidence, Portalis defended Catholicism on grounds that would persuade: that the Church was the surest guardian of moral and social stability. And it did appeal to the mentality of the Corsican prodigy, who had said at Malmaison in a conversation on August 18, 1800, "If I governed a Jewish people, I should reestablish the Temple of Solomon."[19] Hostile to the plan of Catholic reestablishment, the tribunate showed its displeasure by electing as its head Danou, one of the first consul's open opponents. Then Talleyrand, peremptory in disbelief and recriminatory in guilt, did all he could to further undermine the Concordat. Portalis' chief accomplishment was to secure official acquiescence.

Had Napoleon followed his own predelictions from the start, he would have chosen the constitutional Church, but he decided it had "good maxims but no reputation". Boulay de la Meurthe estimated that the constitutionalists numbered no more than seven thousand by 1796; in some *départements* there were only a couple of hundred, in a few practically none. The peasant sagacity of the Vianney family in those years, as they passively resisted the constitutional clergy sent to them, is representative of a large segment of the rural sentiment. Napoleon had the choice either to attempt a constitutional Church based on the civil constitution (the constitution had not erected

---

[19] Ibid., 83.

a formal Church in its provisions), or to reestablish Roman Catholicism. Expecting the advantages of a client Pope, he decided his course.

Rome saw an opportunity to repudiate the Gallican errors in these same proceedings. The distorted Gallican ecclesiology was more significant to the long sweep of Church, and more damaging to the Church's supernatural witness, than the proximate political questions. In a letter to the Pope, Cardinal Martiniana related a conversation in which Napoleon, in Verceil on his return to Paris from Marengo, expressed eagerness to end the old Gallican strivings. His plan for a Concordat would be a unique initiative of Paris and the Holy See independent of the Gallican Declarations. On July 10, 1800, the Pope communicated his good will to Martiniana.

Writing to Cardinal Doria on July 2, 1801, Consalvi was certain that "the whole body of magistrates, all philosophers, all the libertines and the greater part of the military" were against Napoleon's scheme. The general public by now was weary of the whole matter and apathetic in their response. They certainly showed little support for the loyalist clergy, who were compelled to begging and secular trade. For lack of funds, the Pope could not afford private couriers and had to entrust his confidential pouches to friends who happened to be traveling to Paris. Consalvi obtained a pontifical decree on July 28 forming a little congregation of five cardinals, five bishops, and an equal number of assistants to expedite negotiations, replacing the unwieldy congregation that had been created in September 1790 to study the civil constitution.

The Holy See rejected the formal draft of the Concordat, called the Fifth Project, which not only recognized the appointment of bishops who had been consecrated without papal consent but also assented to divorce and to married priests; these issues may be taken as symbols of bad faith whenever the supernatural grace and prophetic mission of the Church are discussed. Nor would the Sacred College agree to a national episcopal conference with canonical executive authority independent of the Holy See.

It says something of Napoleon's limited introduction to theology that he counted on prompt approval by Rome. But there was one consideration for Rome to ponder, though Gallican historians such as Debidour may exaggerate the subtlety of the Holy See in perceiving it: by acceding to Napoleon's request for the deposition of the bishops of the *ancien régime,* the papacy would be exercising a prerogative that those Gallican aristocrats had repudiated for well more than a century. There would have been mixed feelings, of course: Rome was obliged to the four score loyalist bishops. "It would be strange indeed", wrote Spina to Bernier in Paris, "to hoist anew in the provinces the standard of our Holy Religion on the ruins of eighty columns of faith, overthrown and destroyed by the same arm of Peter which sought to sustain and protect them."[20]

Meanwhile, Grégoire and his fellow constitutionals gathered in a second national council at Paris and warned Napoleon on July 4, 1801, against compromising the Gallican case. From the other side, Talleyrand, though still privately unhappy with the Concordat, was not inclined to let even unworthy principle interfere with the unworthier pursuit of his private interests. Having committed himself to the emperor's cause, he urged docility on Rome; if the Concordat were not accepted, he warned, then the Pope would have to rely on the military

[20] Ibid., 43.

support of two apostate nations, England and Russia, against the wayward but nonetheless eldest daughter of the Church. It was an argument designed to infuriate as well as persuade, and it seems to have done both.

Having secured more concessions, Consalvi signed the final text on July 15, 1801. Napoleon even allowed the agreement to be announced in the form of a papal bull. The Pope had instructed the nonjuring bishops to relinquish their sees. Napoleon thought the wording of the letter was too gentle. For the emigrés and Cardinal Maury, *Tam Multa* was an outrageous change of the Holy See's "principles and its clothing". All of these prelates, however, had been noblemen and, given their performance before the Revolution, it is not undue to describe their resistance to the Revolution as complicated by social necessity and affinity, possibly more than by theological principle. Martyrdom was a crowning vindication, but it was to be found most among the lesser clergy, who had little vested social interest in resisting the Republic. The Concordat, in its pristine form, was a triumph of the Holy See over a Gallicanism that had abused the Successor of Peter longer than had the Revolution.

But after all the bulls connected with the Concordat had been published, Napoleon unilaterally attached the organic articles. These unambiguously asserted the initiatives of the state over the church. No briefs or legates were to be received from Rome in the future; no decrees of general councils or national synods could be published in France without government permission; and the four Gallican declarations were to be taught in all seminaries, with seminary professors required to subscribe to them. The Pope made a formal protest in consistory on May 24, 1802, which Napoleon airily dismissed as one of the "customary reservations of the Court of Rome in regard to Gallican liberties".[21]

The sheer opportunism of the French government turned many fair-minded Gallicans into more sympathetic papalists; soon a transformation began throughout the nation, and the French penchant for clear-cut extremes displayed itself in the widespread movement away from Gallicanism as a theory to ultramontanism as a crusade. It would have a profound impact on the entire period of Vianney's pastorate, and far past it. Of course Napoleon could have cared less for the Gallican declarations as historic evidences; he appropriated and amplified them in the organic articles simply to further his own agenda, which meant the humiliation and eventual appropriation of the papacy. This is precisely why he saw no reason to support the old Gallican theory put forward at the councils of Pisa and Constance, which subordinated the papacy to general councils: he would much rather take his chances with one man than with a council of men. He was neither papalist nor conciliarist; the concept of episcopal collegiality was acceptable only so long as he could define what it meant along the way. "He who has put the Koran and the Gospel on the same level", said Maury, "has always just the same respect for the Church as for the Grand Mufti." Meanwhile Grégoire, whose puppet Church was threatened with extinction by the Concordat, likened the agreement to the Concordat of Bologna, which Pope Leo X and Francis I had contracted to nullify the pragmatic sanction of Bourges. For a man compromised as Grégoire, the Concordat was offensive as a betrayal of his betrayal.

21 Ibid., 91.

The apologetical writings of Grégoire present the most deliberate exposition and defense of the Gallican claims in practical application. In his *Essai Historique,* the traditional liberties are not a special donation to the Church in France: they are the common heritage of all Christendom. The other Christian nations of Europe simply had lacked the courage to preserve them. The line of argument resembled the makeshift patristical analysis of the Tractarians later in England, and it seems positively sober compared with some of the weaker treatises on collegiality that have emanated since Vatican II, oblivious to papal corrections. Grégoire objected to the canonization of Pope Gregory VII as a judgment against his theory: he was unwilling to be judged and found wanting by a saint. Disposed to courting popularity by professing to be unpopular, he presented himself to the republicans as a man sore oppressed, when in fact he enjoyed the patronage of the new social establishment. On October 3, 1801, in the *Annales de la religion,* he advertised implacable hostility to the 1791 and 1792 briefs of Pius VI. He must stand as less of a hypocrite than as a deluded man whose convoluted ecclesiology Napoleon could not understand and no Catholic could support. Charles II of England said that Puritanism is no religion for a gentleman and Anglicanism is no religion for a Christian; along those lines one could say that the Gallicanism of Grégoire was no religion for anyone.

The Concordat prevailed, reconciling the refractory clergy to the national obedience, ending the schism, and reassuring the purchasers of Church property that their deeds would remain intact. In return, the Pope was assured possession of his temporal domains in Italy, though without regaining the legations ceded in the Treaty of Tolentino.[22] In keeping with some of his protestations to Cardinal Martiniani at Verceil, Napoleon assumed the right to nominate the bishops, while the Pope would have the right to assent and consecrate. The old investiture controversy was resolved by a compromise more ancient than Gallicanism and with no obeisance to the declarations of 1682.

With an eye ever turned to the future, Napoleon left deliberately vague a "police clause" to permit his supervision of every detail in the execution of the agreement. Then he turned to the legislature. Strengthened by the papal ratification in December 1801, he made the daring move of persuading the Senate to retire one-fifth of the tribunes and members of the legislative body. By designating the candidates for dismissal, he gave the legislature an unmistakable warning. But Napoleon had paid a price that he was not prepared to measure in the heady flush of his immediate triumph. By cooperating in the stabilization of the government, the bishops garnered a new prestige for themselves; no longer were they the languid breath of the old order or props in a useless play. Clerical power increased and was capable of influencing prefects and other officials quite before the Restoration, evidence of how "Napoleon could be subdued by the tools with which he worked".[23]

With quiet resignation, and with time on his side, for Popes think in terms longer than emperors, Pius VII made no further objections to the organic articles save to remain neutral in

[22] Brinton, 31.

[23] Geoffrey Bruun, *Europe and the French Imperium* (New York: Harper & Row, 1963), 238.

the renewed European war. He was obliged to settle on a treaty with the Italian republic, but all things considered, he fared better here than with Germany, which afforded no settlement after its secularization of Church properties in 1803. The delicate concord shattered when Napoleon occupied Rome on February 2, 1808, and then annexed the remaining papal states on May 17, 1809, this in retaliation for the Pope's refusal to support the continental blockade of England. The work of missions suffered; the first bishop of New York was unable to leave for America and died in Naples without setting eyes on his diocese. As the Church expanded in the other continents, the Pope was obliged to endure domestic confinement and obstinacy from those he had long counted his own. Acting on the seizure of the papal properties, he excommunicated "all robbers of Peter's patrimony" and was interned as a prisoner near Genoa in what amounted to solitary confinement.

This was the year and these the circumstances when Jean Marie Vianney was conscripted for military service. His problematic army career has to be understood against the background of these complexities and compromised loyalties; to do less is to be polemical or ignorant of the conditions. Three years later, the Holy Father was removed to Fontainebleau, exhausted and confused, where he was forced to sign a new Concordat granting the emperor his claims over papal territories and privileges. But three months later, renewed in strength, on March 24, 1813, the Pope withdrew his signature; and a year later to the day, he returned to Rome, Napoleon having been weakened by reverses on the battlefield. After a brief exile to Genoa occasioned by the escape from Elba, the Pope returned to the Vatican on June 7, 1815, laden with the moral

ornaments of docile suffering and the sympathies of populations shaken by the obloquies he had endured. Vianney, a
seminarian at the time, was an unknown witness to one of the
most dramatic rehabilitations in papal history. By his equanimity and persistence, Pius had revived the fortunes of the
papacy from their nadir; the later nineteenth century would
become the most expansive and evangelistic in history.

The experience of the Church in the shadow of the Enlightenment is a sobering account of how many professed believers
would sell out the vineyard to Ahab rather than wander for a
time with Elijah. So it was, for example, that Athanasius did
not take much of the city out to the wilderness after him; and
so it was that Saint John Fisher was alone among the bishops
of his nation in his affliction. "Will you also go away?" asked
Christ, and Peter gave the answer. But there were not many
ravens to feed Peter, and those have not always been many
who sustained his successors in times of lonely witness. The
nobility of the common Catholic man in France of the Revolution remains as a mute indictment of those many clerics and
others who drew with bloodless calculation on selfish claims
to justify their retreat with the rest of the crowd. The bitter
fruit of Gallicanism embarrassed and morally bankrupted the
parallel theory in Germany, the Febronianism of Johann von
Hontheim. Today it would be somewhat like the steadily
increasing number of non-Catholics who are coming to realize,
through the evidences of moral apostasy and social chaos, the
indispensability of the papal charism in guiding philosophical
discourse. In the wake of unleashed reality, Anglicanism, for
example, has disintegrated in the late twentieth century as
Febronianism did in the eighteenth century; at the same time,
some evangelical bodies initially constituted out of an antipapal

spirit are beginning to see the Pope as the abiding guarantor of a consistent cosmology and ethics. And the various modernist misinterpretations of Vatican II have similarly proved futile to solve the enormous social dilemma of a world that has vindicated the truth of the authentic Magisterium by defying it. Certainly public awareness of the papacy has enlarged since the day Pius IX's death was reported in a few brief lines on an inside page of the *New York Times*.

As the Keys of Peter are a promise as well as a power, there is every hope for priests such as Father Balley and families such as the Vianneys in every generation who will maintain the plausibility of an ancient truth. In 1814, as Saint Jean Vianney dutifully neared the end of his studies at Ecully under the refractory Balley, his Pope was emerging victorious over his emperor, who had thought Christians like them were hopeless and pesky idealists. The French ordeal assured that any later petitions against papal fortitude, even by men so well intentioned as Dupanloup and Gratry, would not stand. The perdurability of Catholic reason in the face of unsystematic rationalism and the willingness of souls to undergo slow-motion martyrdom in the languid flames of secularism, a torment more trying than the direct thrusts of false doctrine and schism, have had an incalculable and increasingly hopeful effect on the right understanding of both Vatican Councils. Unknown figures such as Vianney were part of the history that is having its repercussions in humane society today.

Appendix 2

RETREAT AT ARS FOR PRIESTS, DEACONS, AND SEMINARIANS

October 6, 1986

Pope John Paul II

THE FIRST MEDITATION

1. *"As the Father sent me, I too send you. . . . Receive the Holy Spirit"* *(Jn 20:21–22).*

Dear brothers, it is Christ who chooses us; he sends us as he was sent by the Father, and he imparts the Holy Spirit to us. Our priesthood is rooted in the missions of the Divine Person, in their mutual gift in the heart of the Holy Trinity. "The grace of the Holy Spirit . . . continues to be transmitted by episcopal ordination. Then, through the sacrament of orders, the bishops make the sacred ministers sharers in this spiritual gift" (see Encyclical *Dominum et Vivificantem,* no. 25). Priests and deacons too share in this grace.

Our mission is a mission of salvation. "God sent his Son into the world, so that the world might be saved through him" (Jn 3:17). Jesus preached the Good News of the Kingdom; he chose and formed his apostles; he accomplished the work of redemption by the Cross and the Resurrection. Following the apostles, we are associated in a particular manner with his work of salvation, to make it present and effective everywhere in the world. Saint Jean Marie Vianney went so far as to say, "Without the priest, the death and passion of our Lord would be of no use. It is the priest who continues the work of Redemption on earth" (*Jean-Marie Vianney, Curé d'Ars, sa pensée, son coeur,* presented by Fr. Bernard Nodet, Le Puy, 1958, p. 100; hereafter cited as Nodet).

It is this that we must put into effect: it is, accordingly, not our work, but the design of the Father and salvific work of the Son. The Holy Spirit makes use of our mind, of our mouth, of our hands. It is our especial task to proclaim the Word unceasingly, in order to spread the gospel, and to translate it in such a way that we touch people's hearts without altering it or diminishing it; and it is ours to perform once again the act of offering that Jesus made at the Last Supper and his acts of pardon for sinners.

2. It is not only a commission that we have received, a significant function to carry out in the service of the people of God. People can speak of priesthood as of a profession or function, including the function of presiding over the eucharistic assembly. But we are not reduced by this to functionaries.

This is so first of all because we are marked in our very souls through ordination with a special character that configures us to Christ the Priest, so that we are made capable of acting personally in the name of Christ the Head (cf. decree *Presbyterorum Ordinis,* no. 2). Certainly, it is true that we are taken from among men and that we remain close to them, "Christians with them", as Saint Augustine said. But we are "set apart", totally consecrated to the work of salvation (cf. ibid., no. 3): "the function of the priest, in that it is united to the episcopal order, shares in the authority with which Christ himself builds up, sanctifies and governs his Body" (ibid., no. 2). It is the Second Vatican Council that recalls this to us.

We are at one and the same time in the Christian assembly and in front of it, to signify that the initiative comes from God, from the Head of the Body, and that the Church receives it. Sent in the name of Christ, we have been sanctified by him with a particular qualification: this remains, and profoundly touches our existence as baptized persons. The Curé d'Ars had extremely direct formulations to speak of this: "It is the priest whom God puts on earth as another mediator between the Lord and the poor sinner" (Nodet, p. 99): we should say today that he participates in a specific way in the mission of the sole Mediator, Jesus Christ.

This implies a consequence in our life each day. It is normal that we seek continually to conform ourselves to Christ, whose ministers we are, not only in our ministerial acts but also in our thoughts, the attachment of our heart, and our conduct, as disciples who go to the extent of reproducing the mysteries of his life, as Father Chevrier says. Obviously, this presupposes a genuine intimacy with Christ, in prayer. All our person and all our life refer to Christ. *Imitamini quod tractatis.* All the baptized are called to holiness, but our consecration and our mission make it a particular duty for us to aim at holiness, whether we are diocesan or religious priests, by means of the riches inherent in our priesthood and the requirements of our ministry within the people of God.

It is true that the sacraments derive their efficacy from Christ, not from our dignity. We are his poor and humble instruments, who must not attribute to ourselves the merit of the grace that is transmitted; but we are responsible instruments and, by the holiness of the minister, souls are better disposed to cooperate with grace.

In the Curé d'Ars we see precisely a priest who was not

satisfied with an external accomplishment of the acts of redemption; he shared in this in his very being, in his love of Christ, in his constant prayer, in the offering of his trials or his voluntary mortifications. As I said already to the priests at Notre Dame in Paris, on May 30, 1980, "The Curé d'Ars remains for all countries an unequaled model both of the carrying out of the ministry and of the holiness of the minister."

3. In other words, dear friends, we may well admire the splendor of the ministerial priesthood, and likewise the vocation to the religious life, because there is a certain relationship between the two. You know the saying of the Curé d'Ars: "Oh, the priest is something great! If he knew it, he would die" (Nodet, p. 99). Indeed, what a wonderful thing it is to exercise our threefold priestly ministry as bishops or priests, a ministry that is indispensable to the Church:

—the ministry of the one who proclaims the Good News: to make Jesus Christ known; to put men into a true relationship to him; to watch over the authenticity and fidelity of the Faith, so that it may neither be lacking nor changed nor sclerotic; and also to keep alive in the Church the impulse of evangelization, and to form apostolic workers.

—the ministry of the one who dispenses the mysteries of God: to make them present in an authentic manner, especially to make present the paschal mystery by means of the Eucharist and of forgiveness of sins; to permit the baptized to have access to these, and to prepare them for this. The laity will never be able to be delegated to such ministries; a priestly ordination, which permits one to act in the name of Christ the Head, is necessary.

—the ministry, finally, of the pastor: to build up and maintain the Communion among Christians, in the community that is entrusted to us, with the other diocesan communities, all linked to the successor of Peter. Before any specialization in view of his personal competences, and in accord with his bishop, the priest is in fact the minister of Communion: in a Christian community that often risks rupture or closing in on itself, he ensures both the gathering together of the family of God and its openness. His priesthood confers on him the power to lead the priestly people (cf. Letter of Holy Thursday 1979, no. 5).

4. Thus the specific identity of the priest appears clearly. In any case, after the debates of the last twenty years, this is now less and less a matter of discussion. Yet the very small number of priests and of priestly ordinations in many countries could lead certain faithful, or even priests, to be resigned to this shortage, on the pretext that the role of the laity had been better rediscovered and put into practice.

It is true that the Council had the happy intuition of locating the ministerial priesthood again in the perspective of the apostolic mission within all the people of God. It prevented priests from making their priesthood an independent possession, detached from this people. It emphasized the fundamental task of proclaiming the Word, which prepares the ground for faith, and thus for the sacraments. It gave a better expression to the relationship between the priesthood of the priest and that of the bishop, and showed its relationship to the ordained ministry of the deacons and to the common priesthood of all the baptized, thanks to which all can and must have access to the riches of grace (adoption as sons, life of Christ, the Holy Spirit, the sacraments), and make their life a spiritual offering, bear witness to Christ in the world as disciples, and take their part in the apostolate and the services of the Church.

However, precisely in order to exercise fully this prophetic, priestly, and royal role, the baptized need the ministerial priesthood. By means of it, in a privileged and tangible manner, the gift of the Divine Life received from Christ, the Head of the all the Body, is communicated to them. The more Christian the people become, the more they become aware of their dignity and of their active role in the Church, and the more they feel the need of priests who are truly priests. And this is true also in de-Christianized regions and in social milieus cut off from the Church (cf. discourse at Notre Dame, Paris, May 30, 1980, no. 3). Laity and priests can never be resigned to see the number of priestly vocations and ordinations reduced, as is the case today in many dioceses. This resignation would be a bad sign for the vitality of the Christian people and would put its future and its mission at risk. It would be ambiguous to organize the Christian communities as if they could very largely do without the priestly ministry, under the pretext of facing the near future with realism. On the contrary, let us ask ourselves if we are doing all that is possible to awaken in the Christian people the awareness of the beauty and the necessity of the priesthood, to awaken vocations, to encourage them and bring them to maturity. I am happy to know that your vocations directors are taking new initiatives to issue the call again. Let us not weary in asking for prayers, so that the Lord of the harvest may send laborers.

Dear brothers, let us remain modest and humble, because this is a grace of the Lord, received for the service of others, and we are never truly worthy of it. The Curé d'Ars said, "The priest does not exist for himself, he exists for you" (Nodet, p. 102). But, like him, let us not cease to wonder at the greatness of our priesthood and to give thanks each moment.

And may you, dear seminarians, aspire even more to this sublime service of the Lord and of his Church, in joy and hope!

Prayer

Lord, like the Apostle Peter, we have all felt in our inmost lives the call to leave the tranquil banks and put out on the deep, to leave the nets of a human profession in order to be fishers of men;

You have called us through the Church, you have consecrated us and anointed us with your Spirit; you have sent us on ahead of you, to act in your name, at the service of all the members of the People of God, so that they may receive your message and your divine life more and more;

Make us constantly engaged in thanksgiving, and attentive to conform our whole life to the holiness of this ministry, you who live with the Father and the Holy Spirit for ever and ever.

THE SECOND MEDITATION

5. *"I have made myself all things to all men, in order by all means to save some"* (I Cor 9:22).

The word *salvation* is one of those used most frequently by the Curé d'Ars. What does it mean for him? To be saved is to be delivered from the sin that separates from God, dries up the heart, and risks eternal separation from the love of God — which would be the worst unhappiness of all. To be saved is to live united to God, to see God. To be saved is likewise to be reintroduced into a true communion with others, because our sins very often consist in wounding the love of neighbor, justice, truth, the respect for his goods and his body: all this is contrary to the will of God. There is a profound solidarity among all the members of the Body of Christ: one cannot love him without loving his brothers. Salvation therefore permits one to rediscover a filial relationship to God and a fraternal relationship to others.

The redemption of Christ has opened for all the possibility of salvation. The priest cooperates in redemption, preparing souls for it by preaching conversion and by giving pardon for sins. It was for their salvation that the Curé d'Ars wanted to be a priest: "To win souls for the Good God", as he said when he announced his vocation at the age of eighteen, as Saint Paul had said, "to win the greatest number" (1 Cor 9:19). It was for this that Jean Marie Vianney spent himself to the point of exhaustion and undertook to do penance, as if to wrest from God the graces of conversion. He feared for their salvation and wept. And when he was tempted to run away from his heavy charge as parish priest, he came back, for the salvation of parishioners. We read in Saint Paul, "The love of Christ constrains us . . . now is the day of salvation" (2 Cor 5:14; 6:2). "The priesthood", as Jean Marie Vianney also said, "is the love of the heart of Christ" (Nodet, p. 100).

Dear brothers, many of our contemporaries seem to have become indifferent to the salvation of their souls. Are we sufficiently concerned about this loss of faith, or do we just resign ourselves?

Certainly, we have every reason to insist today on the love of God, who sent his Son to save and not to condemn. We have every reason to emphasize love rather than anxiety and fear. This is what the Curé d'Ars did, too.

Besides this, men are free to adhere or not to faith and salvation; they claim this freedom with loud voices, and the

Church for her part wishes them to take the step of faith in freedom from external constraints (see *Dignitatis Humanae,* no. 3), while safeguarding the moral obligation on each one to seek the truth and to hold onto it and to act in accordance with his conscience.

Finally, God himself is free with his gifts. Conversion is a grace. In the encyclical *Dominum et Vivificantem* (pt. 2, no. 47), I have shown that only the Holy Spirit permits us to become aware of the gravity of sin and of the tragedy of the loss of the sense of God, and gives the desire for conversion.

But our love for mankind cannot be resigned to seeing them deprive themselves of salvation. We cannot directly produce the conversion of souls, but we are responsible for the proclamation of the Faith, of the totality of the Faith and of its demands. We must invite our faithful to conversion and to holiness; we must speak the truth, warn, advise, and make them desire the sacraments that reestablish them in the grace of God. The Curé d'Ars considered this a formidable but necessary ministry: "If a pastor remains dumb when he sees God outraged and souls wandering away, woe to him!" We know with what care he prepared his Sunday homilies and his catechesis, and with what courage he recalled the requirements of the gospel, denounced sin, and invited men to make good the evil they had committed.

To convert, to heal, to save: three key words of our mission. The Curé d'Ars obviously stood truly in solidarity with his sinful people: he did everything to snatch souls from their sin and torpor and to lead them back to love: "Grant me the conversion of my parish, and I am ready to suffer whatever you wish for the rest of my life." It has been said that he had "a vision of salvation full of pathos": it may be that some expressions and a severe tone were inspired in him by Jansenism. Yet he was able to overcome this rigorism. He preferred to insist on the attractive side of virtue and on the mercy of God, for whom our sins are "like grains of sand". He showed the tenderness of the God who had been offended. His appeals followed the direct line of the appeals of the prophets (see Ezek 3:16, 21), of Jesus, of Saint Paul, and of Saint Augustine on the importance of salvation and the urgency of conversion. He feared that the priests might become apathetic and accustomed to the indifference of their faithful. How could we neglect his warning today?

6. *"Let yourselves be reconciled to God."*

This sentence of Saint Paul defines perfectly the ministry of Saint Jean Marie Vianney. He is known in all the world as the one who heard confession for ten to fifteen hours a day or even longer, and was still doing this up to five days before his death. Doubtless, we cannot transpose this literally into the rhythm of our priestly lives, but his attitude and his motivations challenge us vigorously.

The essential thing in his ministry of salvation was to offer forgiveness to repentant souls, at the price of an effort that does not cease to impress us. Do we accord the same importance to the sacrament of reconciliation? Are we ready to consecrate time to it? Do we look hard enough in our cities and villages for the practical means to offer them the possibility of this sacrament? Do we try to renew the celebration of the sacrament, in conformity with the suggestions of the Church (confrontation with the gospel, communal preparation made periodically, and so on), without ceasing to envisage the personal act of confession, at least for grave sins? In the last case, do we try to make people understand that this is a condition for participation in the Eucharist and also for the worthy celebration of the sacrament of marriage (see the apostolic exhortation *Reconciliatio et Paenitentia*, no. 27)? Do we appreciate the marvelous opportunity offered to us in this way to form consciences and to guide souls to a spiritual progress?

I know, dear friends, that many priests, with their bishop, have tried to take this practice up again, after a difficult period. I encourage you in this with all the force I possess. This was the object of the postsynodal document *Reconciliatio et Paenitentia*.

I know too that you encounter many difficulties: the shortage of priests, and above all the loss of affection on the part of the faithful for the sacrament of forgiveness. You say, "For a long time now, they no longer come to confession." That is indeed the problem! Does this not conceal a lack of faith, a lack of the sense of sin, of the sense of the mediation of Christ and the Church, and low esteem for a practice known only in the deformations of routine?

Let us note what his vicar-general said to the Curé d'Ars: "There is not much love of God in this parish: you will put it there." The holy parish priest also found penitents without much fervor. However, because of his priestly attitude of holiness, a considerable crowd grasped the importance of the sacrament of forgiveness. What was the secret with which he attracted both believers and unbelievers, holy people and sinners? The Curé d'Ars, who was so hard in some sermons in order to castigate sin, was—like Jesus—very merciful in the encounter with each sinner. Father Monin said of him that he was a "fire of tenderness and mercy". He burned with the mercy of Christ.

We have here an extremely important aspect of evangelization. From the evening of Easter onward, the apostles were sent out to forgive sins. The gift of the Holy Spirit is bound to this power. And the Book of Acts continually comes back to the forgiveness of sins as the grace of the New Covenant (see Acts 2:38; 5:31; 10:43; 13:38). This is the *leitmotiv* of the preaching of the apostles: "Let yourselves be reconciled."

These words are addressed to us, too, dear friends. Are we personally faithful in receiving forgiveness through the mediation of another priest?

7. It was to the Eucharist that Jean Marie Vianney wished to lead his penitent faithful. You know the central place that the Mass occupied in each of his days, and with what care he prepared himself for Mass and celebrated it. He was well aware that the renewal of the sacrifice of Christ was the source of the graces of conversion. He emphasized also Communion, inviting those who were properly prepared to receive Communion more frequently, contrary to the pastoral praxis of the time. You know, again, that the Real Presence of Christ in the Eucharist fascinated him, in the Mass and outside it. He was found so often before the tabernacle, in adoration! His poor parishioners in turn were not slow to come and greet Christ and adore him in his Blessed Sacrament. The Council has happily allowed us to renew our eucharistic celebrations, to open them to a participation of the community, to make them living and expressive. I think that the Curé d'Ars would have been happy at this. Yet we see that, despite this, not everything has progressed. The notable diminution of religious practice, due to multiple causes that I do not wish to analyze here, is a fact that causes great concern. Our faithful must learn again its capital importance in the life of

the Christian. This was an essential catechesis for the Curé d'Ars. Besides this, the dignity of the celebration and the spirit of recollection are values that have not always been respected. The Curé d'Ars insisted on creating in his church a whole climate of prayer, which was accessible to the people and tended to promote adoration even outside of Mass. Who would not desire to promote this taste for silent prayer in our churches, this sense of the interior life?

One thing more impresses us: the Curé d'Ars worked hard to restore the sense of Sunday, so that mothers of families and servants would be free to come to the eucharistic assembly. I encourage you to continue to promote the Christian Sunday.

I leave you to meditate on this grace which the Lord gives us, of forgiving sins in his name and of offering his Body in nourishment to our brothers and sister. "A savior with Christ!"

Prayer

Lord Jesus Christ, who gave your life so that all might be saved and have life in abundance, keep alive in us the desire for the salvation of all whom you entrust to our ministry. Renew our readiness to offer them reconciliation with God and with their brethren, like Saint Paul and Saint Jean Marie Vianney.

We thank you for your Body and Blood, which you permit us to offer each day for the salvation of the world, to receive within ourselves, to give to our brothers and sisters, and to venerate in our churches. Do not permit our hearts to become accustomed to this gift: let us, like the Curé d'Ars, discern in it your love that goes to the ultimate lengths. You who reign with the Father and the Holy Spirit for ever and ever.

THE THIRD MEDITATION

8. *"We carry this treasure in earthen vessels, so that this extraordinary power may be from God, and may not come from ourselves"* (2 Cor 4:7).

Dear brothers, we had to begin first by meditating on the splendor of the priesthood, on the "extraordinary power" of salvation that God entrusts to us. Yet how could we be unaware of the tribulations of the ministry, which Saint Paul himself experienced? How could we fail to recognize the weaknesses of our "earthen vessels"? I should like to help you to live then in hope and to encourage your efforts to find the sources of help. The Curé d'Ars said, "Do not be afraid of your burden. Our Lord carries it with you."

The difficulties of the apostle can come from outside, when he is faithful in serving Jesus Christ alone. He suffers mockeries and calumny, and his freedom is shackled; as Saint Paul says, he may even be "harassed on every side", "persecuted", "brought low". In some countries, very many priests and Christians suffer these persecutions in silence. Often they have the effect of stimulating and purifying the faith of the faithful. But what a trial! And what an obstacle to the ministry! Let us remain in solidarity with these brothers in their trials.

In the countries of the West, there are other difficulties. You encounter a widespread spirit of criticism, of bad faith, of secularization, even of atheism, or simply of exclusive concentration on material concerns; the message that you wish to bring in the name of Christ and of the Church is relativized or rejected. In the fifties Cardinal Suhard well described the sign of contradiction constituted by the priest in a society that fears his message (see *Le prêtre dans la cité*) and classes him among those who belong to the past, or among the utopians. Since then, in many dioceses, the priests have become fewer and the average age has grown higher. This pyramid of ages sometimes makes the integration of the young priests difficult.

The discouragement can even find nourishment in our mentalities as priests. Some may let themselves be conquered by gloominess, by bitterness in the face of failures, or by endless discussions; sometimes there is a hardening of heart that comes from ideologies foreign to the Christian and priestly spirit; sometimes there is even a spirit of systematic distrust with regard to Rome. All of this has weighed and continues to weigh on the dynamism of priests. I have the impression that the young priests are more free vis-à-vis such mentalities. I encourage them, and I invite them also to appreciate the preceding generations of priests who were put to the test but remained faithful; they have borne the burden of the day and the heat, in the midst of many changes, and they have carried out their charge very often in the spirit of the gospel.

Finally, each of you knows his own difficulties: of health, of solitude, of family worries, and also the temptations of the world that enter into you; sometimes there is the sentiment of a great spiritual poverty or even humiliating weaknesses. We offer to God this fragility of our "earthen vessels".

It is good for us to know that the Curé d'Ars too knew many trials: the miseries of his body, which was ill treated by the efforts of his ministry and by his fasts, the misunderstanding and calumnies of his parishioners, the critical suspicions and jealousies of his confreres, and more mysterious spiritual trials: what Father Monnin called a certain "supernatural melancholy", spiritual desolations, anguish about his own salvation, an implacable struggle against the spirit of evil, and a certain darkness. Generous and spiritual souls are rarely exempt from these. Yet, despite his keen sensitivity, the Curé d'Ars was not seen to be discouraged. He resisted these temptations.

9. You too know the way of salvation and the means to refresh your strength.

I would say first of all: a spiritual renewal.

How could we bring a remedy to the spiritual crisis of our time, unless we ourselves grasp the means of a profound and constant union with the Lord, whose servants we are?

In the Curé d'Ars, we have an incomparable guide. He said, "The priest is above all a man of prayer.... We need reflection, prayer, union with God."

It was with good reason that our spiritual directors insisted on a time of prayer given each day freely, in the presence of the Lord, in the daily listening to the Word of God, in the praise and intercession we make in the name of the Church through the prayer of the liturgy of the hours, in the manner of celebrating the Eucharist every day, in prayer to Mary. What admiration the Curé d'Ars had for our Lady: "My oldest affection"! What confidence: "It is enough to turn to her, to be heard"!

I think further, of regular periods of retreat, to permit the Spirit of God to penetrate us, to "verify" us, and to help us to discern what is essential in our vocation.

It is obvious that we must integrate into our prayer the daily encounter with human beauty and misery in our ministry; it can nourish our prayer, provided that we refer everything to the Lord, "for his glory".

All our priestly commitments take on a new relief in the light of this spiritual vitality:

—celibacy, the sign of our unlimited availability to Christ and to others.

—a real poverty, which is a share in the life of the poor Christ and in the condition of those who are poor, as Father Chevrier showed.

—obedience, which is shown in our service in the Church.

—the asceticism necessary to every life, beginning with that of the ministry carried out day by day.

—the acceptance of the trials that come, and even voluntary mortifications offered with love for souls: the Curé d'Ars knew by experience the truth of that word of the Lord, "There are demons that are cast out only by fasting and prayer."

But you will ask, Where is one to find the energy for all this? Certainly, we are not dispensed from the necessity to be men of courage. However, "the yoke is sweet and the burden is light", if our courage relies on the belief and hope that the Lord will not abandon those who have consecrated themselves to him: "God is greater than our heart" (1 Jn 3:20).

And more than this, we shall find joy: the emaciated face of the Curé d'Ars seemed always to smile!

10. *"I have become all things to all men: to the weak I became weak"* (1 Cor 9:22).

The priestly ministry, then, living in a state of union with God, is the daily place of our sanctification.

This is how Jesus prayed to the Father for his apostles: "I do not pray that you should take them out of the world, but that you should guard them from the evil one" (Jn 17:15). The Council recommended to pastors that they should never be strangers to the existence and conditions of life of their flock (see *Presbyterorum Ordinis,* no. 13). In France, many priests of the generation of the Council, and even earlier, have had this concern to a very high degree. This attitude of welcoming, listening, understanding, and sharing is always necessary, so that evangelization may be carried out in a language that is audible and credible. I say this especially to the new generations of seminarians. Father Chevrier made himself poor with those who were poor. It is necessary to penetrate in the same manner the new mentalities of the milieus that are to be evangelized, rich or poor, cultured or not. It is necessary that the missionary vigor of those older than you be maintained through you in today's world. Yet precisely for this reason, the Council adds that priests shall not forget that they are the dispensers of a life other than earthly life, and that they must not model themselves on the present world, but must issue the challenge of the gospel to it. It is not their task to back up the material or political options of their faithful (even when these are legitimate), so that their ministry may be open to all, and clearly oriented toward the Kingdom of God.

II. The spiritual and apostolic quality of the priests of tomorrow is prepared today, and I cannot omit a mention of this formation.

Dear seminarians, what a joy it is for me to see you all gathered together here! I greet in you the next generation of the clergy of France. Even if you are still the little flock of which the gospel speaks, I am full of hope when I see you. And I count on your joy in consecrating your lives to the Church, so that many other candidates will be encouraged to come forward. I believe that you are ready too to accept the demands of this service.

Many of you enter the seminary at a more mature age than in the past, after experience in work or studies. However, as a recent study shows, it is very often the case that your path to the priesthood began before you were thirteen years old. Accept the conditions of discernment and maturity that are proper to your vocation. If God calls you and if the Church so judges, then do not let yourselves be discouraged by the trials through which you pass. I imagine that you know the innumerable difficulties that the young Jean Marie Vianney encountered before he became a priest: the lack of instruction and of contact with educated people, delay because of the French Revolution, the necessity of working on the farm, the distracting fact of military service, and above all the difficulty of learning Latin, the lack of memory, the hesitations of the authorities in the seminary, the late ordination, in solitude, in an occupied country. Certainly, he benefited from graces: a Christian climate in his family, the effective and tenacious help of Father Balley of Ecully. Yet his path to the priesthood will encourage all those who know trials in the maturing of their vocation.

Your seminaries must be able to welcome different kinds of sensitivity, in a great mutual respect; generous souls must not be held back by the fear of others, nor must they judge them a priori. The bond with the bishop is fundamental, and the accompaniment by a personal spiritual director and the judgment of a team of educators are the guarantee of the vocation. One does not acquire the priesthood: one is called to it by those who judge you suitable, in the name of the bishop.

My desire is that your seminaries may prepare you as well as possible for the priestly life that has been continually before your eyes today. When I received the bishops of this Eastern Central region in their *ad limina* visit in 1982, I said that you must pursue a profound philosophical reflection that includes the metaphysical level, without remaining in an "impressionistic haze"; theology must be approached in the intellectual, scholarly, and spiritual attitude of the most complete initiation possible into the mystery of salvation; listening to the Word of God must take the first place in your houses; formation in the spiritual life, with adequate meetings and the assiduous reading of the great authors, is obviously indispensable. At the same time, you must have the experience of a fraternal community life and of a deepened liturgical and personal prayer. There is room also for a certain apprenticeship of the ministry: how to know the world of today as it is, how to approach it in a pastoral dialogue that is a dialogue of salvation. On the threshold of the priestly life, you must be open to the diversity of the priestly tasks that are necessary for a diocese, and you must be ready for the task that will be entrusted to you.

Happily, many students today seem to desire these demands of seminary life; they represent also a great responsibility for the directors and professors. I pray that the Lord will help them in this very important service of the Church.

12. You priests likewise have need of intellectual refreshment and of the support of the community.

You understand well the necessity of intellectual work, of a kind of permanent formation that will deepen your theological, pastoral, and spiritual reflection (see the Code of Canon Law, can. 279). How impressive it is to note that the Curé d'Ars, despite his harassing days, tried to read each day, choosing one of the four hundred books that remained in his library!

I wish also that a true fraternity may unite you, deeper than all the differences, a fraternity that is sacramental and also exists on the level of feelings. Father Chevrier wished to associate other priests and laity with himself.

The religious priests find support in their confreres. The diocesan priests live in a greater solitude, and I think that the priests of the younger generations will find it hard to live alone like the Curé d'Ars. It is certain that many will find a great support and a stimulus to their reflection and their prayer in the associations of priests. I know that these are regaining vitality in France, and I give them my encouragement.

Certain persons or associations of laity, such as the Word of the Countryside, undertake also to help isolated and poor priests. This is very praiseworthy.

However, what I wish to emphasize is the ever-more-intense collaboration between priests and laity in the ministry. There is a great hope for the apostolate in this, and I would say also a great stimulus for the priest himself, if he knows how to trust the laity in their own initiatives and how to help them to discern what is appropriate, and how to preserve his own identity as a priest. Even in this field, the Curé d'Ars knew how to obtain the collaboration of his parishioners and to give them greater responsibility.

13. My reflections this morning concern you closely, dear deacons, because you are the collaborators of the priestly order. I cannot speak of your task without thinking of the attitude of Jesus on Holy Thursday: he rises from table and washes the feet of his disciples, and, at the moment when he institutes the Eucharist, he indicates the service of others as the royal way. The bishop associates you as permanent deacons with the priests, by means of an ordination that puts you forever at the service of the people of God in a manner that is proper to you (see *Lumen Gentium,* no. 29). The Church counts greatly on you, especially for the proclamation of the Work and for catechesis, for the preparation for the sacraments,

for the administering of baptism and giving Holy Communion, for presiding over the prayer of the community in certain circumstances, to ensure other services of the Church, and above all, for bringing the testimony of charity in many sectors of the life of society. I am happy to bless you and to bless your families.

14. At the close of this long meditation, I come back to the missionary aspect of our priesthood. Like a good shepherd, we must go to people where they are. There are many kinds of apostolic approaches for this: the discreet and patient presence in friendly closeness, sharing the conditions of life and sometimes of work too in the world of the workers, in the world of those who work intellectually, or in other milieus when these seem to be cut off from the Church and need the daily and credible dialogue of a priest who is in solidarity with their searching for a world that is more just and more brotherly. In this case, priests are less able to exercise the ordinary ministries of their confreres who are parish priests or chaplains. May they know that they have the esteem of the Church, inasmuch as their motivation is apostolic and they renew themselves in the spiritual life regularly, and in the cases where this corresponds to a mission received from the bishop. May they always give an authentic testimony to the gospel, considering this a priestly function, a preparation of a more complete evangelization! May their membership of one single presbyterate, with which they shall actively seek to maintain frequent and close links, permit them to keep alive in themselves the responsibility of those entrusted with the mysteries of Christ; and may all priests feel themselves in solidarity with their ministry in the service of spreading the gospel! Besides this, the changes that the gospel must cause in society are

normally the work of the Christian laity, linked to the priests.

It remains true that all the pastoral efforts of priests must converge, as in the Curé d'Ars, on the explicit proclamation of the Faith, on the forgiveness of sins, on the Eucharist.

Above all, as Paul VI said to your bishops in 1977, never separate mission and contemplation, mission and worship, mission and Church, as if there were on the one hand some who exercise a missionary activity toward those who are on the margins of the Church and, on the other hand, some who prepare for the sacraments and prayer and build up the institution of the Christian Church. Mission is the work of the whole Church: it is inspired by prayer and draws its strength from holiness.

Mission cannot limit itself to the needs of your own country, however great these may be. It is open to the other Churches, to the universal Church that continues to count on the aid of French priests, following in the path of the marvelous missionary generosity that has been alive for a century and a half. The French dioceses that pursue this endeavor of solidarity, even in their present poverty, rediscover a missionary dynamism for themselves.

15. However, I do not want to limit my appeal to France. There are priests and bishops here who have come from more than sixty countries of the world. They feel themselves at home in Ars, where the priesthood has shone out with a special brilliance. The example of Saint Jean Marie Vianney continues to give an impetus to parish priests in the whole world and to all the priests who are involved in the very varied tasks of the apostolate.

From this noble place that contrasts with the previous simplicity of the original village, I give thanks to Jesus Christ for this unheard-of gift of the priesthood, that of the Curé d'Ars and that of all the priests of yesterday and today. They prolong the sacred ministry of Jesus Christ throughout the world. In the Christian communities that are like the frontier posts of the mission, they work often in difficult, hidden, thankless conditions, for the salvation of souls and for the spiritual renewal of the world, which sometimes honors them and sometimes ignores them, disregards them, or persecutes them.

Today, in union with all the bishops of the world, my brothers in the episcopate, whose immediate co-operators are the priests, I pay them the homage that they deserve, praying God to sustain them and reward them. I invite all the Christian people to join me in this.

To this word of thanks, I join an urgent appeal to all priests: whatever may be your interior or exterior difficulties, which the merciful Lord knows, remain faithful to your sublime vocation, to the various priestly commitments that make you men wholly available for the service of the gospel. In critical times, remember that no temptation to abandonment is fatal before the Lord who has called you, and know that you can count on the support of your confreres in the priesthood and of your bishops.

The only decisive question that Jesus puts to each one of us, to each pastor, is the one he put to Peter: "Do you love me, do you love me truly?" (see Jn 21:15).

So, dear brothers, have no fear. If the Lord has called us to work in his field, he is with us through his Spirit. Let us be drawn onward by the Holy Spirit, in the Church.

To each of you, seminarians, priests, and deacons and to all those whom you represent, I give my affectionate Apostolic Blessing.

Now we are going to pray to Mary in the Angelus. The Curé d'Ars consecrated this parish to Mary conceived without sin. May she help us to cooperate in the best way possible in the mission of her Son, the Savior!